Absolutely
on
Music

were listening to music and talking about one thing or another when he told me a tremendously interesting story about Glenn Gould and Leonard Bernstein's 1962 performance in New York of Brahms's First Piano Concerto. "What a shame it would be to let such a fascinating story just evaporate," I thought. "Somebody ought to record it and put it on paper." And, brazen as it may seem, the only "somebody" that happened to cross my mind at the moment was *me*.

When I suggested this to Seiji Ozawa, he liked the idea immediately. "Why not?" he said. "I've got plenty of time to spare these days. Let's do it." To have Seiji Ozawa ill with cancer was a heart-wrenching development for the music world, for me personally, and of course for him; but that it gave rise to this time for the two of us to sit and have good, long talks about music may be one of those rare silver linings that are not in fact to be found in every cloud.

As much as I have loved music over the years, I never received a formal musical education, have virtually no technical knowledge of the field, and am a complete layman where most things musical are concerned. During our conversations, some of my comments may have been amateurish or even insulting, but Ozawa is not the sort of person to let such things bother him. He gave each remark serious thought and responded to each question, for which I was tremendously grateful.

I handled the tape recorder, transcribed our conversations myself, and presented the manuscript to him for corrections.

"Come to think of it, I've never really talked about

music like this before, in such a focused, organized way." This was the very first thing Ozawa said to me after reading the finished manuscript. "But wow, my language is so rough! Do you think readers are going to understand what I'm saying?"

It's true, the maestro does speak his own special brand of Ozawa-ese, which is not always easy to convert to standard written Japanese. He gesticulates grandly, and many of his thoughts emerge in the form of songs. Still, whatever "roughness" there may be in the way he expresses himself, the feeling he seeks to convey comes through with startling immediacy, overarching the "wall of words."

Despite being an amateur (or perhaps because of it), whenever I listen to music, I do so without preconceptions, simply opening my ears to the more wonderful passages and physically taking them in. When those wonderful passages are there, I feel joy, and when some parts are not so wonderful, I listen with a touch of regret. Beyond that, I might pause to think about what makes a certain passage wonderful or not so wonderful, but other musical elements are not that important to me. Basically, I believe that music exists to make people happy. In order to do so, those who make music use a wide range of techniques and methods which, in all their complexity, fascinate me in the simplest possible way.

I tried my best to preserve this attitude when listening to what Maestro Ozawa had to say. In other words, I tried my best to remain an honest and curious amateur listener on the assumption that most of the people reading this book would be amateur music fans like me.

At the risk of sounding somewhat presumptuous, I confess that in the course of our many conversations, I began to suspect that Seiji Ozawa and I might have several things in common. Questions of talent or productivity or fame aside, what I mean here is that I can feel a sense of identity in the way we live our lives.

First of all, both of us seem to take the same simple joy in our work. Whatever differences there might be between making music and writing fiction, both of us are happiest when immersed in our work. And the very fact that we are *able* to become so totally engrossed in it gives us the deepest satisfaction. What we end up producing as a result of that work may well be important, but aside from that, our ability to work with utter concentration and to devote ourselves to it so completely that we forget the passage of time is its own irreplaceable reward.

Secondly, we both maintain the same "hungry heart" we possessed in our youth, that persistent feeling that "this is not good enough," that we must dig deeper, forge farther ahead. This is the major motif of our work and our lives. Observing Ozawa in action, I could feel the depth and intensity of the desire he brought to his work. He was convinced of his own rightness and proud of what he was doing, but not in the least satisfied with it. I could see he knew he should be able to make the music even better, even deeper, and he was determined to make it happen even as he struggled with the constraints of time and his own physical strength.

The third of our shared traits is stubbornness. We're patient, tough, and, finally, just plain stubborn. Once we've decided to do something in a certain way, it doesn't matter what anybody else says, that's how we're going to do it. And even if, as a result, we find ourselves in dire straits, possibly even hated, we will take responsibility for our actions without making excuses. Ozawa is an utterly unpretentious person who is constantly cracking jokes, but he is also extremely sensitive to his surroundings, and his priorities are clear. Once he has made his mind up, he doesn't waver. Or at least that is how he appears to me.

I have met many different people in the course of my life, some of whom I have come to know pretty well, but where these three traits are concerned, I had never encountered anyone before Seiji Ozawa with whom I found it so easy and natural to identify. In that sense, he is a precious person to me. It sets my mind at ease to know that there is someone like him in the world.

Of course, we are also different in many ways. For example, I lack his easy sociability. I do have my own sort of curiosity about other people, but in my case it rarely comes to the surface. As a conductor of orchestras, Ozawa is quite naturally in touch with a large number of people on a daily basis and has to act as the guiding member of a team. But no matter how talented he might be, people would not follow him if he were constantly moody and difficult. Interpersonal relations take on a great significance. A conductor needs like-minded musical colleagues, and he is often called upon to perform social and even entrepreneurial tasks. He has to give much thought to his audiences. And as a musician, he has to devote a good deal of energy to the guidance of the next generation.

By contrast, as a novelist I am free to spend my life hardly seeing or talking to anyone for days at a time, and never appearing in the media. I rarely have to do anything that involves teamwork, and while it's best to have some colleagues, I don't especially need any. I just have to stay in the house and write—alone. The thought of guiding the next generation has never crossed my mind, I'm sorry to say (not that anyone has ever asked me to do such a thing). I'm sure there are significant differences in mentality that come from such differences in our professional functions, not to mention innate personality differences. But I suspect that on the most basic level, deep down in the bedrock, our similarities outnumber our differences.

Creative people have to be fundamentally egoistic. This may sound pompous, but it happens to be the truth. People who live their lives watching what goes on around them, trying not to make waves, and looking for the easy compromise, are not going to be able to do creative work, whatever their field. To build something where there was nothing requires deep individual concentration, and in most cases that kind of concentration occurs in a place unrelated to cooperation with others, a place we might even call *dämonisch*.

Still, letting one's ego run wild on the assumption that one is an "artist" will disrupt any kind of social life, which in turn interrupts the "individual concentration" so indispensable for creativity. Baring the ego in the late nineteenth century was one thing, but now, in the twenty-first century, it is a far more difficult matter. Creative professionals constantly have to find those realistic points of compromise between themselves and their environment.

What I am trying to say here is that while Ozawa and I of course have found very different ways to establish those points of compromise, we are likely headed in pretty much the same direction. And while we may set very different priorities, the *way* we set them may be quite similar. Which is why I was able to listen to his stories with something more than mere sympathy.

Ozawa is a thoroughly honest person who is not given to pleasantries just to make himself look good. And even now, past the age of seventy-five, he retains qualities that you know have been with him since birth. He answered most of my questions candidly and at length. That should be clear to anyone who reads this book. Of course, there were many things he chose not to talk about for one reason or another, some of which I could guess at and some of which I could not. With regard to both the spoken and the unspoken, in all cases, however, I felt a strong sense of identification.

In that sense, this is not a standard book of interviews. Nor is it what you might call a book of "celebrity conversations." What I was searching for—with increasing clarity as the sessions progressed—was something akin to the heart's natural resonance. What I did my best to hear, of course, was that resonance coming from Ozawa's heart. After all, in our conversations I was the interviewer and he was the interviewee. But what I often heard at the same time was the resonance of my own heart. At times that resonance was something I recognized as having long been a part of me, and at other times it came as a complete surprise. In other words, through a kind of sympathetic vibration that occurred during all of these conversations, I may have been simultaneously discovering Seiji Ozawa and, bit by bit, Haruki Murakami. Needless to say, this was a tremendously interesting process.

Let me give an example of what I'm talking about. As someone who has never seriously read a musical score,

I could not fully comprehend that process in concrete detail. But as I listened to Ozawa talk about it, observing his facial expression and tone of voice, I came to understand the deep importance of the act to him. Music does not take shape for him until he has read the score, burrowing into it with complete determination until he is satisfied that he has mastered every last detail. He stares at the complex symbols amassed on a two-dimensional printed page, and from them he spins his own three-dimensional music. This is the foundation of his musical life. And so, early in the morning, he gets out of bed, shuts himself up alone in his own private space, and reads scores for hours with total concentration, deciphering cryptic messages from the past.

Like Ozawa, I also get up at four in the morning and concentrate on my work, alone. In winter, it's still pitch dark, with no hint of sunrise and no sound of birds singing. I spend five or six hours at my desk, sipping hot coffee and single-mindedly tapping away at the keyboard. I've been living like this for more than a quarter of a century. During those same hours of the day when Ozawa is concentrating on reading his scores, I am concentrating on my writing. What we are doing is entirely different, but I imagine we may well be the same when it comes to the depth of our concentration. It often occurs to me that this life of mine would not exist if I lacked the ability to concentrate in this way. Take the concentration away, and it would no longer be my life. I suspect that Ozawa feels the same way.

Thus, when Ozawa talked about the act of reading a score, I could grasp what he was saying concretely and vividly, as if he had been talking about me. This happened at any number of points in our discussions.

Between November 2010 and July 2011, and in several different places (Tokyo, Honolulu, Switzerland), I seized the opportunity to conduct the interviews compiled in this book. It was a decisive period in Seiji Ozawa's life, when his primary activity consisted of recuperation. He had a number of follow-up surgical procedures, and he was going to the gym, working hard on his rehabilitation to regain the strength he had lost after his original surgery for esophageal cancer. He and I belong to the same gym, so I saw him in the pool now and then, soberly performing his exercises.

In December 2010, Ozawa performed a dramatic comeback concert at Carnegie Hall with the Saito Kinen Orchestra, the orchestra he co-founded in 1984 to honor his mentor Hideo Saito (1902–74). ("Kinen" means "memorial.") I could not attend the concert, unfortunately, but judging from the recording, I found it a wonderful, inspired performance, though the extreme physical toll it took on Ozawa was obvious to all observers. After six months of recuperation, Ozawa then directed the Seiji Ozawa International Academy Switzerland, which is held every summer in the town of Rolle on the banks of Lake Geneva; and after intensively training a select group of young musicians, he took to the podium again in Geneva and Paris, conducting the academy's orchestra in two highly successful concerts. This time, I accompanied Ozawa to observe the entire ten-day period of training and performance. I was simply awestruck by the fierce intensity with which he threw himself into the work. I could not help worrying about his health, however, and how it would hold up under such a strain. All the music I heard was wonderful and moving, but it was Ozawa who really made it possible, and he did so by using up every last bit of energy that he had to give.

As I watched him in action, however, one thing dawned on me: *He can't help himself; he has to do this.* His doctor, his gym trainer, his friends, and his family could all try to stop him (and of course they did try, to a greater or lesser degree), but this was something he had to do. For Seiji Ozawa, music was the indispensable fuel that kept him moving through life. Without periodic injections of live music into his veins, he could not go on living. There was only one way in this world for him to feel truly alive, and that was for him to create music with his own hands and to thrust it as a living, throbbing thing into the faces of an audience: "Here!" Who could possibly tell him to stop? I too wanted to say to him, "You really ought to hold off a little, take some time to recover, and start performing *after* you've got your strength back. I understand how you feel, but you know what they say— 'Slow and steady wins the race.'" Really that was the only reasonable response, but I couldn't bring myself to say it to him when I saw him wringing every ounce of strength out of his body to stand upright on the podium. I felt that those words would become a lie once I spoke them. To put it simply, this man was living in a world that transcended reasonable ways of thinking, just as a wolf can only live deep in the forest.

The interviews in this book were not undertaken to comprise a sharply chiseled portrait of Seiji Ozawa. They are intended neither as reportage nor as a theory of what makes one person tick. My only purpose in this book was for me, as a music lover, to have a discussion of music with the musician Seiji Ozawa that was as open and honest as possible. I simply wanted to bring out the ways that each of us (though on vastly different levels) is dedicated to music. That was my original motive, and I like to think that, to some extent, I have succeeded. The experience has left me with the deep satisfaction of knowing that I spent several delightful days with Seiji Ozawa listening to music. Perhaps the most accurate title for the book would have been *My Afternoons with Seiji Ozawa*.

It will be clear to anyone who reads this book that there are some breathtaking gems scattered among Ozawa's many pronouncements. He speaks plainly, and the words he chooses flow naturally as part of the conversation, but among them lurk finely honed fragments of a soul as keen as a blade. To put it in musical terms, these are like subtle "inner voices" that you would fail to catch in a piece of music if you were only half-listening. In that sense, Ozawa was an interviewee with whom it was impossible to relax. I had to stay constantly alert in case I might miss some furtive tone that I knew would be there. If I missed those subtle cues, the very meaning of what he said could be lost.

In that sense, Seiji Ozawa is simultaneously an unschooled "child of nature" and a fountain of deep, practical wisdom; a man who must have what he wants immediately and who can be infinitely patient; a man with bright confidence in the people around him who also lives in a deep fog of solitude. To emphasize just one side of this complex man would present a distorted portrait. In this book I have tried to reproduce what he told me as fairly as possible, in written form.

In any case, the time I spent with Seiji Ozawa was

tremendously enjoyable for me, and I hope through this book to be able to share some of that joy with my readers. I would like to express my deep thanks here to Seiji Ozawa himself for having granted me so much time. Continuing these interviews at regular intervals over a long period involved many logistical difficulties, but my greatest reward came when the maestro told me: "Come to think of it, I've never really talked about music like this before, in such a focused, organized way."

I hope with all my heart that Ozawa continues to give the world as much "good music" as he can for as long as possible. Like love, there can never be too much "good music." The number of people who use it as a fuel to recharge their appetite for life is beyond counting.

Here I would like to thank Koji Onodera, who helped in many ways with the editing of this book. Because my own technical knowledge of music is limited, I benefitted greatly with regard to both terminology and factual information from the advice of Mr. Onodera and his deep familiarity with classical music.

HARUKI MURAKAMI

Absolutely
on
Music

Mostly on the Beethoven Third Piano Concerto

We had our first conversation on November 16, 2010, in my home in Kanagawa Prefecture, to the west of Tokyo. Together we simply pulled LPs and CDs off my shelves and talked about the music as it played. My plan for each session was to keep the discussion from wandering by setting a tentative theme. The central topic for our first session was the Beethoven Third Piano Concerto in C minor. We got to this by way of discussing the Gould and Bernstein performance that he had mentioned to me earlier, but it so happened that Ozawa was scheduled to perform the Beethoven with Mitsuko Uchida the following month in New York.

In the end, due to a chronic back problem aggravated by the movement of the airplane and to a case of pneumonia brought on by the severe cold wave that struck New York that winter, Ozawa unfortunately had to cede the

baton to a replacement, but on this particular afternoon
we were able to spend a full three hours in a conversation
that centered on the concerto. We took occasional breaks
to prevent Ozawa from tiring and enable him to take in
the periodic nutrition required by his medical condition.

Beginning with
the Brahms Piano Concerto no. 1

MURAKAMI: I remember you once told me about a 1962
performance of the Brahms Piano Concerto no. 1 by
Glenn Gould with Leonard Bernstein conducting the
New York Philharmonic. Before the performance,
Bernstein turned to the audience and briefly
announced that they were about to play the concerto
according to Mr. Gould's interpretation, with which
he did not agree.

OZAWA: Yes, I was there. As Lenny's assistant conductor.
All of a sudden, before they started playing, Lenny
came out on the stage and started talking to the
audience. I couldn't catch his English, so I asked the
people around me what he was saying, and I got the
general idea.

MURAKAMI: The speech is included in this live recording
that I have here.

Bernstein's speech:

Don't be frightened, Mr. Gould is here. [*Audience
titters.*] He'll appear in a moment.

I'm not, as you know, in the habit of speaking on any concert except the Thursday-night previews, but a curious situation has arisen, which merits, I think, a word or two. You are about to hear a rather, shall we say, unorthodox performance of the Brahms D-minor Concerto, a performance distinctly different from any I've ever heard, or even dreamt of for that matter, in its remarkably broad tempi and its frequent departures from Brahms' dynamic indications. I cannot say I am in total agreement with Mr. Gould's conception, and this raises the interesting question: "What am I doing conducting it?" [*Audience murmurs, tittering.*] I'm conducting it because Mr. Gould is so valid and serious an artist that I must take seriously anything he conceives in good faith, and his conception is interesting enough so that I feel you should hear it, too.

But the age-old question still remains: "In a concerto, who is the boss—the soloist [*audience laughter building*] or the conductor?" [*More laughter.*] The answer is, of course, sometimes one, sometimes the other, depending on the people involved. But almost always, the two manage to get together by persuasion or charm or even *threats* [*laughter*] to achieve a unified performance. I have only once before in my life had to submit to a soloist's wholly new and incompatible concept, and that was the last time I accompanied Mr. Gould. [*Audience roars with laughter.*] But this time the discrepancies between our views are so great that I feel I must make this small disclaimer.

Then why, to repeat the question, am I conducting it? Why do I not make a minor scandal—get a substitute soloist or let an assistant conduct it? Because I am fascinated, glad to have the chance for a new look at this much-played work. Because, what's more, there are moments in Mr. Gould's performance that emerge with astonishing freshness and conviction. Thirdly, because we can all learn something from this extraordinary artist, who is a thinking performer. And finally, because there is in music what Dimitri Mitropoulos used to call "the sportive element," that factor of curiosity, adventure, experiment, and I can assure you that it has been an adventure this week collaborating with Mr. Gould on this Brahms concerto, and it's in this spirit of adventure that we now present it to you. [*Sustained applause*]

OZAWA: That's it, that's it. But you know, at the time I felt that saying something like this before a performance was not the right thing to do. I still feel that way.

MURAKAMI: But he does it with so much humor, and the audience, while taken aback, is laughing quite a lot.

OZAWA: Well, sure, Lenny was such a good talker.

MURAKAMI: And there's nothing grim about the speech. He just wanted to make it clear beforehand that it was Gould's wish to set the tempo, not his.

The music begins.

MURAKAMI: Hmm, it *is* slow, isn't it? Kind of strange. I can see why Bernstein wanted to explain himself to the audience.

OZAWA: This part is clearly in large duple time, two beats with the counts *one* two three/*four* five six. But Lenny is conducting this as six beats because duple would be too slow to maintain a consistent interval between beats. He has no choice but to conduct with six beats. Usually it's *one* and and/*two* and and, conducted as *one* . . . *two* . . . Sure, there are lots of different ways to do it, but just about everybody does it like that. Here, though, at this slow tempo, he couldn't maintain a consistent interval between beats, so he has to go *one* two three/*four* five six. That's why the flow isn't right and tends to get bogged down like this.

MURAKAMI: How about the piano?

OZAWA: I'm sure it'll be the same.

The piano part begins. (4:29).

MURAKAMI: Really, the piano is slow, too.

OZAWA: Yes, but it sounds perfectly fine, especially if you've never heard anyone else play it. You just assume that's the way the piece goes. Kind of like a relaxed tune from the countryside.

MURAKAMI: But it must be hard for the performer to stretch it out like this.

OZAWA: Yes. Listen, though. When it gets to this part, you can't help beginning to wonder.

MURAKAMI: Around here—

The volume grows, the timpani enter (5:18)

—the orchestra sounds as if it's beginning to come apart.

OZAWA: True. This wasn't recorded at Manhattan Center, was it? At Carnegie Hall?

MURAKAMI: Right. It's a live recording from Carnegie Hall.

OZAWA: I thought so. That's why the sound is so dead. You know, they did a proper studio recording of the performance the next day in Manhattan Center.

MURAKAMI: Of the same Brahms piece?

OZAWA: The same one. But the record was never released.

MURAKAMI: No, I'm pretty sure it's not available.

OZAWA: I was there for that one, too. As assistant conductor. Where Lenny said in his speech that he could have let an assistant conduct it—that's *me*! [*Laughs.*]

MURAKAMI: Meaning, if negotiations had broken down

between the two of them, *you* might have conducted the piece instead of Bernstein . . . Still, this performance does have a good deal of tension to it.

OZAWA: Sure, sure. It's a little unpolished, though.

MURAKAMI: Played this slowly, it sounds as if it could fall apart at any moment.

OZAWA: Yes, it's right on the edge.

MURAKAMI: Come to think of it, when Gould played with the Cleveland Orchestra, he and George Szell couldn't agree and an assistant took over for Szell. I read that somewhere.

The solo piano section of the first movement begins (5:56).

OZAWA: It's strangely slow, but playing it like this, Gould makes it work. It doesn't feel wrong at all.

MURAKAMI: He must have such an acute sense of rhythm. I mean, to be able to keep stretching it out like that, adjusting his sound inside the framework of the orchestra . . .

OZAWA: He's got an absolutely solid grasp of the flow of the music. But Lenny's got it absolutely right, too. He's putting his heart and soul into it.

MURAKAMI: But isn't this piece usually played as a big, passionate outburst?

OZAWA: True, with a lot more passion. You're right, this performance is not what you'd call passionate.

The piano plays the first movement's beautiful second theme (7:35).

OZAWA: Here, the slow tempo is just fine. With this second theme. Good, don't you think?

MURAKAMI: It really is.

OZAWA: Before, the loud section was maybe a little sluggish or unsophisticated, but this really grabs you.

MURAKAMI: Before, you said, "Lenny's got it absolutely right . . . He's putting his heart and soul into it," but you also said you thought it was not a good idea to get up like that and give a speech before a performance.

OZAWA: No, I don't think it's a good idea. But from Lenny, people were willing to accept it, I suppose.

MURAKAMI: I guess you mean it's better to present music as music, without any added preconceptions. But from his point of view, Bernstein probably wanted to make it clear just who decided on the concept of the performance.

OZAWA: I suppose so.

MURAKAMI: Ordinarily, though, in a concerto, who *is*

"the boss"—the soloist or the conductor?

OZAWA: In the case of a concerto, it's mostly the soloist who does the heavy rehearsing. The conductor begins working on it maybe two weeks or so before the performance, but the soloist can be wrestling with it for six months or more. The soloist gets totally inside the piece.

MURAKAMI: Okay, but don't you have situations where the conductor is so far above the soloist that he decides everything without consulting the soloist?

OZAWA: Maybe so. Take the violinist Anne-Sophie Mutter, for example. Maestro Herbert von Karajan discovered her and right away had her recording Mozart and Beethoven concertos. You listen to those, and it's overwhelmingly Karajan's world. So then they thought it would be a good idea for her to play with a different conductor for a change, and Karajan chose me. "Do the next one with Seiji," he said. So we recorded Lalo's Spanish something-or-other. She was barely twenty years old at the time.

MURAKAMI: Edouard Lalo's *Symphonie espagnole*. I'm sure I've got a copy of that somewhere.

Rustling sounds as I hunt for the record, which finally turns up.

OZAWA: This is it! This is it! Wow, I haven't seen this thing for years. The French radio orchestra [Orchestre National de France]. I can't believe you

have *this*. Even I don't have a copy. I used to have
a bunch of them, but I gave them away or people
borrowed them and never brought them back . . .

Gould and Karajan,
Beethoven Piano Concerto no. 3 in C Minor

MURAKAMI: The main thing I wanted you to listen to
today was the Karajan and Gould performance of the
Beethoven Third Piano Concerto. It's not a studio
recording. It was recorded live at a 1957 performance
in Berlin. With the Berlin Philharmonic.

*The orchestra's long, weighty introduction ends, Gould's
piano enters, and the interplay of the two begins (3:19).*

MURAKAMI: Right here, the orchestra and piano are not
together, are they? (?:??)

OZAWA: No, you're right, they're out of sync here. Oh,
here, too, they come in differently. (?:??)

MURAKAMI: Does this mean they haven't completely
worked things out in advance during the rehearsals?

OZAWA: No, I'm sure they must have. But in passages
like this, the orchestra is usually *supposed* to adjust to
what the soloist is playing . . .

MURAKAMI: In those days, Karajan and Gould were
musicians of very different status, I guess.

OZAWA: Well, sure, it was 1957—that was probably not long after Gould's European debut.

MURAKAMI: Tell me if I'm wrong, but that whole first three and a half minutes or so, where it's just the orchestra playing, sounds really Beethovenian to me, tremendously German. But then the young Gould comes in, and it seems he kind of wants to get away from that and loosen it up and make his own music. So then the two sides never quite get together, or they just coolly go off in their own directions and get farther and farther apart. Not that it seems wrong or anything . . .

OZAWA: Gould's music is very free. Also, maybe it stems from the fact that he's Canadian, a non-European living in North America. That might make for a big difference, too. That he doesn't live in the German-speaking world. By contrast, Maestro Karajan's got Beethoven solidly rooted inside him and it's not going to budge. He might as well be out there playing a symphony. Plus he has absolutely no intention of cleverly adapting his style to fit Gould's.

MURAKAMI: Kind of like, "I'm going to make my music the way it's supposed to be made and you can do the rest of it any way you choose." So then in Gould's solo parts and cadenzas and stuff, he's creating his own world. But the two never quite meet—they feel like they're slightly out of kilter.

OZAWA: Which doesn't seem to bother Maestro Karajan at all, wouldn't you say?

MURAKAMI: No, not at all. He's totally immersed in his own world. And Gould's going along at *his* own pace as if he's given up any hope of working together right from the start. It's as if Karajan is building his music straight up from the ground, and Gould's looking out at the horizon the whole time.

OZAWA: Interesting, though, isn't it, listening to it like this? I don't think there's any other conductor who could perform a concerto with such complete confidence as though it were a symphony, not giving any thought to the soloist.

Gould and Bernstein,
Beethoven Piano Concerto no. 3 in C Minor

MURAKAMI: Now I'm going to put on an LP of the same Beethoven concerto, but this time it's a studio recording made in 1959 by Gould and Bernstein with the Columbia Symphony Orchestra (composed of members of the New York Philharmonic), two years after the one with Karajan.

The orchestral introduction. It has a kind of directness, like hurling clay at a stone wall.

OZAWA: This is totally different from Maestro Karajan's, isn't it? It's certainly not a symphony. But the sound of the orchestra is *so* old-fashioned!

MURAKAMI: I never thought of this performance as old-fashioned before, but listening to it right after the

Karajan, it does have a kind of antique sound about it. It's a newer recording, too.

OZAWA: No, it really is old-fashioned.

MURAKAMI: Could it be the recording?

OZAWA: Well, maybe, but it's not just that. For one thing, they've got the mikes too close to the instruments. Everybody used to do it that way in the States. Maestro Karajan's recording captures the orchestra's overall sound.

MURAKAMI: Maybe American listeners preferred that—a forceful, deadish kind of sound.

Gould's piano enters (3:31).

OZAWA: This is two years later than the other one?

MURAKAMI: It's three years before the fuss over the Brahms, two years after the performance with Karajan. What a contrast with the Karajan!

OZAWA: Yes, this one is much more Glenn-style. A lot more relaxed. But to tell you the truth . . . hmmm . . . I wonder if it's okay for me to say this . . . I really shouldn't start comparing Karajan and Bernstein. I'm thinking of the word "direction"—the direction of the music. In Maestro Karajan's case, he had it from birth—the ability to make long phrases. It was something he taught us, the ones who studied with him. Lenny was more what you'd call a genius.

He had an instinctive ability to make long phrases,
but he couldn't do it consciously, intentionally. In
Maestro Karajan's case, he would set his desires in
motion by sheer force of will—inBeethoven, say, or
Brahms. So when Karajan was conducting aBrahms,
for example, his will had this overwhelming
strength. And he would give it priority even if
that meant sacrificing details of the ensemble. He
demanded the same thing from us disciples.

MURAKAMI: Sacrificing details of the ensemble . . .

OZAWA: Meaning if the specific details didn't all work
together, you didn't let it worry you. The most
important thing was to maintain this long, bold line.
In other words, "direction." In music, direction
involves elements of linking. You have detailed
direction and long direction.

*The orchestra plays an ascending three-note figure behind the
piano (4:08-4:19)?? {41.8}.*

OZAWA: These three notes are a case of direction, too:
"La, la, la." Some people can make them as they go
along and some people can't, these parts that flesh
out the music.

MURAKAMI: So in Bernstein's case, regarding what you
call "direction," it's not so much mental calculation
as instinct, something almost physical.

OZAWA: Something like that, I suppose.

MURAKAMI: And when he does it well, it's fine, but when he doesn't, things can come apart.

OZAWA: Right. By contrast, Maestro Karajan sets up the direction clearly beforehand, and he clearly demands it from the orchestra.

MURAKAMI: The music has already formed inside him before the performance.

OZAWA: Pretty much.

MURAKAMI: But Bernstein's not like that.

OZAWA: Maybe not. He's doing it more on the spot, instinctively.

The recording continues. Gould takes a relaxed approach with the solo. (4:33–5:23)

OZAWA: Here, Glenn is being truly free with the music.

MURAKAMI: You mean, compared with the Karajan performance we just heard, Bernstein lets his soloist play more freely—and to some extent he makes his music conform to the flow of the piano? Is that it?

OZAWA: There is some of that, I'd say—in this piece, at least. But with the Brahms, it's not so easy to do, so they had that problem we talked about—especially with that particular piece, the First Piano Concerto.

In the solo, Gould slows his phrasing way down and draws it out (5:01–5:07).

OZAWA: Now *that's* Glenn Gould, where he *slo-o-o-ws* it down like that.

MURAKAMI: He changes the rhythm so freely. That's his style—if he were a writer, I might say it's the way he delivers his sentences. It must be hard to accompany.

OZAWA: Yes, of course it's hard.

MURAKAMI: So in rehearsal, that means you have to understand his breathing and try to match it?

OZAWA: Well, yes, but when you're dealing with musicians of this caliber, they can do it in the actual performance, too. Both sides carefully calculate their moves, though it's not so much a question of calculation as it is of trust. I tend to be on the receiving end of that trust—they take me too seriously. [*Laughs.*] So, often, soloists will do anything they like with me. [*Laughs.*] When a performance like that goes well, though, it's fantastic. The music sounds so free.

The piano plays a descending passage, at the end of which the orchestra enters (7:07–7:11).

OZAWA: Did you notice that? Near the end of the descending passage, just before the orchestra entered, Glenn added a kind of *pon!* sound to the note. (7:10)

MURAKAMI: Added?

OZAWA: Sending a signal to the conductor, saying, "Come in *here*." An accent that is not in the written score. It's just not there.

The piano begins the famous long cadenza near the end of the first movement (13:06).

OZAWA: He's down low, on that low chair of his, playing like this. [*He sinks down in his chair.*] I'm not sure what that's all about.

MURAKAMI: Was Gould already popular back then?

OZAWA: Yes, he was. I was thrilled the first time I met him, of course. But he wouldn't shake hands. He always had gloves on.

MURAKAMI: He was a real eccentric, I guess.

OZAWA: I heard all kinds of weird stories about him when I was music director of the Toronto Symphony Orchestra [from 1965 to 1969]. He invited me to his house, too . . .

Murakami note: Unfortunately, some of the anecdotes revealed at this point cannot be committed to print.
    Final part of the cadenza. The pacing of the notes undergoes dizzying change (??:??-??:??) {44}.

MURAKAMI: His interpretation here is absolutely free, isn't it?

OZAWA: Pure genius. Utterly convincing. But it's very different from the score. Still, it doesn't sound at all strange.

MURAKAMI: When you say things are not in the score, you don't mean just in the cadenza or other solo parts, do you?

OZAWA: No, not just there. That's what's so great about this.

The first movement ends (17:11). I lift the needle.

MURAKAMI: You know, I first heard this Gould and Bernstein recording when I was in high school, and ever since then, this version of the C Minor Concerto has been one of my favorites. I like the first movement, of course, but in the second movement there's that wonderful part where Gould backs up the orchestra with arpeggios.

OZAWA: You mean, where the woodwinds are playing . . .

MURAKAMI: Right, right. An ordinary pianist would make it sound like a straightforward accompaniment, but with Gould you get the feeling that he's playing in direct counterpoint with the orchestra. I've always liked that part for some reason. It's totally different from other pianists' performances.

OZAWA: He would have to be overwhelmingly self-confident to do something like that. Let's listen to it. It just so happens I'm working on this piece now. I'm going to be playing it soon with Mitsuko Uchida. In New York. With the Saito Kinen Orchestra.

MURAKAMI: I'm looking forward to that. I wonder how that performance will go.

I turn the record over and start the second movement, but first we take a short break to drink hot hōjicha tea and eat rice crackers.

MURAKAMI: I would guess that this second movement is difficult to conduct.

OZAWA: It is!

MURAKAMI: I mean, it's so slow! It's beautiful, though.

The piano plays solo. The orchestra enters quietly (1:19).

MURAKAMI: The orchestra's sound is a lot less hard than it was in the first movement.

OZAWA: Yes, it's much better.

MURAKAMI: Maybe they were tense before?

OZAWA: Maybe.

MURAKAMI: The first movement has a real tension running through it. At first it sounded as if there was maybe a duel going on between the soloist and the conductor. Judging from various performances, there seem to be two distinct approaches to the first movement: a confrontational mode and a collaborative mode. Take the 1944 live recording of Rubinstein and Toscanini—it sounds as if the two are fighting. Have you heard it?

OZAWA: No, never.

The woodwinds play, and Gould adds his arpeggios (4:19–5:27)??.

OZAWA: Here it is—the part you were talking about.

MURAKAMI: Yes, this is it. The piano is supposed to be accompanying the orchestra, but Gould's touch is so clear and deliberate.

OZAWA: No, this is certainly not an accompaniment—not in Glenn's mind, at least.

Gould ends a phrase, takes a brief pause, and moves on to the next phrase (5:40)??.

OZAWA: Now that—where he took that pause—that's absolutely Glenn at his freest. It's the hallmark of his style, those perfectly timed empty spaces.

The piano and orchestra intertwine beautifully for a while (?:??–?:??).

OZAWA: Now, we're completely in Glenn Gould's world. He's totally in charge now. In Japan we talk about *ma* in Asian music—the importance of those pauses or empty spaces—but it's there in Western music, too. You get a musician like Glenn Gould, and he's doing exactly the same thing. Not everybody can do it—certainly no ordinary musician. But somebody like him does it all the time.

MURAKAMI: Ordinary musicians don't do it?

OZAWA: No, never. Or if they do, the spaces don't fit in as naturally as this. It doesn't grab you—you don't get drawn in as you do here. That's what putting in these empty spaces, or *ma,* is all about, isn't it? You grab your audience and pull them in. East or West, it's all the same when a virtuoso does it.

MURAKAMI: I know of only one recording that you made of this concerto—with Rudolf Serkin and the Boston Symphony in 1982.

OZAWA: Yes, that was it. We recorded the complete Beethoven piano concerti. We were supposed to do the complete Brahms, too, but he became ill and died not much later.

MURAKAMI: That's a shame.

The orchestra plays a long, quiet phrase (?:??).

MURAKAMI: It must be tough for the orchestra to draw out a long, slow note like this.

OZAWA: It is, very tough.

Piano and orchestra intertwine at a slow tempo.

OZAWA: Oh! They're not together here. (?:??)

MURAKAMI: You're right, they're coming apart.

OZAWA: I was just counting the beat, and maybe he *is* being a little too free.

MURAKAMI: The Karajan and Gould performance we heard had some pretty disjointed parts, too, didn't it?

An extraordinarily slow piano solo (?:??).

MURAKAMI: There can't be too many pianists who can play this second movement without making it sound draggy and boring.

OZAWA: No, it's true.

The second movement ends (10:47).

OZAWA: The first time I ever conducted this concerto, it was with the pianist Byron Janis. We performed it at the Ravinia Festival in Chicago.

MURAKAMI: Oh, yes, I've heard of Byron Janis.

OZAWA: The next was Alfred Brendel. I played the Beethoven Third with him in Salzburg. The next one was probably Mitsuko Uchida. And Serkin came after that.

Serkin and Bernstein, Beethoven Piano Concerto no. 3 in

C Minor

MURAKAMI: I'd like you to listen to one more recording of the Third Piano Concerto.

OZAWA: Fine.

The first movement begins. Opening passage. Uptempo orchestra.

OZAWA: Now, this feels completely different again. It's fast. Wow, it is really fast! They're galloping.

MURAKAMI: Is it rough?

OZAWA: It *is* rough, and they're galloping along.

MURAKAMI: There's a nervous energy in the ensemble playing, too, wouldn't you say?

OZAWA: I would.

The orchestral introduction ends, and the piano charges in at breakneck speed (3:08).

OZAWA: They're both going at it with tremendous gusto. They're perfectly matched.

MURAKAMI: Full speed ahead for both of them! But still, they're gliding along smoothly.

OZAWA: The conductor is clearly using duple time, conducting in 2/2 rather than 4/4.

MURAKAMI: You mean, because the tempo is too fast, he can't help conducting it in 2/2 time?

OZAWA: There are some old printed scores that have it in 2/2, though nowadays 4/4 is considered correct. But the opening of this performance is clearly in 2/2. That's why it sounds as if it's gliding along.

MURAKAMI: You mean to say they decide to do it in 2/2 or 4/4 depending on the speed of the piece?

OZAWA: That's right. If you're going to slow it down somewhat, you have to do it in 4/4. Current research seems to indicate that 4/4 is correct, but back when I was studying it, you could go either way.

MURAKAMI: I didn't know that. This performance is by Rudolf Serkin and Leonard Bernstein with the New York Philharmonic. It was recorded in 1964, five years after the recording with Gould.

OZAWA: It's kind of an inconceivable performance.

MURAKAMI: Why are they in such a hurry?

OZAWA: I can't imagine.

MURAKAMI: I don't think of Rudolf Serkin as a speed demon on the piano. Were performances like this in fashion at that time?

OZAWA: Maybe so. But 1964 . . . hmm . . . Back then, there was a lot of attention paid to the influence on

performance styles by early music, and those tended
to be uptempo without many sustained notes. Also,
stringed instruments had shorter bows. Maybe that
has something to do with it. "Breathless" would be a
way to describe this. It's so un-German!

MURAKAMI: Did the New York Philharmonic tend to be
that way?

OZAWA: Well, sure, compared with the Berlin
Philharmonic or the Vienna Philharmonic, it
couldn't help missing some of that German sound.

MURAKAMI: And I suppose the Boston Symphony
Orchestra is different in its own way.

OZAWA: That's true. Boston has a milder sound. They
don't do performances like this. The musicians
wouldn't like it.

MURAKAMI: Is the Chicago Symphony Orchestra closer to
New York Philharmonic?

OZAWA: Yes. But the Cleveland Orchestra would never
do a performance like this. Cleveland is more like
Boston, even milder. This is way too wild for them.
But the orchestra aside, I can hardly believe this is
Serkin at the piano, just gliding along.

MURAKAMI: Do you think this was Bernstein wanting to
resist the Karajan version of the Beethoven world?

OZAWA: Maybe so. But Lenny made the last movement of

Beethoven's Ninth incredibly slow! It might not be available on record. I saw it on television—one he did in Salzburg, probably with the Berlin or Vienna Philharmonic. It was so slow, I was thinking, "No way!" You know what I'm talking about—the vocal quartet at the end. That part.

I Really Wanted to Do German Music

MURAKAMI: You were saying before that you were with the New York Philharmonic. Did you go to Berlin after that?

OZAWA: Yes. After my first time in Berlin, I was Lenny's assistant with the New York Philharmonic, and then I was called back to Berlin by Maestro Karajan. That's where I debuted. I had my first paying job conducting there. I conducted orchestral works by Maki Ishii and Boris Blacher and a Beethoven symphony—the First or the Second, I'm not sure which.

MURAKAMI: How long were you in New York?

OZAWA: Two and a half years: 1961, 1962, part of 1963. I conducted the Berlin Philharmonic in 1964.

MURAKAMI: Back then, the sound of those two orchestras was as different as night and day—the New York and the Berlin.

OZAWA: Well, sure, they were totally different. They still

are. Even now, with communications so developed, with performers moving so freely among orchestras, and the globalization of culture, they're still totally different.

MURAKAMI: But the sound of the New York Philharmonic in the first half of the sixties was especially hard and aggressive.

OZAWA: Yes, that was Lenny's time. Take his Mahler recordings: they have a hard edge. But this performance we just heard: I've never heard anything of his glide along like that.

MURAKAMI: The Gould we heard before doesn't glide along smoothly like that, either. It's got a pretty hard sound. Do you think it was something that American listeners preferred?

OZAWA: No, not really.

MURAKAMI: But the sound is radically different.

OZAWA: You know how people say that the sound of an orchestra changes with the conductor? That tends to be truer of American orchestras.

MURAKAMI: You mean, European orchestras don't change that much?

OZAWA: You can put a different conductor in front of the Berlin or the Vienna, and the musicians hardly let go of their own special coloration.

MURAKAMI: But all kinds of people took over the New York Philharmonic after Bernstein left—Zubin Mehta, Kurt Masur . . .

OZAWA: And Pierre Boulez . . .

MURAKAMI: I never got the impression the sound of the orchestra changed all that much.

OZAWA: No, I suppose not.

MURAKAMI: I heard the New York Philharmonic a few times playing under other conductors, but it wasn't all that impressive. Why do you think that is?

OZAWA: Well, Lenny wasn't the kind of conductor who used rehearsals to train the orchestra intensively.

MURAKAMI: He was busy doing his own thing.

OZAWA: Hmm, I guess so—a certain kind of genius. Training the orchestra was just not one of his strong points. He was an outstanding educator, that's for sure, but he probably wasn't all that suited to the nitty-gritty of imposing discipline.

MURAKAMI: But isn't the orchestra the same thing for a conductor as literary style is for a novelist? It's natural for a writer to want to perfect his style, so wouldn't a conductor naturally want to work on improving *his* style? At least he demanded a certain level of performance from them, I suppose?

OZAWA: Yes, of course he did.

MURAKAMI: Is it a question of "direction" of the sort we were discussing before?

OZAWA: Yes, to some extent, but Lenny never taught them how to play.

MURAKAMI: Never taught them how to play?

OZAWA: How to play their instruments. He didn't pay a lot of attention to the ensemble approach. Maestro Karajan always used to do that.

MURAKAMI: Practically speaking, what's involved in the "ensemble approach"?

OZAWA: It's all about how you go about making the orchestra sound as an ensemble. Lenny didn't—couldn't—teach us that. By nature. He had a different kind of genius.

MURAKAMI: Are you saying that he couldn't provide practical guidance—"Do this," "Do that"—when he had the musicians there, right in front of him, playing their instruments?

OZAWA: Practically speaking, a good conductor, a professional, instructs his musicians. He'll say, "Listen to this instrument right here," and "Now listen to *this* instrument," and the sound of the orchestra comes together.

MURAKAMI: And each time he does that, then, the musicians concentrate on listening to one instrument, then another . . .

OZAWA: Exactly: "Now listen to the cello." "Now listen to the oboe." Like that. Maestro Karajan was an absolute genius on that front. He would make these points very clearly to the musicians during rehearsal. Lenny could never train an orchestra that way. Or rather, it never really interested him.

MURAKAMI: But he must have had a sound in mind that he wanted the orchestra to produce, didn't he?

OZAWA: Yes, he did, of course.

MURAKAMI: But he couldn't create that sound through his conducting.

OZAWA: And the weird thing is, Lenny was such an outstanding educator. For example, when he delivered the Norton Lectures at Harvard, he did all the necessary preparation for them and delivered a marvelous series of lectures. They're famous. They were made into a book. But in dealing with an orchestra, where you'd expect him to do the same sort of thing, he didn't. He had no concept of "teaching" an orchestra.

MURAKAMI: That *is* weird.

OZAWA: And he was the same with us assistants. We thought of him as our teacher and wanted to learn from him, but he didn't see it that way. You are my *colleagues,* he used to tell us, so if you notice something that needs correcting, I want you to tell me about it, and I'll do the same with you. He had that good American's desire for equality. The way the system was set up, he was supposed to be the boss, but he insisted that he was not our teacher.

MURAKAMI: Not at all European, was he?

OZAWA: No, not the least bit. And he adopted the same attitude toward the orchestra, so he could never really *train* the musicians. Or rather, it took a *long time* to train them to do any one thing. And so, using this egalitarian approach, you wouldn't have the usual situation where the conductor blows up at the musicians, but just the opposite, with the musicians blowing up at the conductor. I saw it happen on several occasions. And they weren't joking around, either: they'd talk right back at him in all seriousness. This was inconceivable with other orchestras.

I had a similar kind of thing happen to me much later on, after we started up the Saito Kinen Orchestra. Most of the members of that orchestra were old friends of mine. There aren't too many of them left now, but the first ten years or so, the others would tell me exactly what they thought straight to my face. That was the kind of atmosphere we had, but some people hated it. Musicians who came from the outside. They couldn't get used to it. They'd complain that it would take forever if we worked out every little thing that way. I was the maestro, after all: I didn't have to let every single musician have his say. But that was exactly what I wanted to do. I used to make a point of asking them to tell me what they thought.

In Lenny's case, though, he wasn't dealing with an orchestra made up of friends who came together of their own volition to play together but rather an old, established professional organization. When he treated them as equals, one thing after another would come up, so rehearsals took much longer than they had to. I can't tell you how many times I saw this happen.

MURAKAMI: They wouldn't just do what he told them.

OZAWA: I suppose he was trying to be a "good American," and maybe sometimes he overdid it.

MURAKAMI: Egalitarianism aside, I'm sure he felt terribly frustrated if he couldn't actually get the orchestra to produce the sound he wanted.

OZAWA: I'm sure he did. Everybody called him "Lenny." They call me by my first name, too, but it was way more extreme with him. Some musicians would assume, as a result, that they could get away with anything, and they'd yell stuff like, "Hey, Lenny, that must be wrong." Keep that up, and your rehearsals won't go anywhere. They won't end on time, for one thing.

MURAKAMI: No, but I imagine you get some real

excitement and some great music when things go well—and kind of a mess when things don't.

OZAWA: True. The music can lose its coherence. That would happen now and then. Back when Saito Kinen was just getting started, we had people calling me "Seiji" and people calling me "Mr. Ozawa," and people calling me "Maestro." It was pretty confusing. That's when it struck me—it must have been like this for Lenny.

MURAKAMI: I don't suppose it was like that with Maestro Karajan.

OZAWA: No, he never listened to anybody. If the sound he wanted and the sound the orchestra was producing were different, it was strictly the orchestra's fault. He'd make them do it over and over until they played the way he wanted it.

MURAKAMI: All very clear and precise.

OZAWA: In Lenny's case, the musicians would talk with each other during rehearsals. That always bothered me. So during my rehearsals in Boston, if somebody started talking, I would stare straight at them, and the private conversations would stop. Lenny would never do that.

MURAKAMI: How about Maestro Karajan?

OZAWA: At first I thought he kept a tight lid on stuff like that. But then, one time, near the end of his career, when he brought the Berlin Philharmonic to Japan, he was putting them through a rehearsal of Mahler's Ninth, to be performed after they got back to Germany. In other words, this was not a piece the orchestra was to play the next day, so they were not really into it. I was in the hall, listening to the rehearsal, and the musicians were all talking to each other. At one point, the maestro stopped the music to point out something to them, and they just kept on talking. So he turned and yelled to me, "Hey, Seiji, have you ever heard an orchestra make such a racket during rehearsals?" [*He laughs.*] So what was *I* supposed to say?

MURAKAMI: Maybe he had lost some of his authority by then. I seem to recall there were some problems with the Berlin Philharmonic in those days.

OZAWA: Yes, but they made up in the end, so by then, that was all in the past. But things were pretty bad for a while.

MURAKAMI: When I watched your rehearsals, I often noticed you sort of cuing the orchestra with subtle facial expressions—kind of like, "All right, now I'm going to show you *this* face."

OZAWA: Hmm . . . I wonder . . . I'm not sure what you mean.

MURAKAMI: You will agree that the Boston's sound changes a lot with its conductors.

OZAWA: Yes, it does.

MURAKAMI: For a long time the conductor was Charles Munch, then Erich Leinsdorf, and then, I think, it was you, am I right?

OZAWA: After Leinsdorf came William Steinberg.

MURAKAMI: Oh, right.

OZAWA: Maybe three or four years after I stepped in, the sound changed—to the clear, concentrated German style I call "into the strings." The players put the bow in deep. It makes for a heavier sound. Until then the Boston sound was always light and beautiful. That's because they used to concentrate on French music. Munch and Pierre Monteux had a major influence. Monteux wasn't music director by that point, but he was there all the time. And Leinsdorf wasn't all that German, either.

MURAKAMI: So when your time came, the orchestra changed its sound.

OZAWA: I really wanted to do German music. I wanted to do Brahms and Beethoven and Bruckner and Mahler. So I had them play "into the strings." The concertmaster resisted, and he ended up quitting. Joseph Silverstein. He was also assistant conductor, and he hated that style of playing. He thought it muddied the sound. He strongly objected, but finally, I was the conductor, so all he could do was resign. He became independent after that and was appointed music director of the Utah Symphony.

MURAKAMI: But you also led the Orchestre de Paris for a while. Does that mean you could do both kinds of music?

OZAWA: Not really. I studied with Maestro Karajan, so my music is basically German. I loved Munch, though, after I went to Boston, so I played a lot of French music. I conducted the complete works of both Ravel and Debussy. Recorded them, too. I learned French music after going to Boston. I didn't learn any of that from Maestro Karajan—oh, maybe *Afternoon of a Faun*.

MURAKAMI: No kidding? I always thought French music was your first specialty.

OZAWA: No, not at all. Never before Boston. The only thing of Berlioz's I ever did until then was his *Symphonie fantastique*. I'm pretty sure that everything else I did of his was at the request of the record company.

MURAKAMI: Isn't Berlioz difficult? Sometimes when I'm listening to him I can't tell what's going on.

OZAWA: Difficult? His music is crazy! Sometimes I don't know what's going on, either! Which may be why his music is suited to being performed by an Asian conductor. I can do what I want with it. Once a long time ago I conducted Berlioz's opera *Benvenuto Cellini* in Rome. Wow, I just let myself go and did anything I felt like. The audience loved it.

MURAKAMI: There's no way you can do that with German music, I suppose.

OZAWA: No, no. Oh, and Berlioz has this Requiem . . . what was it called? . . . oh, yes, *Grande Messe des Morts,* the one that uses eight sets of timpani. Talk about taking a free hand with a piece of music! I conducted it first in Boston, then went all over the place with it. When Munch died, I performed it in Salzburg in his honor, conducting the ensemble that he had put together, the Orchestre de Paris.

MURAKAMI: So when you were playing all that French music in Boston, it was not because you chose it, but because the record company requested it?

OZAWA: That's true. Also, the musicians wanted to play French music. To use it to "sell" the orchestra. So I found myself conducting lots of pieces for the first time in my life.

MURAKAMI: The music you did while you were in Germany, you say, was overwhelmingly German music?

OZAWA: Right. Maestro Karajan did almost nothing else. Well, they did have me doing some Bartók and things, too.

MURAKAMI: But after you took up your post in Boston, you spent a lot of time introducing the "into the strings" technique, creating an environment in which you could perform German music?

OZAWA: Yes. So then a number of German conductors—[Klaus] Tennstedt, Masur—took a real liking to Boston and came as guest conductors almost every year.

Fifty Years Ago,
I Went Crazy Over Mahler

MURAKAMI: When did you start conducting Mahler?

OZAWA: I started liking Mahler under Lenny's influence. My time as his assistant just happened to coincide with the time he was recording the complete Mahler symphonies. I learned them while I was with him, and after I left for Toronto and San Francisco, I got started trying the complete Mahler right away. Once I settled in Boston, I went through all the symphonies twice. While I was in Toronto and San Francisco, though, Lenny was the only conductor anywhere doing the complete Mahler symphonies.

MURAKAMI: Karajan didn't do much Mahler, did he?

OZAWA: No, hardly any, for a very long time. Which is why he had *me* conducting a lot of Mahler while I was in Berlin. I did a lot with the Vienna Philharmonic, too. That way, I concentrated pretty heavily on Mahler at first. The Vienna is visiting Japan now, you know, and if my health weren't so bad, I was supposed to conduct the Mahler Ninth. That and the Bruckner Ninth.

MURAKAMI: Incredible. That's heavy lifting!

OZAWA: On this trip, they performed the Bruckner Ninth, but not the Mahler. They're saving it for when I get better.

MURAKAMI: You've got to put all your energy into rehabilitation.

OZAWA: You said it. [*Laughs.*] But anyway, back then I was absolutely crazy about Mahler. That was fifty years ago!

MURAKAMI: With all that behind you, it's no wonder German music is so central to the Saito Kinen Orchestra.

OZAWA: True. The first time we ever did French music was the Berlioz *Fantastique* three years ago.

MURAKAMI: They also did that Poulenc opera [*Les Mamelles de Tirésias*].

OZAWA: Oh, right, right! That's two French pieces. We also did Honegger. He's Swiss, not French, but his stuff is like French music. Finally, though, Saito Kinen does Brahms best.

MURAKAMI: Yes, they're very good.

OZAWA: Professor Saito's teaching had a lot to do with that, and a lot of the people who spent time abroad were in Germany and Austria. The people who got together in Matsumoto to form the Saito Kinen had usually been in Berlin or Vienna or Frankfurt or Cologne or Düsseldorf. Places like that. Some had been to the States, too, come to think of it.

MURAKAMI: The Saito Kinen Orchestra sounds a lot like the Boston Symphony, don't you think?

OZAWA: That's so true! Absolutely.

MURAKAMI: How do you describe it? Silky? Open? Elastic? I was in Boston from 1993 into 1995 and attending Boston Symphony performances near the end of your time with the orchestra, and I had the impression that the sound had been cooked down to its essence, that it had become somehow denser than what I had heard before, quite different from the earlier Boston sound.

OZAWA: You may be right about that. I was pouring myself into it in those days, doing everything I could to raise the level of the orchestra's precision. I was determined to make it one of the ten greatest orchestras in the world. I wanted to bring the finest possible guest conductors to Boston. To do that, I knew I would have to improve the orchestra. And in fact, the orchestra did win the favor of a lot of conductors, who agreed to come and perform for us. Among the young ones, we had Simon Rattle, as well as the [older] ones I mentioned before,

Tennstedt and Masur, and the period-instrument
authority Christopher Hogwood.

MURAKAMI: I came back to Japan after my time in
Boston, and when I heard the Saito Kinen Orchestra
with you on the podium, it struck me how much
more open and buoyant it sounded. I don't know
about its density, but my impression was that it
was tremendously reminiscent of the old Boston
Symphony sound.

What Is the New Beethoven
Performance Style?

MURAKAMI: I'd like to ask you one more thing about
performing Beethoven. In the old days, there was a
kind of standard style, as represented by somebody
like Wilhelm Furtwängler. Karajan more or less
carried on that approach. At some point, though,
people got a little tired of that Beethoven image
and started searching for a new one. Around 1960.
Gould's approach is one of those, I guess—keeping
the framework intact but trying to move the music
around freely within it. Kind of like dislodging
various elements, pulling them apart and putting
them back together again. There were several
different movements like that, but no definable
new format ever took shape—one that could stand
up against the orthodox performance style. Am I
making sense here?

OZAWA: Sure, sure.

MURAKAMI: It seems to me, though, that lately things have started to change. For one thing, the sound has tended, in fact, to grow thinner, hasn't it?

OZAWA: Yes, you see less of the old tendency to do Beethoven the way you do Brahms—putting together a huge string section to make a thick, heavy sound. This probably has a lot to do with the rise of the period-instrument people.

MURAKAMI: I bet you're right. They're using fewer string players these days. And in concerto performances, too, the soloist doesn't have to work so hard anymore to make a big sound. Even if they don't go so far as to use a period fortepiano, the performer can play a modern piano to get a quieter, fortepiano sound. With the overall sound smaller and thinner, the performer can move more freely within a narrower dynamic range. That way, the Beethoven performance style has begun to move away from what it once was.

OZAWA: That's definitely true in the case of the symphonies. Instead of using the orchestra as one big, powerful unit to make music, the style has changed so as to make each part, each component, more audible.

MURAKAMI: So you can hearthe inner voices.

OZAWA: Right, right.

MURAKAMI: The Saito Kinen's Beethoven performances

feel very much like that.

OZAWA: Because Professor Saito was like that. So when I conducted the Berlin Philharmonic, I was often criticized for making the orchestra sound thin. Maestro Karajan used to tell me that, too, at first. He often made fun of me. The first time I conducted Mahler's First, Maetro Karajan attended the concert. I was cueing everybody. You know, telling every musician where to come in—"You come in here . . . You come in *here*." Doing that makes you very busy.

MURAKAMI: *Very* busy, I would think!

OZAWA: So Maestro Karajan says to me, "Seiji, you don't have to work so hard with my orchestra. Just do the overall conducting, and they'll take care of the rest." But, you know, by cueing them like that, I made the sound of the orchestra more open and transparent. The cues made each of the musicians come through more clearly. True, the overall conducting is very important, but it's also important to bring out the details. The maestro admonished me the day after the concert, at breakfast. He was pretty angry. "Stop cueing the musicians," he said. "That is not the job of the conductor." I remember how scared I was conducting that night's concert. I figured he wouldn't come again, but I was shaking in my boots, wondering what I should do if he did. As it turned out, he never showed. [*Laughs.*]

MURAKAMI: In the old days, it was okay for the orchestra to have one, larger sound.

OZAWA: Right. The recordings were like that, too, of course. Maestro Karajan had a particular Berlin church he liked to record in. And when recording in Paris, he would always specify a hall where the sound echoed as in a church—places like the Salle Wagram, a big old dance hall.

MURAKAMI: A church and a dance hall! [*Laughs.*]

OZAWA: That was mainstream recording back then, to do it in a place with a good echo. The selling point of the space was, like, how many seconds a reverberation lasted. They tried to capture the sound as a single whole. In New York, too, they would do studio recordings in Manhattan Center, another hall with a good echo. Recordings of live performances were not that popular. Instead, everybody would choose a place with a big echo and do their recordings there.

MURAKAMI: Boston's Symphony Hall has that kind of sound, too, doesn't it?

OZAWA: That's right. In the old days, they would take out half the seats to record, and have the orchestra perform where the seats would have been. To get a really nice echo. In my time, though, we tried to get a truer sound by playing in the normal position on stage.

MURAKAMI: So each voice could be heard.

OZAWA: Well, for that, too, but mainly so people could

hear a performance that sounded as though an actual orchestra in performance was playing—without all the echo, keeping the reverberation as short as possible.

MURAKAMI: Now that you mention it, the Gould/ Karajan performance we heard before had rich reverberations.

OZAWA: Maestro Karajan always gave the recording engineer detailed instructions regarding the way he wanted things to sound. Then he would adjust the phrasing to work within the framework of the sound. He knew just how to create the music so that the swelling of the phrase would come out between reverberations.

MURAKAMI: Like singing in the shower.

OZAWA: Sure, if you want to put it that way!

MURAKAMI: What kind of space does the Saito Kinen record in?

OZAWA: A very ordinary theater, the Matsumoto Bunka Kaikan in Nagano Prefecture. The sound there is hard, with very little reverberation.

MURAKAMI: So that's why it's possible to hear all the fine movements in the sound.

OZAWA: That's it. But maybe it's a little *too* clean. I'd like to have just a touch of an echo, but it's hard to find the perfect hall. The best space in Japan now is that place in Tokyo . . . what is it? . . . Sumida Triphony Hall. That's the best hall to record in in Tokyo.

MURAKAMI: Moving back to the subject of modern performances of Beethoven, does this involve reducing the number of stringed instruments—or if not actually reducing them, at least thinning down the sound?

OZAWA: Maybe it's more a matter of splitting up the various sounds so you can hear everything from within the overall sound more clearly. That's probably the dominant tendency these days, and it's absolutely something that has come from period-instrument performances.

MURAKAMI: I suppose orchestras in Beethoven's day had fewer strings.

OZAWA: Yes, of course. So for example in the Third Symphony, the *Eroica,* some conductors will cut the number of strings way down, with, like, six first violins. I don't go that far.

Beethoven with Period Instruments, Immerseel at the Fortepiano

MURAKAMI: Now let's listen to Beethoven's Third Piano Concerto played on period instruments.

OZAWA: This has such a strong reverberation! Listen,

right here, the way the next note comes in before the previous one dies. That shouldn't be happening, ordinarily.

MURAKAMI: The reverberation *is* strong.

The three-note figure sounds in the orchestra's introductory part {72} (?:??).

OZAWA: Now here, Maestro Karajan would have played that *tahn, taahn, taaahn,* adding "direction," but this orchestra just goes *tahn, tahn, tahn.* It's a huge difference. Of course, this is interesting in its own way.

MURAKAMI: You can hear the sound of each instrument independently.

OZAWA: Right. Like that—the sound of the oboe stands out. That's how it's done.

MURAKAMI: It's getting close to chamber music.

OZAWA: Exactly. This kind of performance has its own persuasiveness.

MURAKAMI: The Saito Kinen Orchestra tends to be like this, too.

OZAWA: It does. Everybody has his say—each of the instruments.

MURAKAMI: In many subtle ways, it sounds very different

from earlier orchestras.

OZAWA: Yes, but you can't hear the consonants in *this* orchestra we're listening to.

MURAKAMI: The consonants?

OZAWA: The leading edge of each sound.

MURAKAMI: I still don't get it.

OZAWA: Hmm, how can I put it? If you sing *a-a-a,* it's all vowel. But if you add consonants to each of the *a*'s, you get something like *ta-ka-ka* or *ha-sa-sa.* It's a question of which consonants you add. It's easy enough to make the first *ta* or *ha,* but the hard part is what follows. If it's all consonant—*ta-t-t*—the melody falls apart. But the expression of the notes changes depending on whether you go *ta-raa-raa* or *ta-waa-waa.* To have a good musical ear means having control over the consonants and vowels. When the instruments of this orchestra talk to each other, the consonants don't come out. It's not unpleasant, though.

MURAKAMI: I see what you mean. But if they didn't have the reverberation, it might be tiring to listen to.

OZAWA: True. Which may be why they chose the hall they did for recording.

MURAKAMI: I do find period instrument performances fresh and interesting, but you don't actually hear many of them aside from genuine baroque music, especially with a Beethoven or a Schubert. More often, you hear orchestras using modern instruments that have been indirectly influenced by period performances.

OZAWA: You may be right. In that sense, these are interesting times for music.

On Gould Again

MURAKAMI: What interests me when I'm listening to Gould is the way he deliberately brings contrapuntal elements into performances of Beethoven. He doesn't just try to harmonize with the orchestra but deliberately overlays their music with his, and, as a result, creates a natural tension between the two. This was a fresh interpretation of Beethoven.

OZAWA: That's true, but what's strange is that no one has emerged since his death to carry on and develop that stance of his. Really, no one. I guess Gould was a genius. He may have influenced others, but the way I see it, there is nobody like him, nobody with that kind of courage.

MURAKAMI: Even those few who bring a lot of invention to their performances seem to do so without a genuine sense of necessity and substance.

OZAWA: Mitsuko Uchida is a courageous pianist. And Martha Argerich has a lot of that quality.

MURAKAMI: Do you think female pianists have more of it?

OZAWA: Yes, the women are bolder.

MURAKAMI: There's a male pianist named Valery Afanassiev.

OZAWA: Never heard of him.

MURAKAMI: He's a contemporary musician who brings a lot of inventiveness to his playing—and he performs this Third Piano Concerto. *Very* interesting, intellectual, passionate—unique. But you get tired listening to him. His second movement is just *too* slow. "All right, I get it, I get it!" you want to say. He thinks too much. Gould never had that. Even when his playing is weirdly slow, he makes you listen to the end. You don't get tired of him halfway through. His inner rhythms must be terrifically strong.

OZAWA: It's those empty moments of his—the way he puts in *ma*. He's amazing. Listening to him today for the first time in a long time, I realized all over again how well he does that. It's sheer guts, something he was born with, and absolutely not an act.

MURAKAMI: But there's no one like him. You watch a video of him playing, and he'll suspend a hand in the air and twitch his fingers slightly to add vibrato to the sound of the piano—which is of course a physical impossibility.

OZAWA: There's no question he was an eccentric. When

I first met him, I was just getting started, and my
English was terrible. Thinking back on it now, it
seems like such a wasted opportunity! If only I could
have talked to him more! I could even have had
conversations with Bruno Walter back then if my
English had been halfway decent. Think of all the
things I could have talked about with Glenn! What a
shame! Lenny was a tremendously kind man and he
could accommodate my broken English, so we had
wonderful long conversations.

Rudolf Serkin and Ozawa, Beethoven Piano Concerto no. 3 in C Minor

MURAKAMI: Now I'd like to listen to your 1982 recording
of the Third Piano Concerto with Rudolf Serkin.
You don't mind, do you?

OZAWA: No, not at all.

MURAKAMI: Because some people don't like to listen to
recordings of their own performances.

OZAWA: No, I'm fine. I haven't heard it for a long time,
so I don't remember what it was like. It'll probably
sound heavy to me now.

MURAKAMI: No, it's not heavy at all.

OZAWA: I wonder.

I lower the needle to the record. The orchestra's introduction begins.

OZAWA: Very quiet opening, isn't it?

*The tranquil opening gradually begins to modulate (?:??)
{77}.*

OZAWA: Now, *this* is "direction." Hear those four notes?
Tahn-tahn-tahn-tahn. It's the first fortissimo of the
piece. I put it together that way quite consciously.

*The orchestra swells and comes to the foreground (?:??)
{77}.*

OZAWA: I should have done more of that, given it still
clearer "direction"—like *tah-tah-taahn* with a more
emphatic accent, more boldly. Of course the score
doesn't say "more boldly" anywhere. You have to
read that in for yourself.

*The orchestra creates a clearer musical structure {78.1}
(?:??).*

OZAWA: There, the "direction" is taking shape, though
it's still not bold enough.

The piano enters (3:22).

MURAKAMI: Serkin is really moving the sound along, isn't
he—taking a very positive approach toward adding
his own articulation? {78.5 ??}

OZAWA: Yes, he knows that this is probably his last

performance of this piece, that he won't have another chance to record it while he's alive, and so he's going to play it the way he wants to. Period.

MURAKAMI: The mood is totally different from the high-strung performance he gave with Bernstein, isn't it?

OZAWA: Pure elegance, his sound.

MURAKAMI: But your approach here with the orchestra is very serious, isn't it?

OZAWA: You think so? [*Laughs.*]

MURAKAMI: Serkin is making music the way he wants to.

Behind the piano, the strings play in spiccato (with lightly springing bows) (?:??).

MURAKAMI: Isn't this a little too slow, this part?

OZAWA: True, both of us are playing too cautiously— both Serkin and I. This should be livelier, as if we're chatting with each other.

The cadenza begins (12:50).

MURAKAMI: I'm particularly fond of Serkin's approach to this cadenza. It's like he's climbing a hill with a load on his back. There's nothing fluent here; it's almost as though he's stuttering—you have to admire him for it. Will he be okay? Will he make it all the way to the top? You worry for him as you listen, and the music gets to you.

OZAWA: Nowadays, everybody just tears right through it. It's nice to have one like this, too.

The pianist's fingers seem to falter for a split second (14:56)??.

MURAKAMI: Ooh, he was kind of flirting with danger there, wasn't he? That can be nice, too, though.

OZAWA: Ha ha, really, it was touch-and-go.

The cadenza ends, and the orchestra slowly begins to play (16:02).

MURAKAMI: The orchestra's entry here is so delicate, I tense up.

OZAWA: Mmm, I see what you mean. But the timpanist here is excellent. He's very good—Vic Firth. He was with the Saito Kinen Orchestra for almost twenty years—from the beginning until three years ago.

The first movement ends (16:53).

OZAWA: It was a lot better toward the end.

MURAKAMI: I think so. Really working together.

OZAWA: Fine cadenza, though, you're right.

MURAKAMI: I get this sudden wave of exhaustion

whenever I hear it. It's good, though. It brings out his personality.

OZAWA: How many years before his death was this, I wonder?

MURAKAMI: Well, the recording was made in 1982, and Serkin died in '91, so nine years before. He was seventy-nine at the time.

OZAWA: So he died at eighty-eight.

MURAKAMI: Who set the tempo in this recording, I wonder—him or you?

OZAWA: He was the old maestro in this one, of course, so we did it exactly as he wanted it. Straight through from rehearsals. I did my best to match his approach from the very first *tutti*. Here, I'm conducting strictly as an accompanist.

MURAKAMI: Did you do a lot of rehearsing?

OZAWA: Two solid days. Then the performance, and then we recorded.

MURAKAMI: So what you're saying is that Mr. Serkin decided a lot of stuff beforehand.

OZAWA: The most important thing is the character of the piece. That was for him to decide. But listening to it again now, I can see I wasn't bold enough. I should have plunged right in. It's such a well-defined piece, I should have taken a more positive approach, but I don't know, it's not that I was too restrained, exactly . . .

MURAKAMI: As a listener, it did seem to me to have a certain indefinable air of restraint about it.

OZAWA: Well, it's true I was trying not to overdo it. But listening to it now, with him playing so freely, making exactly the kind of music he wanted to do, I can't help thinking I should have tried more to match him, to conduct with a little more freedom.

MURAKAMI: He's like an old master of classical *rakugo* storytelling, just going along with his instincts.

OZAWA: Yes, he's completely at ease, not the least bit concerned if his fingers stumble a little. That part where you said he was kind of flirting with danger—he really was. But that just adds to the overall flavor when you're that good.

MURAKAMI: When I first heard this recording, I worried that his action or touch or whatever you call it was just a bit slower than it used to be—but, strangely enough, the more I listened to it, the less it bothered me.

OZAWA: That's because a musician's special flavor comes out with age. His playing at that stage may have more interesting qualities than at the height of his career.

MURAKAMI: That was certainly true of Rubinstein when he recorded the complete Beethoven piano concertos with Barenboim and the London Philharmonic in his eighties. His touch is the tiniest bit slower than it used to be, but the music is so rich you eventually forget about that.

OZAWA: Speaking of Rubinstein, he was very fond of me.

MURAKAMI: I didn't know that.

OZAWA: I went all around the world with him for maybe three years, conducting accompaniment for him. It was while I was still in Toronto, so it was a very long time ago. I remember he played a recital at La Scala that I conducted using the La Scala Orchestra. Hmm, let's see, what did we play then? A Tchaikovsky concerto and maybe a Mozart or the Beethoven Third or Fourth. He would usually play a Tchaikovsky after the intermission, though sometimes it would be a Rachmaninoff. No, I think it was a Chopin concerto, not Rachmaninoff. Yes, we went all over, performing together. He'd always take me with him. We'd meet at his place in Paris and leave from there. It was always quite a trip, but the pace was relaxed—say, a whole week at La Scala. We went to San Francisco, too. We would go to places he liked, have two or three rehearsals with the local orchestra, and give a performance. I always had the most marvelous meals with him.

MURAKAMI: So you were always playing with different orchestras. Isn't that hard?

OZAWA: No, no, I got used to it. It's fun being a hired conductor. As I said, I think I did it for three years. I especially remember one Italian vermouth . . . Carpano . . . Punt e Mes Carpano. I learned about it from him.

MURAKAMI: He enjoyed living well, didn't he?

OZAWA: Very much so. He had this personal secretary he took everywhere with him, a tall, slim woman. His wife was always complaining about his ways. He was quite the ladies' man. And he loved to eat well. In Milan he'd go to this incredibly high-end restaurant and order stuff they made especially for him. I never had to look at the menu—I'd just let him do all the ordering, and they'd bring out these special dishes. That's when I learned what real luxury living could be.

MURAKAMI: He was probably very different from Serkin.

OZAWA: Like night and day. They were complete opposites. Serkin was totally serious, a man of simple tastes. He was a devout Jew.

MURAKAMI: You're close to his son Peter, aren't you?

OZAWA: Peter was a real rebel in his youth and caused his father a lot of problems. So Rudolf asked me to look after him. I saw a lot of Peter from the time he was eighteen or so. I guess Rudolf had faith in me, felt that I'd know how to deal with his son. Peter and I did a lot of things together at first. We're still friends, but in those days we'd go to Toronto or Ravinia and places like that every year and perform together. We often performed the Beethoven Violin Concerto arranged for piano.

MURAKAMI: There's a recording of that, with the New Philharmonia Orchestra.

OZAWA: Hmm, now that you mention it, there *was* a recording, wasn't there? That was the first and last time I did that, it's such an odd piece, the Piano Concerto op. 61a.

MURAKAMI: You never recorded with Rubinstein, did you?

OZAWA: No, never. I was so young then, and I wasn't signed to any record company. I hardly recorded anything in those days.

MURAKAMI: It'd be nice to have some new recordings of the Beethoven piano concertos with the Saito Kinen Orchestra. Come to think of it, though, I can't think of an appropriate pianist offhand. Lots of people have already done the complete concertos.

OZAWA: How about Krystian Zimerman?

MURAKAMI: He was doing the complete concertos with Bernstein—and the Vienna Philharmonic, I think. Bernstein died before they could finish, though, so he did double duty on the rest of them, both playing and conducting. He ended up doing all the concertos. They're on DVD, too.

OZAWA: Now that you mention it, I heard him play a
Brahms piano concerto with Bernstein in Vienna.

MURAKAMI: I didn't know they did that. But in the
Beethoven concertos they recorded together,
Bernstein is the one who sets the pace virtually all
the way through. Zimerman's piano is formally
perfect and quite wonderful, but he is not the kind
of musician who takes command, so the orchestra is
pretty much in control—or so it sounded to me, as if
Zimerman was in perfect agreement with Bernstein.

OZAWA: I got very friendly with Zimerman in my Boston
days. He liked Boston a lot, too, and he was talking
about buying a house and moving there. I thought
it was a great idea and urged him to do it, but after
two fruitless months of looking all over for a house,
he gave up. It was really a shame: he was saying
he'd rather live in Boston than Switzerland or New
York, but he just couldn't find a house where he
could freely play the piano without disturbing the
neighbors.

MURAKAMI: He's a tasteful, rather intellectual pianist.
I went to hear him once a long time ago when he
came to Japan. He was *so* young! And his Beethoven
sonatas sounded new and fresh.

OZAWA: You're right, though, if you exclude the pianists
who have already done the complete Beethoven
concertos, I really can't think of someone I'd like to

record them with.

Mitsuko Uchida and Kurt Sanderling, Beethoven Piano Concerto no. 3 in C Minor

MURAKAMI: Now, finally, let's listen to Mitsuko Uchida's performance. I love the way she plays the second movement, and we're running out of time, so let's take a different approach and start with that.

The movement begins with a soft, tranquil solo.

OZAWA [*as soon as the music begins*]: Her sound is truly beautiful. She has such a great ear.

Soon the orchestra steals in (1:19).

MURAKAMI: This is the Royal Concertgebouw Orchestra.

OZAWA: That's a fine hall, too.

The piano and orchestra intertwine (2:32).

OZAWA [*deeply moved*]: It's wonderful to think that Japan has produced such a marvelous pianist.

MURAKAMI: Her touch is so clear. You can hear everything so clearly—every strong note, every quiet note. She plays with total mastery: there is nothing vague in her performance.

OZAWA: She's utterly confident.

The solo piano continues with long, evocative pauses [ma] (5:11).

OZAWA: Listen to that, those perfect moments of silence. This is exactly the passage where we heard Gould using those tiny silences.

MURAKAMI: That's true, now that you mention it. The way she puts in those silent intervals, is it? Her free spacing of the notes is somehow reminiscent of Gould.

OZAWA: Yes, very similar.

The piano's incredibly subtle solo ends, and the orchestra glides in again. This is truly miraculous music making. The two listeners groan simultaneously (5:42).

OZAWA: What an ear she has for music!

The piano and orchestra intertwine again for a time.

OZAWA: Three measures back, the piano and orchestra were out of sync. I'll bet Mitsuko is pretty angry right about now. [*Laughs.*] (??:??)

Beautiful piano solo unfolds, like an ink painting in space. A string of notes, perfectly formed and brimming with courage, each note thinking for itsel. (8:39–9:33).

MURAKAMI: I could listen to this part and never tire of it. The tension never lets up no matter how slowly it's played.

The piano solo ends, and the orchestra enters (9:33).

MURAKAMI: This re-entry of the orchestra seems hard to do.

OZAWA: They should have done better.

MURAKAMI: Really?

OZAWA: It can be done better.

The second movement ends (10:27).

OZAWA [*deeply moved*]: Wow, this is just amazing. Mitsuko is an incredible pianist. When did they record this?

MURAKAMI: In 1994.

OZAWA: Sixteen years ago, huh?

MURAKAMI: I don't know how many times I've listened to it, it never gets old. So graceful, so transparent.

OZAWA: Of course, this second movement itself is a very special piece of music. I don't think Beethoven ever did anything else quite like it.

MURAKAMI: To draw out a slow piece of music like this takes tremendous power, I would think—both for the pianist and for the orchestra. Especially those moments where the orchestra re-enters. As an observer, those seem especially tough.

OZAWA: They *are* tough. The hard part is making the breaths match. The strings, the woodwinds, the conductor, everybody has to be breathing together. It's not easy! You just heard an example of what happens when it doesn't go very smoothly.

MURAKAMI: I suppose you can work all that out in rehearsal—"We come in here, with this exact timing"—but a different flow takes over in the actual performance. Things like that must happen.

OZAWA: Yes, of course they do. And then the orchestra's entry can be thrown off.

MURAKAMI: When you've got an empty moment and you have to glide into it, the musicians all watch the conductor, I suppose?

OZAWA: That's right. I'm the one responsible for putting it all together in the end, so they're all looking at me. In that passage we just heard, the piano goes *tee* . . . and then there's an empty space [*ma*], and the orchestra glides in, right? It makes a huge difference whether you play *tee-yataa* or *tee* . . . *yataa*. Or there are some people who add expression by coming in without a break: *teeyantee*. So if you do it by kind of "sneaking in," as they say in English, the way we heard, it can go wrong. It's tremendously difficult to make the orchestra all breathe together at exactly the same point. You have all these different instruments in different positions on the stage, so each of them hears the piano differently, and that tends to throw off the breath of each player by a little. So to avoid that kind of slip-up, the conductor should come in with a big expression on his face like this—*teeyantee.*

MURAKAMI: So you indicate the empty interval [*ma*] with your face and body language.

OZAWA: Right, right. You show with your face and the movement of your hands whether they should take a long breath or a short breath. That little bit makes a big difference.

MURAKAMI: So the conductor has to decide how to proceed on a moment-to-moment basis?

OZAWA: Pretty much. It's not so much a matter of calculation as it is the conductor's coming to understand, through experience, how to breathe. You'd be amazed, though, how many conductors can't do that. They never get any better.

MURAKAMI: Can the musicians and conductor understand each other through eye contact?

OZAWA: Yes, of course. Musicians love conductors who can do that. It makes it a lot easier for them. Say in this second movement, the conductor has to become the representative of the players and make the final decision of how they're going to come in—whether it's going to be *haa* or *ha* or, more ambiguously, with emotion, . . . *ha* . . . And then he has to convey his decision to everybody else. Doing it that last way is a little dangerous, I suppose. But you make everybody properly aware of the danger, and then you all go in together—you can do it that way, too.

MURAKAMI: The more you tell me, the more I see how hard it is to conduct an orchestra. Writing a novel all by yourself is way easier than that. [*Laughter.*]

On Manic Record Collectors

OZAWA: Now, you might find this a little offensive, but I've
never liked those manic record collectors—people with lots
of money, superb music reproduction equipment, and tons
of records. Back when I was poor, I occasionally went to
the homes of a few people like that. You go in, and they've
got everything ever recorded by Furtwängler, say, but the
people themselves are so busy they can't spend any time
at home listening to music.

MURAKAMI: People with money are usually busy.

OZAWA: True. But throughout our conversations, I've been so
impressed by how deeply you have listened to each piece
of music. Or so it seems to me. In your case, you *have*
collected a lot of records, but you don't listen to them like
one of those collectors.

MURAKAMI: Well, I've got lots of free time and I'm mostly at
home, so luckily I can listen to music from morning to night,

not just collect records.

OZAWA: You're not concerned with the record jackets—you're listening to what's inside them. That's what I've been finding so interesting in our talks, right from the first discussion of Glenn Gould. I found myself thinking, "Hey, this is not bad." The other day, though, I had to go to a major record store in downtown Tokyo, and after looking around for a while, I felt the old distaste coming back.

MURAKAMI: Distaste? You mean, toward records and CDs and stuff as *things*—as commodities?

OZAWA: Yes. I had let myself forget all about those things. I don't have anything to do with them anymore. But spending time in the record store, I felt that old, unpleasant feeling coming back. Now, you are not a musician, and if anything, you're closer to one of those record collectors, wouldn't you say?

MURAKAMI: It's true. I just collect records and listen to them. Sure, I go to a lot of concerts, but since I don't actually make music, I'm more or less a dilettante.

OZAWA: But I'm enjoying talking to you about music like this because your perspective is so different from mine. It's that difference that has been making it a learning experience for me, something fresh and unexpected.

MURAKAMI: I'm very glad to hear that. Listening to recorded music has been one of the greatest joys of my life.

OZAWA: It occurred to me while I was in the record store that I don't want to have these conversations be for record collectors. I want them to be something that people who really love music will enjoy reading. I'd like that to be our guideline.

MURAKAMI: Absolutely! Let's make sure to keep our conversations as *un*-interesting as possible for collectors! [*Laughter.*]

Murakami note: I thought about this afterward and realized that part of me has always derived a lot of joy from collecting records, which maybe makes me like one of those "manic record collectors" that Ozawa was talking about. I don't see my own collecting as "manic," but I'm fairly obsessive, so I do have a tendency to become more or less obsessed with certain *things.* For example, in my teens I fell in love with Mozart's String Quartet no. 15 in D Minor (K. 421), one of the six "Haydn" quartets, in a set recorded by the Juilliard String Quartet, and for a time I listened to it exclusively, again and again. So even now, if someone mentions K. 421, I automatically start hearing the Juilliard's keen-edged performance in my head and picture the album cover. It's imprinted there, and it tends to be the internal standard by which I judge other performances. Records were expensive back then, and I would give my undivided attention to each precious disc, so in my mind (and with a degree of fetishism) a piece of music and the material *thing* on which it was recorded often comprised an indivisible unit. This may not be entirely natural, but since I didn't play music myself, it was the only way I could engage with it. Once I had made a little money, I started buying other records and enthusiastically attending concerts. Then I discovered the joy of comparing performances by different musicians—of relativizing the music, in other words. In this way, over time, I gave shape to what each piece of music meant to me.

By contrast, when one relates to music, as Ozawa does, primarily by reading scores, music must become purer, more internalized. Or at least it is not so readily identified with tangible *things.* The difference may be quite substantial. I imagine that relating to music like that must be very free and open. It may be a bit like the enjoyment and freedom of being able to read foreign literature in the original, rather than in translation. Arnold Schoenberg has said that "music is not a sound but an idea," {97a.1-3 source?} but ordinary people can't listen to it that way. When I told Ozawa that I envied his ability to do so, he suggested that I study to the point of being able to read a score. "Music would become even more interesting for you than it is now," he said. I took some piano lessons many years ago, so I can read a simple piece of music, but I would be lost in a complex score such as a Brahms symphony. "If you studied for a few months with a good instructor, I'm sure you could learn to read that well," he urged me, but I'm not ready to go that far. I do feel I'd like to give it a try someday, but I have no idea when that will happen.

We were chatting along these lines one day before an interview session when it struck me, in a precise, three-dimensional way, that there is a fundamental difference that separates the way we understand music. This was an extremely important realization. It's hardly for me to point out how very high the wall is that separates the pro from the amateur, the music maker from the listener. The wall is especially high and thick when that music maker is a world-class professional. But still, that fact doesn't have to hamper our ability to have an honest, direct conversation. At least that's how I feel about it, because music itself is a thing of such breadth and generosity. Our most important task is to search for an effective passageway through the wall—and two people who share a natural affinity for an art, any art, will be sure to find that passageway.

Brahms at Carnegie Hall

This second conversation took place during two hours spent in my Tokyo office on January 13, 2011. Ozawa was scheduled to undergo endoscopic surgery on his lower back a week later. Unable to remain seated for long, he would often leave his chair and talk while he walked slowly around the room. He also needed to periodically stop to eat. His December performances at Carnegie Hall with the Saito Kinen Orchestra had been an overwhelming success, but this apparently had come at great cost to him physically.

The Emotionally Charged Carnegie Hall Concert

MURAKAMI: I recently listened to the live CD of your performance of the Brahms First Symphony at

Carnegie Hall, and it was truly wonderful—so
full of life, so perfect in every detail. You know, I
actually heard you conduct the Brahms First when
you brought the Boston Symphony to Tokyo in 1986.

OZAWA: No kidding?

MURAKAMI: That was twenty-five years ago, but I
remember what a great performance that was. The
sound was beautiful in every way, and the music
seemed to rise up vividly before my eyes. I can still
hear it. But to tell you the truth, I felt this recent
performance was still more amazing. It had a special
something, a kind of passionate urgency that felt like
a once-in-a-lifetime experience. Quite honestly, I
was worried that your recent illness might have left
you physically weakened, and that would have an
adverse effect on the music, but . . .

OZAWA: No, it was just the opposite. Something had been
building up inside me and it burst out all at once. For
a long time before that performance, I was dying
to make music, but I couldn't. I had badly wanted
to conduct at the Matsumoto music festival in the
summer, but I didn't have the strength. All that was
building up inside me.

There was also the fact that the orchestra had been
charging ahead without me. We had a full four-
day rehearsal in Boston before the Carnegie
performance, during which time the orchestra
made very minute adjustments in their work
schedule to accommodate my strength and

physical restrictions—to a degree that was almost inconceivable with a professional orchestra. For example, we'd rehearse for twenty-five minutes and take a fifteen-minute break, or work for twenty minutes and break for ten. Their concern was really something special. We couldn't use Symphony Hall for the rehearsals, so we practiced in a small classroom at the Boston Conservatory.

MURAKAMI: You've played the Brahms First at the Matsumoto festival, too, with the Saito Kinen Orchestra, haven't you?

OZAWA: Yes, we've done all four Brahms symphonies, but the First we did way back in the early period of the orchestra. It must have been a good twenty years ago.

MURAKAMI: So the membership of the orchestra at Carnegie Hall must have been very different from that time.

OZAWA: Oh, sure, very different, practically a different orchestra. There are a few string players left, but I wonder about the wind instruments. Hmm, maybe one or two left, that's about all.

MURAKAMI: Speaking of wind instruments, I thought the horn player was awfully good in the Carnegie recording.

OZAWA: Yes, he's great. His name is Radek Baborák. He's a real genius, probably the best horn player in

the world. He's Czech. I first met him when he was
still in Munich. After that he moved to the Berlin
Philharmonic as first horn, and he often comes to
play with the Saito Kinen. I think he first came to
Japan the year of the Nagano Olympics—what's
that, 1998? We did the Beethoven Ninth for the
Winter Olympics with him as fourth horn. The
fourth horn is the one with the most solos. That was
his first time, and he's been coming ever since.

MURAKAMI: That horn solo really stuck with me.

OZAWA: Yes, it's wonderful. He comes to Japan to play
with both the Saito Kinen and the Mito Chamber
Orchestra. I get along tremendously well with him.
I've heard he's quit the Berlin and gone back to the
Czech Republic, though.

MURAKAMI: This CD of the Carnegie concert is a live
recording, of course, but they've scrubbed it to
remove stray noises, haven't they? I was amazed the
first time I heard it, it was so quiet. I could hardly
believe it was live.

OZAWA: You're right, it's almost impossible to get
such a clean live recording. They've taken out the
audience's coughs and wheezes and filled the gaps
with rehearsal takes.

MURAKAMI: This feels like backstage gossip, but what
they basically did was patch the blemishes?

OZAWA: That is correct.

MURAKAMI: But you told me that in the introductory part of the fourth movement there are also two unusual spots where they made a switch, for performance reasons, and it was not just to remove background noise. I should explain to our readers that you let me have a copy of the original recording and gave me a kind of homework assignment, asking me to find where it was different from the edited version. So I spent all of yesterday evening comparing the two recordings in every detail. [*Laughter.*]

I put the unedited CD of the symphony on, beginning with the fourth movement. While it plays, Ozawa eats a dried persimmon for nourishment. The orchestra reaches a long, diminishing roll of the timpani (2:28).

MURAKAMI: It starts here, right?

OZAWA: Yes, this is it.

The French horn begins to play the theme of the introductory section. The sound of the horn is deep and soft.

OZAWA: This is Baborák.

MURAKAMI: A beautiful, leisurely sound. How many horn players are there altogether?

OZAWA: There are four horns, but only two are playing here. They're not playing in unison, though, but in alternating measures, and they overlap slightly where one ends and the other begins (2:39–43). That way, there's no break where they take a breath.

Brahms indicated in his score that it should be done that way.

The horn solo ends, and the flute picks up the theme.

OZAWA: Now the flute takes it. This is Jacques Zoon. He was principal flautist in Boston about ten years ago. Now he's teaching in Switzerland. The flutes alternate—the first flute [3:13], and now the second flute takes over [3:17]. Now here's the first flute again [3:21]. Brahms specifies these small details so the audience won't hear the instrumentalists taking a breath.

MURAKAMI: Here the flute solo ends, and now the theme is taken up by a wind ensemble (3:50).

OZAWA: Yes, three trombones, two bassoons, and there's a contrabassoon in the mix, too.

The trombones here are playing for the first time in the movement, as if they have been waiting for their chance. Then, as if rising through a break in the clouds, the horns find their way through the quietly celebratory, majestic wind ensemble for another short solo (4:13).

MURAKAMI: This is where the part that's different in the two versions ends, correct?

OZAWA: We're listening to the first version now, right?

MURAKAMI: That's right. In the first version, the horns seem to come strongly to the foreground, bright and clear.

OZAWA: Yes, while in the revised CD, the horns sound—

MURAKAMI: Farther back.

OZAWA: You've got it.

MURAKAMI: Well, I worked hard at comparing the two.
[*Laughter.*] The horns are pulled back in the edited
version, and the sound is duller and more restrained.

OZAWA: Right. The horns in the original are just a little
too bold, so they replaced this part with another
take, and that's what you hear in the new version.
Actually, though, there's one more part where they
switched takes.

MURAKAMI: That one I couldn't find.

*After a breathtakingly beautiful moment of silence, the
strings ease into the fourth movement's famous main theme
(4:52). The introductory section, centered on the horn solos,
has performed its important role—they lead right into this
famous section.*

MURAKAMI: All right, let's now listen to the revised
version, starting from the roll of the timpani.

The first horn solo begins.

OZAWA: Here is the first horn, then the second, then first,
then second. See what I mean? You can't hear the

horn pausing for breath.

MURAKAMI: Not at all.

OZAWA: Now the flutes. First flute, one measure, second
flute, then first, then second. Right at this point, in
the other recording, you could hear him taking a
breath. The flute actually requires more breath than
the horn, you know. So they switched takes on this
part.

MURAKAMI: Oh, really? I see what you mean. A layman
would never notice something like that.

After the wind ensemble, the horn solo rises up again.

OZAWA: Here, see what I was talking about? The horns
are softer in this recording.

MURAKAMI: They *are* softer. They sound very different.
They were almost brash on the other recording, but
here they have a more restrained, deeper quality.

*Brahms uses the horns with great skill, as if calling the
audience deep into a German forest. The sound carries with
it an important part of Brahms's internal spiritual world.
Behind the horns, the timpani pulsate softly but insistently,
as if secretly waiting for something with great meaning. This
is a part well worth the great care that has been lavished on
its editing.*

OZAWA: The other instruments gradually join with the
soloists.

MURAKAMI: You can hear the strings clearly.

OZAWA: Yes.

The introductory section ends, and the beautiful main theme begins, a melody that almost makes you want to add words.

MURAKAMI: I get the feeling that the switch in the
horn segment somehow improved the balance,
or the coherence of the music, over the unedited
version. But this is something you can only get by
concentrating very closely on every detail. The
first version is also a wonderful performance. I'm
sure I wouldn't have noticed the difference if you
hadn't made me listen for it. In literary terms,
this would be about equivalent to the difference
in nuance introduced by one tiny modifier, which
the overwhelming majority of readers would read
through without noticing a thing. Still, the editorial
skill here is amazing. There's nothing odd going on
in the sound.

OZAWA: No, this is the work of Dominic Fyfe, the
English recording engineer. He's terrific. In any
case, 99 percent of the performance is straight from
the live recording. As I said before, most of the edits
were simply to remove audience noise.

Performing Brahms with the Saito Kinen Orchestra

MURAKAMI: Listening to this CD has made me wonder
if the sound at Carnegie Hall has changed over the

years.

OZAWA: It has. When we recorded this, I hadn't been there for some time, and I'm pretty sure it changed during that time. It got a lot better.

MURAKAMI: I heard it was renovated.

OZAWA: Oh, really? That makes sense. When I brought the Boston Symphony there thirty years ago, you could hear the subway rumbling underground. It passes right underneath. You'd get the subway going by four or five times in the space of one symphony. [*Laughter.*]

MURAKAMI: At least from listening to this recording, it seems to me that the sound is better.

OZAWA: You're right, it's much better than it used to be. The live recording came out a lot better than I thought it would. Hmm . . . when was I last at Carnegie before this? Probably five years ago when I conducted the Vienna Philharmonic there. I remember then thinking that the sound had improved. It certainly hadn't when I was there with the Boston Symphony eight years before that.

MURAKAMI: As I mentioned earlier, I heard you do the Brahms First with the Boston Symphony in 1986; and later with the Saito Kinen Orchestra on DVD. Now there's this new performance at Carnegie Hall, and listening to them all, I get the impression the sound is very different from one recording to the next. Why do you think they're so different?

OZAWA [*after a lot of thought*]: Well, first of all, the biggest difference might be that the Saito Kinen string sound has changed. How should I put it? The strings are more "talkative"? They've brought expression more to the foreground. The strings have made their expression so rich that some people might say they're overdoing it.

MURAKAMI: You mean their expressiveness is more overt?

OZAWA: Yes, and the wind instruments have joined them in being more expressive. For comparison, we listened to the same part of the Brahms First played by Karajan and the Berlin Philharmonic a few minutes ago, and of course it was very fine and well balanced and solidly symmetrical, but the Saito Kinen musicians are not that concerned about balance. Just listen to this Carnegie Hall performance we're discussing, and you can tell their mind-set is probably very different from that of the usual professional orchestra.

MURAKAMI: Their mind-set?

OZAWA: In other words, say you've got a dozen or more people in a section of the orchestra. Each one of them, from the one in front to the one all the way in back, is thinking, "I'm the one who's going to make this work," "I'm number one," and they're playing up a storm.

MURAKAMI: That's incredible. But even if there has been this change in expressiveness, the actual sound of the strings hasn't changed direction all that much since the beginning.

OZAWA: Not at all. It's exactly the same.

MURAKAMI: I'd like to hear a little about the origins of the Saito Kinen Orchestra. It's not a typical permanent orchestra, is it? People who normally work in other places get together once a year and perform as a unit.

OZAWA: That's right.

MURAKAMI: In other words, they take off from work to join forces?

OZAWA: Well, there's the string section, for example. I won't say most of its members, but a good number of them, do not perform in other orchestras. True, we have people such as the concertmaster of a famous orchestra, but I'm pretty sure the greater proportion of our members are people who do not belong to specific orchestras, people who play chamber music or who teach.

MURAKAMI: I guess there are a lot of musicians like that.

OZAWA: I think there are more and more people, especially lately, who want to make music but who don't want to play in an orchestra all year.

MURAKAMI: You mean, they want to make music more

freely—they don't want to submit to the restrictions involved in belonging to a fixed organization.

OZAWA: Right. For example, there's Claudio Abbado's Mahler Chamber Orchestra. It's the same thing with them. A lot of leading musicians gather together from all over to form the group, but most of them are active in music without belonging to specific orchestras.

MURAKAMI: That is an outstanding orchestra, isn't it?

OZAWA: Yes, they're terrific.

MURAKAMI: Lately, it seems, new organizations like that, very high-quality orchestras separate from the established, so-called distinguished orchestras, have been on the increase throughout the world. Since the members of these new groups gather spontaneously, do you think that naturally leads to a certain kind of spontaneity in the sounds they produce?

OZAWA: That could very well be the case, because these are not people who belong to an orchestra and play with the same people week after week. And even if some of them are musicians who play with the same people week after week, they see all new faces in these new groupings, and so they come to the music with a different mind-set. Of course, there are people who call these new orchestras "once-a-year wonders," and not always with a good meaning. [*Laughter.*]

MURAKAMI: Which means the musicians are not your employees, so if they happen not to like the music you are making, they can decide not to participate next time. It's not a job for them that requires them to do work they don't like. They can just up and quit.

OZAWA: Well, true, but we do have people who come all that distance for the chance to work with me. Musicians who normally play in Berlin or Vienna or in some American orchestra will make the trip to the hills of Matsumoto. It's hard for people like that to take time off, and while they're in Matsumoto, they can't do side jobs or take students.

MURAKAMI: Are you saying you can't pay them very well?

OZAWA: We're always struggling to pay them as much as possible, but quite frankly, we have our limits.

MURAKAMI: But still, the number of orchestras worldwide that are organized in such a fluid way, with people freely coming and going, has been increasing, hasn't it? It's quite a contrast to traditional established orchestras operating under a strict management system. And that way the musicians can enjoy spontaneously "talking" with each other.

OZAWA: Yes, Claudio Abbado's Lucerne Festival Orchestra is like that, and so is the Deutsche Kammerphilharmonie.

MURAKAMI: Oh, that's the Bremen orchestra that Paavo Järvi directs, isn't it? I heard it the other day.

OZAWA: Each one of them is active for three or four months out of the year, and after that the musicians have to fend for themselves—"Sorry, everybody, we can't pay your salary while you're away, so you're on your own now." That's the new system.

MURAKAMI: It's different for the conductors, too, I suppose. Your attitude must be a little different when you're conducting one of these orchestras as opposed to conducting an established orchestra—say, when you were conductor of the Boston Symphony.

OZAWA: Oh, yes, very different, of course. You're a little tense, for one thing, and you bring a different kind of enthusiasm to it. Everybody—a group of friends—gets together in the hall for the "once-a-year wonder," so you'd better stay alert or you hear them saying, "You're not your usual self this year, Seiji. Maybe your strength is waning," or "Maybe you haven't been doing your homework." It can be tough. I've had a lot of occasions where they could be pretty nasty—or at least blunt. [*Laughter.*] Well, anyway, most of my buddies from the old days have retired or whatnot. There aren't too many of them left.

MURAKAMI: How do you decide what to play?

OZAWA: At first it was nothing but Brahms. We'd add maybe Bartók's Concerto for Orchestra or Toru Takemitsu's *November Steps*, but the core of the repertory was always the four Brahms symphonies. Sticking close to Brahms, we'd add other pieces little by little. We did one of the four Brahms symphonies each year, and then the Matsumoto music festival began. In Matsumoto, too, we did Brahms and went on to Beethoven.

MURAKAMI: First, let there be Brahms.

OZAWA: Exactly.

MURAKAMI: But why? Why Brahms?

OZAWA: Well, we——or rather I——felt that Brahms best conveyed the sense of Professor Saito. You've heard of the conductor Kazuyoshi Akiyama, I'm sure. He saw things differently. He thought we should be doing a little lighter repertory——Mozart and Schumann. I'm pretty sure he first conducted Schumann with the Saito Kinen. But I thought we should do Brahms. I asked the others about it, and I think that's how we decided. We felt that Brahms was more suited than Beethoven to Professor Saito's idea of "talkative strings," a richer expressiveness in the string section. So then we started touring Europe with the idea of doing the complete Brahms. We've done four European tours now. The first Brahms symphony we played was . . . I'm pretty sure . . . the First.

MURAKAMI: Professor Saito's main repertory consisted of Brahms, Beethoven, and Mozart, I believe.

OZAWA: Yes, and Haydn.

MURAKAMI: Mainly German music.

OZAWA: Yes, and Tchaikovsky, of course. The symphonies and the Serenade for Strings. We had our longest and best training for the Serenade at the Toho Gakuen School of Music. And do you know why? Because the Toho orchestra hardly had any wind instruments! [*Laughter.*] We'd play Mozart with only one oboe and one flute, and the organ would fill in for the rest. Sometimes I played the timpani, and then Professor Saito would conduct; or if it was a piece without timpani, I would conduct. Yes, there really was a time like that!

MURAKAMI: When you say the orchestra was suited to Brahms, how do you mean? Was it the timbre, or the sound?

OZAWA: No, it's not so much the sound as . . . how should I put this? Its style of playing, the string section's use of the bow, theirdirection, their phrasing are probably just suited to Brahms. Professor Saito taught us that music is expression, and that is also my view. When he taught us a Brahms symphony, he was especially fervent about this. He had to be practical, though, and so, in part because of the available instrumentation, he tended to teach pieces such as Tchaikovsky's Serenade for Strings, Mozart's Divertimento, some of Handel's Concerti Grossi, a Bach *Brandenburg concerto,* or Schoenberg's *Verklärte Nacht.*

MURAKAMI: But even with that dearth of wind

instruments, he'd forge ahead energetically with a
Brahms symphony?

OZAWA: That's right. He'd manage, one way or another,
to make up for the thin ranks of wind players.

MURAKAMI: I'm not very knowledgeable about technical
matters, but aren't Brahms's orchestrations a good
deal more complex than Beethoven's?

OZAWA: No, not really. They were working with
practically the same instruments. Something
like the contrabassoon was not so common in
Beethoven's day, but otherwise they were not that
different. There are only the tiniest differences in
orchestration.

MURAKAMI: So what you're saying is that Brahms
and Beethoven are pretty much the same when it
comes to the way they integrate the sounds of the
orchestra?

OZAWA: Yes. There's a lot more breadth to the sound
of Brahms, but for Brahms and Beethoven, the
instrumentation itself is pretty much the same.

MURAKAMI: Why is it, then, that when I listen, their
sound is very different?

OZAWA: That is true. [*Pause.*] Look, Beethoven himself
changes a lot in the Ninth. His orchestrations were
quite limited until he got to his Ninth Symphony.

MURAKAMI: My impression is that when Brahms and Beethoven use a similar group of instruments, the result is still something very different. With Brahms, it's as if a new sound comes in between any two sounds, making the whole thing one level denser. Maybe that's why it's so much easier to grasp the musical structure in a Beethoven piece.

OZAWA: Yes, of course. The structure is much easier to see in a piece by Beethoven. You can hear the winds and the strings talking to each other. But Brahms creates his unique sound by blending the two together.

MURAKAMI: Ah, that helps me understand the difference.

OZAWA: This is clear even in Brahms's First Symphony. That's the reason everybody says that Brahms's First Symphony is like Beethoven's Tenth. That's where the connection lies.

MURAKAMI: So where orchestration is concerned, Brahms continued with the reforms that Beethoven began with his Ninth, and final, Symphony.

OZAWA: That's the idea.

MURAKAMI: And after Brahms, the Saito Kinen goes on to make Beethoven symphonies central to its repertoire.

OZAWA: Yes, and after Beethoven we've been doing Mahler—the Second, the Ninth, the Fifth, and the First, I think. And recently we did our first French piece, the *Symphonie fantastique*. As for opera, we did Poulenc and Honegger. I used to consult with William Bernell, a guy in San Francsisco who made programs. The two of us would get together and decide what to perform. I got his advice when I was in Boston, too, and all the way from the beginning with the Saito Kinen. He died last year at the age of eighty-four. We worked together for almost fifty years.

MURAKAMI: If you ever felt like playing some Sibelius, that would make me very happy. I love his symphonies. I've never heard a Sibelius by you other than the Violin Concerto you recorded with Viktoria Mullova.

OZAWA: Which of his symphonies do you like? The Third? The Fifth?

MURAKAMI: The Fifth is my favorite.

OZAWA: That last movement is good, isn't it? When I was taking lessons from Maestro Karajan in 1960–61, I conducted the finale of the Sibelius Fifth. That and Mahler's *Das Lied von der Erde*. He gave me those as an assignment in big, romantic pieces.

MURAKAMI: Maestro Karajan was very fond of the Sibelius Fifth, wasn't he? I think he must have recorded it four times.

OZAWA: Yes, he liked it a lot. His performances were wonderful, of course, but he also used it to teach his disciples. He always told us that it was the job of the conductor to create long phrases. "Read what's behind the score," he would say. "Don't just read individual measures; read in longer units." We were accustomed to reading four- or eight-measure phrases, but he saw the music in terms of very long units—sixteen measures, or, in extreme cases, up to thirty-two measures. None of this is written in the score, of course, but he insisted that it was the conductor's job to read that way. The composer was always writing with those long phrases in mind, so it was up to us to find them. That was one of the most important things he taught us.

MURAKAMI: Karajan's performances always have this very solid narrative that comes from his creation of those long phrases. I'm often amazed to hear how his old recordings, in particular, have this element of storytelling or persuasiveness that has survived the years without the least sense of aging—though every now and then, I admit, there will be something that strikes me as a little old-fashioned.

OZAWA: There are those moments, it's true.

MURAKAMI: It seems to me that in Karajan's music, there's a fairly clear dividing line between the two. It can go either way, with little compromise in either case.

OZAWA: You may be right. Furtwängler was the same way.

MURAKAMI: Now we're talking about a national treasure.

OZAWA: It's true. [*Laughter.*] And then there was Karl
Böhm. You know, from Vienna. I once saw him
conduct Richard Strauss's opera *Elektra* at Salzburg.
He looked as though he was conducting with little
twitches of his fingertips, barely moving his arms,
but the orchestra—it was really like magic—
produced this *huge* sound. [*Ozawa spreads his arms
wide.*] I'm sure there must have been some special,
historical tie between him and the orchestra. I mean,
he was really old when I saw him, and he conducted
with small movements and no big cues to speak of,
but the sound he got out of them was amazingly
large.

MURAKAMI: Do you think that means he was not keeping
them under tight control but instead letting them
play freely?

OZAWA: Hmm, not even I know the answer to that.
Maybe so . . . I wonder. I wish I had a better
explanation for it. In Maestro Karajan's case, you
could see it happening. Most of the time he would
leave it up to the orchestra to play as they wished,
and he would only take charge at the important
points. But in Maestro Böhm's case . . . hmm . . . he's
up there giving these tiny little cues, but every now
and then this huge phrase leapt out. I don't know
how he did it.

MURAKAMI: Maybe there was something special about the
Vienna Philharmonic?

OZAWA: Maybe so. Or it could have been their great

respect for him. Maybe there was an unspoken understanding between them about the kind of music they would produce. It's tremendously satisfying to see and hear music being made that way.

Follow-Up Interview: The Truth about Horn Players' Breathing

MURAKAMI: I'd like to ask you a little more about the part of the Brahms First Symphony we heard the other day, where the solo horns trade measures in the fourth movement. Afterwards, I saw a video of your performance when you brought the Boston Symphony to Osaka in 1986, and as far as I can tell, the horn players don't appear to be alternating.

We watch the horn solo passage.

OZAWA: Yes, it's true, they are *not* alternating. You're absolutely right. Oh, I remember now. The man playing the horn here is Chuck Kavalovski, a university professor. I think he's a physicist or something, and a super-eccentric guy. Can you show me that part again?

We watch again.

OZAWA: One, two, three . . . there! You can't hear the horn.

MURAKAMI: There's a gap where the horn player takes a breath.

OZAWA: Exactly. The sound cuts out at that point. We're doing a bad thing to Brahms here. That gap shouldn't be there. But Kavalovski insisted on doing it his way. This was a real problem when we recorded. Here, listen to the flute solo that follows.

The horn solo ends, and the same theme is picked up by the flute.

OZAWA: One, two, three . . . there! See, there's no break in the sound. While the first flute is taking a breath, the second flute continues the note, so there's no gap. Which is exactly the way Brahms wrote it. The horns are supposed to do the same thing.

The video shows clearly that the note continues even while the musician takes his mouth from the instrument to breathe. This would not be obvious to anyone listening to the recording.

MURAKAMI: So the second flute plays backup while the first flute breathes. I suppose that is the reason for alternating measures.

OZAWA: Exactly. It's great that you noticed this! Probably because of what I told you the other day.

MURAKAMI: Yes, of course. I never would have noticed on my own. Now let me show you the DVD of the Saito Kinen's 1990 London performance.

OZAWA: One, two, three . . . there! The note continues the way it's supposed to, even while the horn player takes a breath. No gap. And at the head of the second and fourth measures, they're playing in unison, as indicated in the score. Brahms does interesting stuff like this.

MURAKAMI: But the horn player in Boston ignored the instruction, you say?

OZAWA: Yes, he decided on his own, and he absolutely insisted on doing it his way. In other words, he rejected Brahms's little trick.

MURAKAMI: Why do you think he did that?

OZAWA: I'm sure he disliked the change in timbre that came from switching horns. I remember this was a big problem for us at the time. Here, let's look at the score you brought.

Ozawa marks the score with a pencil as he carefully explains each detail to me, clarifying what I had been unable to grasp.

OZAWA: See? Here it is. You have to read this part closely or you could miss it completely. The second horn enters here and plays to here, and while he is playing, the first horn takes a breath. This instructs the first horn to play two beats; and the second to stretch it out to four beats. Look, there's even a dot here.

MURAKAMI: Oh, I see. That's why the same note is written twice in parallel. I was wondering what that was all about.

OZAWA: Brahms was the first one to do this. To bring it off, though, the two horns have to sound the same.

MURAKAMI: Well, sure.

OZAWA: Brahms wrote it like this on that assumption. Before Brahms, though, you probably couldn't make that assumption. That's because everybody was playing the so-called "natural horn," without valves, and the sound could be very different from one instrument to the next. If you tried this trick with different-sounding horns, it could be a mess. Or maybe it was just that nobody thought of doing it. In the end it's a pretty simple matter.

MURAKAMI: It certainly is. So that horn player in Boston was quite the exception, wasn't he? This was not just another way of interpreting the music.

OZAWA: Not at all. You're not supposed to play it that way, but he's a very unusual guy, and he was going to do it that way no matter what anybody said. I wouldn't have recalled that if you hadn't brought it up. He's an absolutely brilliant guy, and we were very close friends when I was in Boston.

The Relationship of Writing to Music

MURAKAMI: I've been listening to music since my teens, but lately I've come to feel that I understand music a little better now than I used to—that maybe I can hear the fine differences in musical detail—and that writing fiction has gradually and naturally given me a better ear. Conversely, you can't write well if you don't have an ear for music. The two sides complement each other: listening to music improves your style; by improving your style, you improve your ability to listen to music.

OZAWA: Interesting . . .

MURAKAMI: No one ever taught me how to write, and I've never made a study of writing techniques. So how did I learn to write? From listening to music. And what's the most important thing in writing? It's rhythm. No one's going to read what you write unless it's got rhythm. It has to have an inner rhythmic feel that propels the reader forward. You know how painful it can be to read a mechanical instruction manual. Pamphlets like that are classic examples of writing without rhythm.

You can usually tell whether a new writer's work is going to last by whether or not the style has a sense of rhythm. From what I've seen, though, most literary critics ignore that element. They mainly talk about the subtlety of the style, the newness of the writer's vocabulary, the narrative momentum, the quality of the themes, the use of interesting techniques, and so forth. But I think that someone who writes without rhythm lacks the talent to be a writer. That's just my opinion, of course.

OZAWA: Do you think we can feel that kind of rhythm when we read it?

MURAKAMI: Yes, the rhythm comes from the combination of words, the combination of the sentences and paragraphs, the pairings of hard and soft, light and heavy, balance and imbalance, the punctuation, the combination of different tones. "Polyrhythm" might be the right word for it, as in music. You need a good ear to do it. You either can do it or you can't. You either get it or you don't. Of course, it *is* possible to extend one's talent for rhythm through hard work and study.

I'm a jazz lover, so that's how I set down a rhythm first. Then I add chords to it and start improvising, making it up freely as I go along. I write as if I'm making music.

OZAWA: I never knew that there could be rhythm in writing. I'm still not that clear on what you mean by it.

MURAKAMI: Well, rhythm is an important element for both reader and writer. If you're writing a piece of fiction and you haven't established a rhythm, the next sentence won't come out, which means the story can't move ahead. The rhythm in the writing, the rhythm of the story: if you've got those, the next sentence will come out naturally. When I'm writing a sentence, I automatically sound it out in my head, and a rhythm takes hold, kind of like in jazz: you ad-lib a chorus, and that leads organically to the next chorus.

OZAWA: I live in the Seijo neighborhood of Tokyo, and I was recently given a pamphlet for a candidate running for office there. I opened it up and found some kind of pledge or manifesto, so I started reading it because I had nothing better to do at the time, and I found myself thinking, "This guy will never make it." And I felt this because I couldn't read more than three lines of this document, no matter how hard I tried. This guy seemed to be saying something important, but I just couldn't read it.

MURAKAMI: And that's probably because his writing had no rhythm to it.

OZAWA: You think so? Is that what it was? What about somebody like Natsume Sōseki?

MURAKAMI: I think Sōseki's style is tremendously musical. It makes for very smooth reading. It's quite wonderful even now, a century after his death. I'm pretty sure he was less influenced by Western music than by the long narrative chants of the Edo period [1603–1868], but he had a great ear. I don't know how deeply versed he was in Western music, but he spent a couple of years studying in London, so I suspect he familiarized himself with it to some degree. I'll look into it.

OZAWA: He was also a professor of English, wasn't he?

MURAKAMI: He probably had a good ear in that sense, too, with a good combination of Japanese and Western elements. Hidekazu Yoshida was another writer with a musical style. His Japanese flows beautifully, is very easy to read, and is quite personal in tone.

OZAWA: You may be right about that.

MURAKAMI: Speaking of professors of literature, I gather your
English professor at the Toho Gakuen School of Music was
the novelist Saiichi Maruya.

OZAWA: That's true. He had us read James Joyce's *Dubliners*.
There was no way I could understand a book like that.
[*Laughter.*] I sat next to a girl who was good at English
and she told me what it was about. I didn't study at all.
Which meant that I didn't know any English when I went to
America [*Laughter.*].

MURAKAMI: So it was just that you didn't study, not that Mr.
Maruya was a bad teacher.

OZAWA: No, I *really* didn't study.

What Happened in the 1960s

The first half of this conversation took place on January 13th, 2011, following the previous section's Second Conversation on the Carnegie Hall concert. There wasn't enough time that day to complete the conversation, so the second half took place on February 10th, also in my Tokyo office. At one point the maestro exclaimed, "I've forgotten so much!" but his recollections were in fact quite vivid and interesting.

Working as Assistant Conductor
Under Leonard Bernstein

MURAKAMI: Today I'd like to focus on your experiences in the 1960s.

OZAWA: I wonder how much I'll remember. I get
the feeling I've forgotten just about everything.
[*Laughter.*]

MURAKAMI: You mentioned before that you had been
assistant conductor under Leonard Bernstein in
New York. I was planning to ask you—but at the
time forgot—exactly what kind of work an assistant
conductor does.

OZAWA: Just about all orchestras have one assistant
conductor, but Bernstein was unusual—he had
three. I suppose they had some extra source of
money to pay for three assistants. Each year they
hired three new people for the position, to stay for
one-year terms. Claudio Abbado did it, and Edo de
Waart, and Lorin Maazel, and lots of other famous
conductors. I was interviewed for the position
while I was still in Berlin, when the New York
Philharmonic happened to come to Germany on
tour. Lenny and maybe ten committee members
did the interview. After a concert, we all piled into
cabs and went to this sort of strange bar called
Rififi where we drank and did the interview. They
used the bar's piano and did a kind of test of my
ear. Lenny had just conducted the Beethoven First
Piano Concerto from the keyboard and was feeling
very relaxed after a job well done. My English was
terrible at the time, so I could hardly understand
what anybody was saying, but somehow I managed
to pass [*laughter*] and become an assistant. The other
two had already been chosen for that year, so I was
the last of the three. The others were John Canarina

and Maurice Peress.

MURAKAMI: So you went from Berlin to New York?

OZAWA: That was in the fall, and six months later, in the spring of 1961, the New York Philharmonic was set to go to Japan. There was some kind of big event going on in Tokyo—"East Meets West" or "West Meets East" or something—and the orchestra was invited to participate. They decided that I should be the assistant conductor to go, which made sense since I was Japanese. Normally each of us was responsible for a third of the repertory—with three assistant conductors, we would each prepare one of Lenny's three performance pieces, in case he got sick and needed someone to fill in.

MURAKAMI: So if something happened, you'd come on stage and conduct in his place.

OZAWA: Right. Also, in those days, often the conductor couldn't make it to a rehearsal. I wonder why, come to think of it. Maybe plane schedules weren't as dependable as they are now. Lenny often didn't show up for the beginning of a rehearsal, so the three of us would decide which of us would go first and rehearse with the orchestra.

MURAKAMI: In his place, you mean.

OZAWA: Yes. Lenny was rather fond of me, so I was often treated better than the others. Long before the Japan trip, the New York Philharmonic had commissioned a work by Toshiro Mayuzumi, who produced his *Bacchanale* for them. Mayuzumi naturally assumed that Bernstein would be conducting it, but Bernstein told me, as the assistant for that piece, to take charge of the rehearsal at Carnegie Hall. So I ran through the rehearsal with both Bernstein and Mayuzumi looking on. I assumed it was just for that one day, and that Lenny would take over after that, but the next day he told me to do it again. So I ended up conducting the work's New York debut.

MURAKAMI: Incredible.

OZAWA: We went to Japan after the New York performance. In my mind, of course Lenny would be conducting the piece in Japan, but on the plane, he told me that I would be conducting it for the Japan performance—that my name was already printed in the program.

MURAKAMI: So they were planning to have you perform it in Japan all along.

OZAWA: And that's exactly what happened.

MURAKAMI: Was that your first public appearance conducting the New York Philharmonic?

OZAWA: I think it was. No, actually, I had done it once before. The orchestra was on a national tour and— was it in Detroit?—I conducted an encore, probably in an outdoor performance. Lenny liked to play the finale of Stravinsky's *Firebird* as an encore. It's a short piece, maybe five or six minutes long. So when he was called back to the stage, he took my hand and led me out and announced to the audience, "Here's a young conductor. I'd love to have you listen to him perform." The audience probably wasn't too happy about that, though fortunately no one went so far as to boo me.

MURAKAMI: You really did get special treatment, didn't you?

OZAWA: It was out-and-out favoritism. And it happened so suddenly that, psychologically, I wasn't the least bit prepared to perform! I almost panicked, but I gave it my best and got terrific applause at the end. It was a great success. The same kind of thing happened two or three times after that.

MURAKAMI: I don't think I've ever heard of anyone conducting just the encore.

OZAWA: No, it never happens. I felt really bad for the other two assistant conductors.

MURAKAMI: What kind of salary does an assistant conductor get?

OZAWA: Next to nothing. I was single when I started, so I got $100 a week. You can't live on that, of course. When I got married, they increased my pay to $150, but that was still not enough. Altogether, I was in New York for two and a half years, in cheap apartments. The first one cost $125 a month, and it was a basement apartment with windows at sidewalk level. When I woke up and opened the window I'd see legs going by. After I got married and my salary went up, we moved into an upper floor. But New York summers are horrendously hot, and of course we didn't have air conditioning, so when we couldn't sleep, we'd go to a nearby all-night movie theater—the cheapest one we could find—and spend the night there. We lived near Broadway, so there were plenty of theaters. But they made you get out of your seat whenever a movie ended, which meant that every two hours we'd have to wake up and go out to the lobby to kill time.

MURAKAMI: Did you have time for a side job?

OZAWA: A side job? I had no time for that. It was all I could do to study each week's music.

MURAKAMI: You must have had a lot to learn if you could be called on at any time to take the stage and conduct.

OZAWA: Sure, you have to prepare every last detail. And then there were the two other assistant conductors. They were in charge of the rest of the program, but there was always the possibility that one of them might not be able to appear. So you had to learn their music, too. I never had enough time for anything.

MURAKAMI: I see what you mean.

OZAWA: I had nothing else to do then, so I'd spend

every spare minute in Carnegie Hall. They used to accuse me of living there! The other two assistant conductors, though, did have other work, I seem to recall. I think they were conducting Broadway musicals and maybe conducting some choruses. So sometimes they'd come to me and ask me to fill in for them. Then I really had a tough time! I'm pretty sure I was the hardest-working of the three of us. If I hadn't taken on their share, and something came up, we'd have had a real mess.

MURAKAMI: It sounds as if you were doing the work of three people.

OZAWA: Well, think of what would have happened if Lenny suddenly became ill when one of his assistants was working on Broadway! We couldn't have had a performance! So I learned all the music. For better or worse, I was always hanging around backstage.

MURAKAMI: By "learning the music," you mean, specifically, closely reading the score, correct?

OZAWA: That's right. They wouldn't let us run the actual rehearsal, so all we could do was read the score until we had it memorized.

MURAKAMI: And I suppose you were there, watching, when Bernstein rehearsed?

OZAWA: Yes, naturally. I'd watch and memorize every little movement of his. There was a small room in the auditorium designed for that purpose. You could

hear everything but the audience couldn't see you.
There's a room like that [at the former Philharmonic
Hall, now David Geffen Hall] in Lincoln Center.
In Carnegie Hall, too, there's one like it, though
not so specialized. It's positioned a little above the
conductor at an angle and has just enough room for
four people to sit. I watched a concert once from that
room with Elizabeth Taylor and Richard Burton.

MURAKAMI: No kidding!

OZAWA: They were there as Lenny's guests. It was at the
height of their popularity, so it would have caused
too great a commotion for them to sit among the
audience. "Why don't you take them in to sit in your
place, Seiji?" Lenny said. So the three of us squeezed
in there—literally [*laughter*]—and watched the
concert. I remember they spoke to me, but my
English was so bad, I didn't know what to say.

MURAKAMI: But anyhow, living like that, so closely
attached to one orchestra, you must have learned a
lot.

OZAWA: It was a tremendous learning experience. I'm just
sorry my English was so bad. For example, Bernstein
had a television series called *Young People's Concerts*
and I would attend the meetings for every broadcast,
but I hardly understood what he was saying. It was
such a wasted opportunity. I still feel bad about it.

MURAKAMI: Yes, you could have learned even more.

OZAWA: Exactly. But when it came to actually
conducting, Lenny gave me lots of opportunities.
Talk about still feeling bad—I still feel sorry for the
other two assistants.

MURAKAMI: Do you know what they're doing now?

OZAWA: Maurice Peress was active on Broadway and did
some big shows. He also performed in London and
New York. John Canarina was conducting a rather
small orchestra in Florida or somewhere. You know,
some people who remain assistant conductors too
long end up as assistants. I did it for two and a half
years. As I mentioned before, we were supposed to
be replaced by new assistants after one year, but none
of us had positions to go to after our first year with
Lenny, so we all stayed on. I even ended up house-
sitting for Lenny when he went on sabbatical.

Close Reading of Scores

MURAKAMI: So it was during that time that you came
to like reading scores? Or at least you put a lot of
energy into reading them?

OZAWA: Well, sure, because I didn't have a choice in the
matter. I didn't have a piano at home, so I'd spend
hours studying scores backstage, using the piano
on hand to sound them out. But come to think of it,
it was the same for me while I was in Vienna, until
quite recently. I didn't have a piano at home, so I'd
go to my room in the opera house nearby and play

until all hours of the night. I had a really good grand piano there. I found it very moving at times, to think back to those days when I was doing the same thing in New York. There was a piano in the conductors' room in Carnegie Hall, and I'd go there late at night and practice to my heart's content. Those were easygoing days, with hardly any security, so you could do something like that rather freely.

MURAKAMI: I'm not too sure what's involved in reading a score, but I think of it in terms of the translation work that I do every day. I sit there reading English books and converting them into Japanese, and sometimes I'll come up against a passage that stumps me. I just can't figure out what it means, no matter how much I think about it. So I'll just sit there with my arms folded, staring at the lines for hours, and sometimes I manage to get it, but other times not at all. So then I'll skip that passage and go on to the rest of the text, and every once in a while, I'll go back and have another look, and after two or three days of doing that, it finally dawns on me, like, "So *that's* what it says," and the meaning will just rise up off the page like nothing at all. At first glance, the hours I spend staring at the passage would seem to be a waste of time, but I think *that's* the time when I'm really getting it. I can't help feeling that reading a score is a similar experience.

OZAWA: A difficult score can often be like that, it's true. Except, well . . . this is kind of like exposing trade secrets, but a musical staff has only five lines, you know. And there's nothing at all difficult about the notes themselves. They're like the letters of the alphabet. But the more they pile up, the more difficult things become. You might know all your letters and be able to read simple words, but the more they're combined into complex sentences, the harder they become to understand and the more background knowledge you need to understand what they mean. It's the same with music, but that "knowledge" part gets really huge. It's precisely because the symbols used to write music are so simple—simpler than the written word—that when you don't understand something, you get seriously lost.

MURAKAMI: I guess that's because explanatory comments are usually kept to a minimum in a musical score, and the rest is indicated with these pure symbolic notations, right?

OZAWA: Sure, there's basically nothing written in words in the score that tells you what to do. The first time I had it really tough was with the opera *Wozzeck*. You know it, I suppose?

MURAKAMI: By Alban Berg.

OZAWA: Right. The first time I conducted that, I read the score and figured I pretty much understood it. And then I started rehearsals. With the New Japan Philharmonic. My schedule wasn't going to allow me much time for rehearsals just prior to the performance itself, so I made special arrangements to rehearse with the orchestra some three or four

months ahead of time. I figured I'd take a few days
to work with them while I was briefly in Japan before
returning to—I think it was Boston, back then.
And then I'd come back to Tokyo just before the
performance, for the actual rehearsals. I was so glad
I did that! Those three or four months in between
were a lifesaver! By which I mean that once I got
started with the orchestra, one thing after another
came up that I didn't know how to deal with. It was
full of stuff that I just couldn't sort out.

MURAKAMI: You mean, you assumed you understood
everything when you were reading the score, but in
fact you didn't?

OZAWA: Right. I understood for the first time that I didn't
understand what I thought I understood.

MURAKAMI: And you came to that understanding when,
at your direction, the orchestra actually produced the
sounds that were in the score?

OZAWA: When I read the score and translated what was
written into the sounds of the piano, I thought I
understood it. But when I made those sounds with
the orchestra, it was one "Oh no!" moment after
another. In other words, I'm conducting, and all the
while the sound is moving around like crazy. And
once that starts to happen, I get totally lost.

MURAKAMI: Huh!

OZAWA: What a shock that was! So in my panic, I started

rereading the score from scratch. And *that's* when I
got it. I had understood the "language" of the music
well enough when I was just reading the score—
what the music was trying to say. And I had been
able to grasp things having to do with rhythm.
But what I didn't understand were the harmonies.
No, I guess I had understood the harmonies, too,
intellectually. But the second they started to move
through time, I was lost. Music, of course, is an art
that occurs through time.

MURAKAMI: Yes, of course.

OZAWA: When I played the music exactly as Berg had
written it, using the tempi that he had indicated in
the score, my ear simply couldn't keep up with the
time. No, not my ear—my ability to understand.
My understanding couldn't keep up. Mind you, we
were playing exactly as Berg had written it down
on paper. And the musicians were all quite capable
of playing the music as written. In spite of that,
there were several passages that I simply couldn't
understand. Not a lot of them, but a significant
number. That was the first time I ever experienced
such a thing, which is what got me to start studying
the score again in such a panic. It was just plain lucky
for me that I happened to have those few months in
between to study the score again.

MURAKAMI: So what you're saying is that there are cases
in which the harmonic flow of a composition can't
be understood unless you sound it out with the
orchestra?

OZAWA: That's the idea. You know, up to about the time
of Brahms, whom we've been talking about, or
Richard Strauss, you can pretty much tell what kind
of harmonies you're going to get just by looking at
the score. From experience. But you get to somebody
like Charles Ives, and you have absolutely no idea
what the harmonies will be like without actually
producing the sound. After all, he was making music
in a deliberate attempt to destroy such things. You
might try to produce the sound of the orchestra
on the piano, but ten fingers on a keyboard are
not enough for some things. You've got to hear
the actual sound. Of course, when you become
accustomed to such music, you kind of get the hang
of which chords to leave out to play it on the piano.
Or, to put it the opposite way, you begin to see which
sounds you *can't* leave out.

MURAKAMI: When do you read scores?

OZAWA: You mean, what time of day?

MURAKAMI: Yes.

OZAWA: In the morning. Very early. I have to
concentrate, and I can't have a drop of alcohol in my
system.

MURAKAMI: I'm not presuming to compare my work with
yours, but I also work early in the morning. That's
when I can concentrate best. I always get up at four
o'clock in the morning when I'm writing a novel.
I prepare myself to get completely absorbed in the

writing while everything is dark.

OZAWA: How long do you work?

MURAKAMI: About five hours.

OZAWA: I can't last that long. I might get up at four o'clock, but by eight o'clock I'm hungry for breakfast. [*Laughter.*] In Boston, rehearsals used to start around ten-thirty, so I'd have to eat by nine at the latest.

MURAKAMI: Is reading scores fun?

OZAWA: Fun? Sure, I suppose so. Especially when it goes well, it's lots of fun. But when it doesn't, I hate it.

MURAKAMI: Can you give me a concrete example of when it hasn't gone well?

OZAWA: When I can't get the music into my head. Say, when I'm tired, or when my understanding or my concentration is off. I may be revealing trade secrets again here, but it often happens that the music you are going to perform at night is very different from the music you need to study that same morning. Say, in Boston, I'd have four programs to play in four weeks, so after the opening night of one program, I'd have to start studying for the next one. That was the toughest thing, now that I think back on it.

MURAKAMI: You get overwhelmed by the schedule.

OZAWA: Ideally, you'd have two weeks between the end of one concert series and the start of the next one to study, but there was never quite enough time for that.

MURAKAMI: I suppose you must have had a lot of busywork—or should I say administrative duties?—as music director of the Boston Symphony.

OZAWA: Yes, of course, a lot. There would be at least two meetings a week, and those would inevitably be long when there were complicated things to discuss. Some of them could be quite enjoyable, though. What I liked most was putting together programs. I also enjoyed the meetings where we'd choose guest conductors and soloists. The worst were discussions of personnel matters—what to do about so-and-so's salary, who gets promoted, who gets demoted: we had to decide things like that. And the Boston Symphony had no mandatory retirement age, which meant that if there were older players members whose playing had begun to decline, I'd find myself in the position of having to urge someone older than me to start thinking about retirement. That was the most painful thing. I had a few cases like that during my time as music director, some of them good friends. That was really hard.

From Telemann to Bartók

MURAKAMI: Let's talk about the sixties again. I believe your first American recording was an accompaniment for the oboist Harold Gomberg. It contains concertos by Vivaldi and Telemann, and the recording date is listed as May 1965. I happened to come across this copy at a used-record store in the US.

OZAWA: How incredible that you found this thing. Wow, it brings back memories!

MURAKAMI: I guess there was still no real consensus back then as to the meaning of "baroque music." Listening to these performances, I got that impression. The oboe's phrasing sounds more romantic than baroque to me.

OZAWA: Well, sure, in those days nobody knew how to perform this music. We knew there was something called "baroque music" and that there were some musicians who played it, but we hadn't really heard the repertory. This was my very first time performing it.

MURAKAMI: To me it seems as if the orchestra is producing something closer to a baroque sound than the soloist. What was this "Columbia Chamber Orchestra"?

OZAWA: That was a made-up name. They were really a bunch of string players from the New York Philharmonic picked by Gomberg to make the recording. None of us had played baroque music before. As an assistant conductor of the New York Philharmonic, I was chosen to conduct.

MURAKAMI: It's hard for me to think of you performing Telemann.

OZAWA: Yes, it might have been the only time for me. I had to work *hard* for this.

MURAKAMI: Did Harold Gomberg make a point of choosing you for the recording?

OZAWA: Yes, I think he liked me personally.

MURAKAMI: After this you recorded two Bartók piano concertos—nos. 1 and 3. They were recorded in July of that same year—two months after the Telemann. Peter Serkin is the soloist. This is a tremendously eye-opening performance!

OZAWA: That was the Chicago Symphony—or was it Toronto?

MURAKAMI: Chicago. And even today the performance sounds fresh and original. There was a certain reserve or uncertainty with the Telemann and Vivaldi, but this one's pretty much wide open.

OZAWA: You think so? I don't remember a thing about that performance. The year before, I was a surprise pick for music director of the Ravinia Festival. It caused a big stir—I even went on a TV show called *What's My Line?*—something like the old NHK quiz show *My Secret*. So the record company came to see me right away and we arranged to make recordings every year after the concert. The next day, we'd drive the half hour to Chicago and record.

MURAKAMI: Chicago's Ravinia Festival is like Boston's
   Tanglewood . . .

*I put the Bartók record on the turntable. The First Concerto.
Breathtakingly sharp sounds come flying out of the speakers,
a vivid aural image brimming with life. The performance is
superb.*

OZAWA: Oh, the trumpet is Herseth, Adolph Herseth.
   He's a legendary trumpeter with the Chicago
   Symphony.

The piano solo begins.

MURAKAMI: The sound of the piano is stunning, too,
   completely free of uncertainty.

OZAWA: Yes, he's really good. Peter was still in his teens.

MURAKAMI: It's a tremendously sharp performance.

The orchestra joins in with the piano.

OZAWA: Oh, I remember this part . . . In those days, the
   Chicago Symphony's brass section was the best in
   the world. Herseth and the rest of them were a stellar
   lineup.

MURAKAMI: Was that when Fritz Reiner was the principal
   conductor?

OZAWA: No, it was Jean Martinon.

MURAKAMI: But what a leap that was for you—from Telemann to Bartók! Talk about variety! *Ozawa laughs.*

MURAKAMI: In December of that same year you also recorded the Mendelssohn and Tchaikovsky violin concertos.

OZAWA: I can't quite recall the name of the fellow who played the violin on that one . . .

MURAKAMI: Erick Friedman.

OZAWA: And the orchestra was the London Symphony . . . ?

MURAKAMI: Yes, the London Symphony. I also found that recording in an American used-record store. Listening to it nowadays, though, there's something kind of old-fashioned about the violin's performance—a little too passionate.

OZAWA: I remember doing the recording, but not much more than that.

MURAKAMI: And just about the same time, again with the London Symphony, you recorded the Schumann Piano Concerto with Leonard Pennario. Also on the record is Strauss's *Burleske*. Then, the following year, yet again with the London Symphony, you recorded the Tchaikovsky Piano Concerto no. 1

with John Browning. That's quite a number of romantic concertos you put together in London with American performers. I haven't heard the recording with Browning, but in retrospect these performers don't seem all that impressive. No one really listens to them anymore.

OZAWA: I'm pretty sure the record company had a massive campaign going to sell both Pennario and Friedman. But I will say this: John Browning was an absolute genius on the piano.

MURAKAMI: I haven't heard much about him lately.

OZAWA: Yes, I wonder what he's doing.

Murakami note: Born in 1933, John Browning was a hot young pianist in the 1960s, but he scaled back his activities in the seventies, citing "overwork" as the cause. He re-emerged in the mid-1990s, playing contemporary American music, but died in 2003.

MURAKAMI: So you go from Telemann straight to Bartók and then swing back to dead center with the romantics. I'm curious how such a wide range of recording commissions came to you. Aside from the Gomberg recording, all are with the RCA Victor label.

OZAWA: I never know where requests like that are going to materialize from. I had had some success at the Ravinia Festival and was more or less in the spotlight at the time. After all, the Chicago Symphony was said to be the strongest orchestra in the world, so the fact that they had singled me out caused quite a stir. I suppose the record company wanted to exploit the publicity surrounding me, so that's how I ended up going to London to make all those recordings.

MURAKAMI: Looking at your discography, I can see you must have been very busy. Then that next summer, in 1966, you recorded Honegger's oratorio *Jeanne d'Arc au bûcher*. Your repertory has such tremendous variety!

Ozawa laughs.

MURAKAMI: What was your policy in those days—to accept any offer that came from a record company?

OZAWA: That's right. I was still not in any position to choose.

MURAKAMI: Was the Honegger also suggested by the record company?

OZAWA: I'm pretty sure it was. There's no way I would have gone to them wanting to do a piece like that.

MURAKAMI: I still can't tell from looking at your discography what the record company had in mind for you.

OZAWA: I have absolutely no idea.

MURAKAMI: Even an outside observer like me can't help

becoming a little confused looking at this lineup.
Next you did Berlioz's *Symphonie fantastique* with the
Toronto Symphony. That was late in 1966. Were you
already their principal conductor by that point?

OZAWA: Yes. I think it was that year. I recorded
Takemitsu's *November Steps* and Messiaen's
Turangalîla Symphony right after becoming
Toronto's music director. I was only there four years
altogether.

MURAKAMI: I see both pieces were recorded in 1967. Were
they your choices?

OZAWA: Yes—oh, not the Messiaen! That was the
composer's idea. I had performed it for him when he
came to Japan—before I was boycotted by the NHK
Symphony. He really liked my work—or should I
say he was crazy about it? He said he wanted me to
do everything of his. I was ready to do the complete
works, but Toronto wouldn't go along with that
plan: they said they'd never sell any tickets. At least
I managed to get the *Turangalîla Symphony* and
Oiseaux exotiques recorded.

The Rite of Spring: Something Like the Inside Story

MURAKAMI: To prepare for this interview, I listened
to—well, not all, but most of the recordings you
made in the sixties, and if I were to choose my
personal favorites, they would include the Bartók
piano concerto we mentioned, the *Symphonie*

fantastique you did with the Toronto Symphony, and Stravinsky's *Rite of Spring*. I thought they were especially wonderful—just as fresh today as ever.

OZAWA: You mean the Stravinsky I did with the Chicago Symphony?

MURAKAMI: Yes.

OZAWA: There's a story that goes along with that recording of *The Rite of Spring*. Stravinsky himself actually rewrote the score just before we made the recording. In his "revised version," he changed the bar lines. It was absolutely incredible. He made it completely different from the version we had studied so hard—a shock for the conductor and the performers alike. I figured there was no way we could do it.

MURAKAMI: What does it mean to "change the bar lines"?

OZAWA: Hmm, let's see, how can I explain this to you? [*He mulls it over for a while.*] It means completely changing how you count the beats. Say you've got 1-2-3, 1-2, 1-2, 1-2, 1-2, 1-2-3, and you change it to 1-2, 1-2, 1-2, 1-2 . . . like that.

MURAKAMI: So he changed irregular meters into regular ones?

OZAWA: Stravinsky said he "streamlined" it—he simplified it. He had an assistant named Robert Craft who was himself a conductor and composer. The score was changed so that if Craft conducted it, even a student orchestra would be able to play it.

MURAKAMI: In other words, it ceased to be a difficult piece.

OZAWA: And that's the version that Stravinsky asked me to record. So I did.

MURAKAMI: You mean, this recording we're listening to is of the revised version?

OZAWA: Well, I did perform the revised version with Stravinsky and Craft in the audience, and I recorded it for RCA. I recorded both the original version and the revised version with the Chicago Symphony.

MURAKAMI: I had no idea. I've never seen any recording of *The Rite of Spring* you did with the Chicago Symphony other than this one. I've always listened to this one on the assumption it was the same *Rite of Spring* I knew.

OZAWA: I'm not sure what happened, but the revised version was probably never released.

MURAKAMI: You mean they shelved it?

OZAWA: I knew it was no good when we played it, and the musicians knew it, too. Lenny said I was the biggest victim. He was furious. He was sure Stravinsky must have revised it to extend the copyright. I had studied the old version like crazy,

I had conducted it any number of times, and I had pretty much mastered it. Now I was having the rug pulled out from under me. Conducting the revised version required a totally different approach. This record we've got here, though, is the original version.

MURAKAMI: I've read the liner notes very closely, and it doesn't say a word about which version it is. They *do* mention that the composer had revised the work in 1967, but they don't say that that is the version being performed on the record. It seems to be deliberately vague. You'd think it would be a good selling point to stress that the record contained the very latest version.

Murakami note: According to the testimony of Robert Craft, who had cooperated with the revision, the main reason Stravinsky revised the work was that he himself had trouble conducting the parts with the irregular meter.
I put the record on the turntable.

OZAWA: Is it okay if I eat this *o-nigiri* rice ball?

MURAKAMI: Please do. I'll make tea.

I make tea.

OZAWA: I was still in London at the time of the 1968 recording. That was the year Robert Kennedy was killed.

MURAKAMI: Was this recording of *Rite of Spring*

something you did because *you* wanted to do it?

OZAWA: Yes, very much so. For one thing, I had already performed it everywhere.

MURAKAMI: So at that point in your career, you were able to take on the works that you wanted to record—not just what the record companies brought you?

OZAWA: Yes, that was more and more the case.

The quiet introduction ends, and the famous wild bam bam bam bam of the first scene, "Harbingers of Spring (Dances of the Young Girls)" takes over.

MURAKAMI: What an intense, edgy sound!

OZAWA: Yes, the Chicago Symphony was at its peak in those days, and I was young and energetic.

MURAKAMI: Let's listen to this same passage with you and the Boston Symphony. It was recorded about ten years later.

I change records, and the introduction begins again.

MURAKAMI: *Very* different mood . . .

OZAWA: Really, a much softer sound.

The bassoon plays the theme.

OZAWA: This bassoonist died, you know. In a traffic

accident. Sherman Walt. He played with the Saito Kinen, too.

We listen to the music, drinking tea and eating o-nigiri.

MURAKAMI: If I may be permitted to express my personal opinion as a music lover, when I hear you performing with the Chicago or Toronto symphonies in the sixties, it sounds as if you've got the music doing a lively dance on the palms of your hands. There's a kind of reckless audacity.

OZAWA: Reckless may be the best way to go sometimes.

MURAKAMI: Then you're with the Boston Symphony in the seventies, and it feels as if you're cupping your hands a little, more enfolding the music. It's easy to tell the difference, listening to all the recordings.

OZAWA: Yes, I see what you mean. The later ones may be a little more subdued.

MURAKAMI: More mature, musically? I'm not sure putting it that way can account for everything that's going on . . .

OZAWA: Well, when you become music director, you get very concerned about the quality of the orchestra.

MURAKAMI: After this 1973 recording with the Boston, you never did another studio recording of *The Rite of Spring*, did you?

OZAWA: No, I never did, though I was asked to any
number of times.

*Again comes the bam bam bam bam of "Harbingers of
Spring (Dances of the Young Girls)."*

OZAWA: Not so raw, is it? Interesting, this one.

MURAKAMI: The feel of the music is a little different from
standard performances of *The Rite of Spring,* though.

Three Seiji Ozawa Recordings
of *Symphonie fantastique*

MURAKAMI: Now I'm going to put on the recording of
the Berlioz *Symphonie fantastique* you did with the
Toronto Symphony. It's from 1966.

*I begin with the fourth movement, "Marche au supplice"
(March to the Scaffold).*

MURAKAMI: What would you say about the level of
playing you found in the Toronto Symphony when
you first arrived?

OZAWA: It was not very good, to tell you the truth. I
made a lot of changes in the orchestra's lineup, which
didn't win me too many friends. I even changed the
concertmaster. The old one came and knocked on
my door to complain. But the new people I hired are
still there today.

MURAKAMI: The sound is a little hard, wouldn't you say?

OZAWA: Yes, it is. We did this recording in Toronto's Massey Hall. It was famous for its bad sound. People used to call it "Messy Hall."

MURAKAMI: Charlie Parker did a famous live recording there. You just have to say "Massey Hall" and jazz fans know what you mean. But in this recording of your performance, the music itself is tremendously lively. It dances.

OZAWA: Yes, it's very free. You can *see* the music. It's much better than I expected. The recorded sound is not very good, though.

I lift the needle at the end of the movement.

MURAKAMI: I agree, it's a very good performance. Just listening to this one, I'm convinced it's the only performance of the piece you'd ever need. But then again, when I listen to the Boston Symphony performance, my opinion changes. The two are so totally different.

OZAWA: They were recorded at such different times, though. The Boston must have been fifteen years later.

MURAKAMI: No, not that much later. Let's see . . . the Boston one is 1973, just seven years after the Toronto.

I put on the Boston recording, again the "March to the Scaffold." The difference in tempo is almost shocking. It is so much heavier.

OZAWA: The orchestra itself is much better here, of course.

MURAKAMI: The sound it produces is very different, isn't it?

OZAWA: Listen to this bassoon passage: it's the Boston at its best. I couldn't have done that with the Toronto. And the timpani—it sounds completely different. In that sense, the Toronto Symphony was a collection of young musicians.

MURAKAMI: But with tremendous enthusiasm.

OZAWA: Yes, they had plenty of enthusiasm!

We listen to the music for a while.

MURAKAMI: It's amazing how different the music is with only seven years separating the performances.

OZAWA: But that was a big seven years for me. I changed a lot. After Toronto, I became the San Francisco Symphony's music director, and then moved to Boston.

MURAKAMI: Different orchestra, different sound: it's only natural for the music to be different.

OZAWA: And the *Fantastique* I just did with the Saito Kinen [December 2010] was, again, totally different. I myself have changed, for one thing. I purposely avoided playing the piece for a long time, to leave some space between performances. This new one might be a little too rich.

MURAKAMI: Too rich?

Ozawa laughs.

MURAKAMI: This next one is a DVD of a live performance of the *Fantastique* by the Saito Kinen in Matsumoto, in 2007.

Again, we hear "March to the Scaffold," and again there are small differences from the previous two. The music still visibly seems to dance, but its "undulation" is different. It has a different "groove," as might be said in jazz.

OZAWA: That trumpeter on the left is first trumpet in Berlin . . . and this person plays third trombone with the Vienna Philharmonic.

Ozawa stands and moves with the music. Looking at himself conducting on screen, he sighs.

OZAWA: This is how I ruined my hips. After I broke my shoulder, I couldn't use it properly, so I forced my body to move in an unnatural posture, which then threw my hips out. *This* body part doesn't move, so *that* one ends up a mess. It's stupid!

MURAKAMI: Your conducting is so dynamic. It's hard work, swaying with the music like that.

OZAWA: But comparing performances this way, they're really different! This is the first time I've ever done anything like this. I'm shocked at how different they are.

MURAKAMI: The differences are very obvious to me, too. You were only thirty-one when you conducted the Toronto in that powerful performance that keeps on surging forward, forward. As I said before with the Stravinsky, the music leaps and dances on the palms of your hands. But then you went to Boston and took over a major orchestra, and it feels as though you're cupping your hands, embracing the music, carefully letting it ripen. And now comes the recent Saito Kinen performance, and I get the impression you're unfolding your hands a little, letting the air in, freeing it up. Possibly you're giving the music itself a chance to develop more spontaneously, kind of like letting out whatever will come, maybe—to put it simply, taking a more natural approach?

OZAWA: Hmm, you may be right . . . but in that sense the December 2010 Carnegie performance of the *Fantastique* went even farther in that direction. It was pretty intense for me.

MURAKAMI: Maybe the sound of the Saito Kinen is more suited to that approach.

OZAWA: True. Watching this performance on the screen,

I'm obviously not worrying about every little detail.

MURAKAMI: Which is exactly what you used to do in your Boston days. As if you were carefully tightening one screw after another.

OZAWA: Right. Like I said before, I'm constantly trying to improve the quality of an orchestra, increasing its value.

MURAKAMI: In the Boston version of the *Fantastique* we heard before, you're constantly adjusting every little detail: the tempo changes from one part to the next, the color of the sound changes. It's marvelous, and though I wouldn't call it ornate, it's like looking at a moving miniature. With the Toronto or the Chicago versions, the music itself breaks into a run before there's any question of adjusting anything.

OZAWA: They're raw, aren't they? I had a lot of energy back then.

MURAKAMI: Listening to these three very different performances of the *Fantastique,* I could feel the three different phases of your musical life.

OZAWA: Well, sure, those things change with age. Your approach to an orchestra changes as you get older. And, in my particular case, as I mentioned before, there was the sheer technical matter, after I broke my shoulder, of not being able to move my arms as energetically as I had in the sixties and seventies.

MURAKAMI: And in the case of Boston, the fact that you were the permanent music director must have meant that you were constantly seeing the same people during the off-season, too. Wouldn't that enhance your relationship with the orchestra and make you want to start tweaking it in all kinds of little ways?

OZAWA: Sure, that's unavoidable.

MURAKAMI: In the case of the Saito Kinen, though, the orchestra is not always together, so you can't do too much tweaking. To some extent, you have to give them their independence and let them run with it. Am I right about that?

OZAWA: You certainly are. But the fact that we get together only for a month in the summer and for occasional concert tours keeps us fresh. We're always surprising each other. Like lovers who can only meet once a year [*Laughter*.].

MURAKAMI: How about your time in Vienna?

OZAWA: Vienna was like best friends getting together to make music. It was so easy for me!

MURAKAMI: You were director of the Vienna State Opera, but its orchestra is essentially the Vienna Philharmonic, isn't it?

OZAWA: Yes, 100 percent the same. But I wasn't the director of the Vienna Philharmonic, just of the Staatsoper. The Vienna Philharmonic doesn't have a music director. Members of the Vienna Philharmonic join the Staatsoper orchestra first, and then they get into the Philharmonic. You can't join the Philharmonic from the outset.

MURAKAMI: Oh, really? I had no idea.

OZAWA: You audition for the Staatsoper orchestra first, and after two or three years you move into the Philharmonic. A few musicians do play for the Philharmonic as soon as they join the Staatsoper, though.

MURAKAMI: So, unlike your time in Boston, you didn't need to deal with management or training?

OZAWA: Correct. Of course I would be there for the auditions, but I was just one vote out of several. I had almost nothing to do with personnel matters. Singers were another matter. I had a lot to say about choosing the company.

MURAKAMI: But you simply used the orchestra you were given?

OZAWA: Correct.

MURAKAMI: In other words, the orchestra was viewed as just one component of opera as a comprehensive art form?

OZAWA: Correct. So that raises the question of exactly what the director of the Staatsoper does. I wish I

had settled in there for a long stay and conducted a
lot more operas, but when my health deteriorated,
I couldn't do very many. But, boy, I enjoyed myself
there! I'm so glad I lived long enough to have that
experience. I think of it as a wonderful opportunity
that the gods gave me. I had no idea what it was like
to be in an opera company. Just finding that out was
terrific in itself. It was so much fun! I love opera,
and they would let me conduct anything I wanted,
unconditionally.

MURAKAMI: I went to Vienna two years ago and heard
you conduct Tchaikovsky's *Eugene Onegin*. The
stage production was very good, of course, but I
was electrified by the polished perfection of the
orchestra. Viewed from the balcony, the orchestra
looked like a single living thing, swaying with the
music. The *Eugene Onegin* you conducted in Tokyo
in 2008 was very enjoyable, but this was something
special. I heard a few other operas in Vienna at that
time—sheer bliss!

MURAKAMI: Getting back to the 1960s, RCA had you
doing a huge variety of recordings, didn't they?
There was Mussorgsky's *Pictures at an Exhibition*
[1967], Tchaikovsky's Fifth Symphony [1968],
Mozart's *Haffner* Symphony [1969], Bartók's
Concerto for Orchestra [1969], Orff's *Carmina
Burana* [1969], Stravinsky's *Firebird* and *Petrushka*
(1969). Add to those the standard coupling of
Beethoven's Fifth and Schubert's "Unfinished"
(1969), and you're all over the map.

OZAWA: True. Ha ha ha. The Mozart was with Chicago, wasn't it?

MURAKAMI: No, that was the New Philharmonia. Most of the others were with the Chicago Symphony, though. But that Beethoven piano concerto with Peter Serkin we talked about before was with the New Philharmonia Orchestra, wasn't it?

OZAWA: Right, right, that odd piece. As I said earlier, I had never played it before and never did it again.

MURAKAMI: This op. 61a was a violin concerto that Beethoven himself revised for piano and orchestra. It's kind of a stretch, sonically, for the piano, don't you think?

OZAWA: Very much so. But Peter was that kind of guy back then—he wanted to play things other than what his father was playing. It was really too bad, because that way he couldn't perform ordinary Beethoven pieces, but he wanted to play Beethoven, so he chose works that his father wouldn't. After his father died, though, he started playing the same pieces—Beethoven's Choral Fantasy, for example.

MURAKAMI: I'm very fond of another performance of yours from this period: Orff's *Carmina Burana*. It's marvelous—lively, colorful.

OZAWA: That was with the Boston, right?

MURAKAMI: Right.

OZAWA: That was before I became the music director.
I also played *Carmina Burana* with the Berlin
Philharmonic, when Maestro Karajan was still there.
I performed it at the famous "Silvester Concert" on
New Year's Eve in 1989, and I brought the entire
Shinyukai Choir from Japan. *Carmina Burana* might
be another good one for the Saito Kinen. We've got
such a good chorus to work with.

MURAKAMI: I'd love to hear it.

How Could Someone Young and Unknown Do Something So Amazing?

MURAKAMI: As we listen to these recordings, many of
which you made when you were young, I feel a
little mystified about something. You were still in
your twenties when you debuted in America in the
mid-1960s, but judging from the records you made
back then, you were already a complete musician.
Your musical world was fully formed, vital and
dynamic—and very exciting. Of course, there was
still room for maturation to come, but at that point
in time, your world was already there in its totality,
with its own autonomous, irreplaceable magnetism.
There was no—how can I put it?—no trial-and-
error. Of course, there was inevitably some variation
in your level of mastery of certain pieces, but there
was no trial-and-error, no tentativeness at any point.
How was such a thing possible? You left Japan,
you went to a foreign country where you had no
connections, and the next thing you knew, you were

conducting the New York Philharmonic and the Chicago Symphony, putting your own musical world on display and captivating foreign audiences. How could someone young and unknown do something so amazing?

OZAWA: Well, ultimately, it's because I had it drilled into me from a very young age by Professor Saito.

MURAKAMI: But surely that can't be the whole explanation. Not all of Professor Saito's students went on to have careers like yours.

OZAWA: Well, *I* can't explain it . . .

MURAKAMI: It seems to me that you must have a tremendous power of organization—a way of turning parts into a unified whole. It's consistently there for you, without a hint of uncertainty. Do you see this as a personal strength?

OZAWA: Look, let me just say this. I've had this technique physically fixed inside me from the time I was young, a technique that was instilled in me by Professor Saito. Most conductors have to work like hell in their youth to internalize their technique.

MURAKAMI: By "technique," do you mean the act of waving the baton?

OZAWA: Sure, sure, the technique of using it to prepare an orchestra for a performance. During the performance itself, it almost doesn't matter how you move the baton. No, that's overstating it, but it's really not *that* important. What *really* matters is how you wave your baton during rehearsals, in order to get the orchestra ready. That's what I learned from Professor Saito. In my case, right from the beginning, I never lost focus on that piece of advice. Oh, I suppose there has been some change as I've aged, but for the most part, it's remained pretty consistent.

MURAKAMI: But there must be a lot of things that a musician can only learn while in the thick of it, through accumulated experience. It's the same with novelists. Do you mean to say that you already had these things in place?

OZAWA: Well, I can say that I never struggled with those things from the start. I rarely felt inadequate, and I suspect that's because I had such a good teacher. So then, when I got to observe Lenny or Maestro Karajan conducting close-up, I pretty much understood what they were doing. I could see what they were trying to do. I could look at them analytically. So it never occurred to me to mimic their techniques. By contrast, someone who still doesn't have his own technique in place ends up imitating someone else's outward form, just superficially copying another person's movements. That didn't happen with me.

MURAKAMI: Is waving the conductor's baton difficult?

OZAWA: Difficult? Hmm, I don't know if it's so difficult.

But I had already internalized the technique in my late teens. Maybe I was special in that sense. I mean, I started conducting in my third year of middle school. I've been at it a long time! Before I ever got to conduct a professional orchestra, I had already been conducting for seven years.

MURAKAMI: You were already studying conducting in middle school?

OZAWA: I conducted the school orchestra.

MURAKAMI: The Toho Gakuen orchestra?

OZAWA: Correct. I had four years of high school and three years of university education. By which I mean I did my first year of high school at Seijo Academy and then again at Toho. There was still no music department at Toho then, so I waited a year until they got it together. Then I went to the university for two and a half years. For that entire seven-year span, I conducted student orchestras, so I had plenty of experience before I ever conducted the Berlin or the New York Philharmonic. Come to think of it, nobody ever gets that much experience under their belt. I'm sure Professor Saito thought it was bound to be good for me.

MURAKAMI: Lots of people play an instrument from the time they're little, but not too many young musicians aspire to be professional conductors.

OZAWA: That's true. I didn't know anybody else like

me. And the reason I was able to communicate with orchestras and convey to them what I wanted them to do—even though I could hardly speak their language—was because I had mastered the fundamental technique that had been drilled into me by Professor Saito.

MURAKAMI: Yes, but even before that—you have to have a clear image in your own mind of exactly what you want to do and how you want to do it. If you're writing fiction, say, it's important to be able to write, of course, but before that you have to have a strong sense in mind of something you are determined to write *about*. As far as I can tell from your records, at least, you always had a strong self-image from the time you were young. Your music always has a very clear, tight focus. It seems to me that the world is full of musicians who don't or can't do that. I probably shouldn't generalize about all Japanese musicians, but I can't help feeling that while they have a high overall level of technical mastery and can perform music that may be technically flawless, they rarely communicate a distinct worldview. They don't seem to have a strong determination to create their own unique worlds and convey them to people with raw immediacy.

OZAWA: That's the worst thing that can happen in music. You start doing that and the very meaning of the music is lost. It's just one step away from elevator music, which, to me, is the most frightening kind.

Follow-Up Interview: Maurice Peress and Harold Gomberg

MURAKAMI: The other day we talked a little about Maurice Peress, one of the other assistant conductors with you under Leonard Bernstein.

OZAWA: Oh, yes, yes, it just so happens I heard from him a short time after our conversation. He sent an old photo to my New York manager's office. It was a shot of the three of us assistant conductors standing in front of Carnegie Hall. It came with a nice note from him inquiring after my health. He heard about the concert I had to cancel in New York and decided to write. It was forwarded to me just yesterday or the day before. A total coincidence.

MURAKAMI: That's nice. I did a little research about Maurice Peress on the Internet after we talked about him. He's Puerto Rican–American and is apparently still quite active. He conducted the Kansas City Philharmonic from 1974 to 1980 and afterward conducted orchestras all over the world. His son is a pretty famous jazz drummer, Paul Peress. He's into fusion.

Ozawa reads the printout that I show him.

OZAWA: Maurice did a lot of conducting in China, too— and the Shanghai Opera!

MURAKAMI: He also wrote a book, *Dvořák to Duke Ellington*.

OZAWA: Yes, he was a good friend of Duke Ellington's. Wow, it's amazing that you can look up stuff like this.

MURAKAMI: It's on Wikipedia, but I don't know how accurate it is. I looked up Harold Gomberg, too. His younger brother is also an oboist. He was the principal oboist for the Boston Symphony.

OZAWA: Right, right. Ralph was the younger brother, played first chair in Boston for a long time. He retired not long before I left. The elder brother was first chair in New York, the younger the first chair in Boston.

MURAKAMI: It's rare for siblings to play the same instrument and for both of them to be so successful at it.

OZAWA: Yes, very rare. And they were both terrific. Ralph's wife was head of the Boston Ballet School. Harold was a lot crazier than Ralph. He had this incredibly beautiful daughter he was scheming to get hooked up with Claudio Abbado.

MURAKAMI: Abbado came after you as an assistant conductor of the New York Philharmonic, didn't he?

OZAWA: Yes, he was still a bachelor then. I got swept up in all that. It was pretty wild. [*Laughter.*]

MURAKAMI: I understand Harold Gomberg enjoyed a performance of yours when you were a young assistant and chose you to conduct one of his recordings.

OZAWA: Yes, he heard me conduct Toshiro Mayuzumi's *Bacchanale* and part of *Firebird* as an encore in place of Lenny, and he got me to conduct his recording.

MURAKAMI: He was first chair in the New York Philharmonic for a very long time, wasn't he? Thirty-four years altogether.

OZAWA: Right, but still, he passed away quite some time ago. Ralph, too, in 2006. Harold's wife, Margret, was a harpist, and she also did some composing. She was quite famous. They loved Italy and had a wonderful old country place in Capri, where they spent their summers. They invited me there once. I was in Europe conducting some French orchestra and had a lot of time on my hands, so they had me visit. I took the train to Naples and the ferry to Capri. They used to paint together. [*He reads from the Wikipedia printout.*] Ah, it's all coming back to me now.

MURAKAMI: It says he died of a heart attack on Capri.

OZAWA: Oh, really? He was twenty years older than me.

Eugene Ormandy's Baton

OZAWA: Eugene Ormandy was a tremendously kind man. He
took a liking to me and invited me many times to guest-
conduct his Philadelphia Orchestra. This was a real help to
me. I had a very low salary at Toronto, but the Philadelphia
Orchestra had lots of money and paid well. He trusted me
and let me use his personal office in the performance hall
whenever I was conducting there.

He once gave me a baton of his, and it was terrific, a special-
order item, very easy to use. I had so little money in those
days, I couldn't afford a custom-made baton. So anyway,
one day I opened his desk drawer and found a whole row
of them. I figured he wouldn't miss a few batons if they
were gone for a while and helped myself to three. But I got
caught right away. [*Laughter.*] He had this scary woman for
a personal secretary. She probably made a habit of counting
the batons in his drawer and she grilled me. "You took

them, didn't you?" "Yes, I'm sorry, I took them."

MURAKAMI: How many batons were there in the drawer?

OZAWA: I don't know, maybe ten.

MURAKAMI: Well of *course* they caught you if you took three out of ten! [*Laughter.*] But you mean to say his batons were so easy to use they were worth stealing?

OZAWA: Yes, they were great batons. This kind of baton was like the tip of a fishing rod cut off with a piece of cork attached for a handle, very flexible, made to his specifications. Later, he told me where I could order them.

MURAKAMI: I'll bet he got a big laugh telling everybody about this. "Once upon a time, Seiji Ozawa stole three batons from my desk drawer!" [*Laughter.*]

On the Music of Gustav Mahler

This conversation took place on February 22, 2011, in my Tokyo office. There was also a short follow-up interview, after which I added a few details. We talked a great deal about Mahler. As we spoke, I realized what an important part of Ozawa's repertory the music of Mahler has been. I myself had a problem getting into Mahler for a very long time, but at a certain stage in my life the music began to move me. Still, I was astounded to hear from Ozawa that a Mahler composition he had never heard before could make a deep impact on him when he read the score. Was such a thing really possible?

Saito Kinen as Pioneer

MURAKAMI: I've been meaning to ask you something

but it slipped my mind last time. The Saito Kinen Orchestra is not a permanent organization—it meets just once a year, with a somewhat different roster each time—but still it seems to have a consistency to its sound, wouldn't you say?

OZAWA: Yes, I would. And I think that as long as I'm conducting it, that consistency will be there. Also, it's s an orchestra that strongly foregrounds the strings. And we choose pieces to play that work well with that sound. Among Mahler pieces, say, the First and the Ninth . . . and the Second is like that, too.

MURAKAMI: Can the sound itself of the orchestra as a whole remain unchanged even though you don't play together regularly?

OZAWA: Well, if anything has changed, maybe it's the oboe. After playing with us for many years, Fumiaki Miyamoto retired a few years ago. He coached his successor for a while, but after he left, we weren't able to settle on a permanent oboist. Then we found a very good French player and recently performed the Berlioz *Fantastique,* so we're getting closer to our original sound.

MURAKAMI: Does the sound of the orchestra change noticeably when someone other than you conducts?

OZAWA: I guess so. That's what they tell me. That it changes a lot. But the strings are firmly established as the tradition of the Saito Kinen. That foundation was built by Professor Saito's former students. There are a few other orchestras in the world that were formed the same way as the Saito Kinen, but that string foundation is what distinguishes the Saito. The string section is an absolutely disciplined unit.

MURAKAMI: The Saito Kinen was the first of these seasonal orchestras, wasn't it?

OZAWA: I think you may be right. I don't think there were any other orchestras like it anywhere in the world at the time. The Mahler Chamber, the Lucerne, the Deutsche Kammer: they were all formed after the Saito Kinen. But you know, back when we got the orchestra started, there was a lot of negative criticism, people saying there was no way that such a thrown-together group could make good music. There was a lot of positive feedback, too, of course.

MURAKAMI: At first, the idea was to make it a one-time appearance, wasn't it?

OZAWA: That's true. In 1984, former students of Professor Saito put the orchestra together to commemorate the tenth anniversary of his death. We performed in Tokyo's Bunka Kaikan and the brand-new Osaka Symphony Hall. Then it was like, "Hey, this is good! We can keep going! We can take this orchestra anywhere in the world!"

MURAKAMI: You mean when you first started, there was never any thought of reorganizing every year and doing foreign performance tours?

OZAWA: Not at all. It never crossed our minds.

MURAKAMI: But eventually the Saito "system" became a worldwide trend. You were truly pioneers, wouldn't you say?

Back When Bernstein Was Grappling with Mahler

MURAKAMI: By the way, you never worked on Mahler with Professor Saito, right?

OZAWA: No, never.

MURAKAMI: Was that just a matter of the period?

OZAWA: Well, you know, very few people were playing Mahler until Bernstein started grappling with him so passionately in the early sixties. Of course you had somebody like Bruno Walter, but almost no other conductors took a positive interest in Mahler besides him.

MURAKAMI: I started listing to classical music in the mid-sixties, but Mahler's symphonies were not at all popular back then. About all you could find in the recording catalogs were the First [the "Titan"], the Second [the "Resurrection"], and *Das Lied von der Erde*. They were not widely listened to, and I think they were rarely performed. Young people nowadays are shocked when I tell them that.

OZAWA: It's true, Mahler was not at all popular. Maestro

Karajan was doing *Das Lied von der Erde,* and he used it to teach us, but he was not playing any of the other symphonies.

MURAKAMI: Böhm wasn't playing the Mahler symphonies either, was he?

OZAWA: No, no, not at all.

MURAKAMI: And neither was Furtwängler.

OZAWA: No, it's true. He was playing everything up to Bruckner . . . You know, I've never heard Bruno Walter's Mahler.

MURAKAMI: The other day I was listening to a 1939 Mahler recording by Willem Mengelberg and the Concertgebouw Orchestra.

OZAWA: Ha, I didn't know such a thing existed.

MURAKAMI: The Fourth Symphony. Not surprisingly, it sounds like a creaky old thing. I also listened to Bruno Walter doing the Ninth Symphony in Vienna in 1938, just before he fled from the Nazis. My main impression of both of them—the Walter and the Mengelberg—was how old they sounded. I don't mean just the quality of the recording, but the tones they produced. Both men were direct disciples of Mahler, and their performances may be historically important, but you listen to them today and they're kind of hard going. Then a new period comes along, and Walter makes stereo recordings and builds the foundation for a Mahler revival, and Leonard Bernstein makes it happen with his passionate recordings.

OZAWA: Which is exactly when I was his assistant conductor, when he was recording the complete Mahler with the New York Philharmonic and the London Symphony.

MURAKAMI: Back then, ordinary music fans were not listening to Mahler, even in America?

OZAWA: No, hardly anybody listened to Mahler. So then Lenny became absolutely relentless, performing Mahler cycles in performance, and recording everything. He may not have done the complete works in performance, but he cycled through nearly everything at least twice. Then he went to Vienna and did the same thing with the Vienna Philharmonic, sometime in the late sixties.

MURAKAMI: After he left the New York Philharmonic?

OZAWA: Yes, but even before that, he went to Vienna and did it with them—when he was on sabbatical.

MURAKAMI: Which reminds me, you said before that you were house-sitting for him when he was on sabbatical. You mean actually taking care of his house?

OZAWA: No, I was "house-sitting" the orchestra.

MURAKAMI: "House-sitting" the orchestra?

OZAWA: That included some conducting, though not a lot. Mainly, I was doing various chores for the orchestra, inviting lots of guest conductors, like Josef Krips, or William Steinberg, or what's-his-name, that handsome American fellow who died young . . . ?

MURAKAMI: Handsome young American conductor . . . ?

OZAWA: You know . . . Thomas . . .

MURAKAMI: Schippers?

OZAWA: That's him. Thomas Schippers. He was an incredibly good-looking guy, a good friend of Lenny's, married to a beautiful young heiress from Florida. He founded the Spoleto Festival with Gian Carlo Menotti, but he died young. I think he was still in his forties. Krips, Steinberg, Schippers, and there was one other conductor . . . I can't remember who . . . but anyway, there were four guest conductors, and I made all the arrangements. For example, when Steinberg did the Beethoven Ninth, I went and arranged for the chorus, that kind of thing. Each of the four guest conductors took the podium for six weeks, and I got to do two of the regular-season concerts that year. So I was both assistant conductor and the one who filled in the gaps. I learned a *lot* from that experience! I became good friends with Thomas Schippers, and Steinberg used to treat me to dinner all the time. And Krips—I think it was because of our time together back then that he recommended me to become conductor of the San Francisco Symphony. Of course, you know I went to Toronto after New York. Krips spent seven years as music director of the San Francisco, and when he left suggested that I succeed him. So I quit as music director of the Toronto Symphony and moved to San Francisco.

MURAKAMI: Was Lenny on a year-long sabbatical?

OZAWA: Yes, he was off for a whole year, the '64 to '65 season.

MURAKAMI: And you were basically managing the orchestra while he was gone.

OZAWA: Right. I was like a replacement music director. But not personnel. I refused to do that. And I didn't do auditions. All I did was the busywork. But that was more than enough, let me tell you!

MURAKAMI: That was before you went to Toronto, right?

OZAWA: Right. I think it was the year before I went to Toronto. I probably got all of that business taken care of before I left.

MURAKAMI: And Bernstein was in Vienna the whole time?

OZAWA: Yes, he supposedly took the year off because he wanted to take a break from conducting and concentrate instead on composing, but in fact he did

a lot of conducting in Vienna. I remember there was
an awful lot of grumbling about that in New York.
Then all of a sudden Vienna made him an offer, and
that was it—he went. It might have been at that time
that he conducted Beethoven's opera *Fidelio*. In an
old theater called Theater an der Wien, which was
where *Fidelio* had had its first performance, in 1805.
I had some kind of work in Vienna at the time of
Lenny's performance, I forget what it was, but I went
to hear it—sitting right next to Karl Böhm!

MURAKAMI: Amazing!

OZAWA: I seem to recall he gave me the ticket. Yes, it was
his wife's. I didn't have any money in those days. I
was traveling to Vienna to conduct, but their fees
were incredibly small, and it cost a lot to go there
from America. Maybe that's why I got a free ticket.
So anyway, after the performance, I went with Böhm
to Lenny's dressing room. I was very curious to hear
what the two of them would talk about, but neither
of them said a word about *Fidelio*. I mean, Böhm was
the world's leading conductor of *Fidelio*, after all.

MURAKAMI: True.

OZAWA: I had worked as his assistant when he came to
Japan and conducted *Fidelio* at the Nissay Theatre,
so I figured they'd have a ton of things to say about
the opera, but neither of them said a word about
it. [*Laughter.*] I don't remember exactly what they
talked about, but I think it was, like, food, and
remarks about the theater, stuff like that.

MURAKAMI: Maybe neither of them wanted to be the first to broach the subject.

OZAWA: I wonder. In retrospect, it seems very strange.

MURAKAMI: So you were saying that Bernstein was playing Mahler in Vienna, too . . . ?

OZAWA: Yes, I think he was. Hmm, come to think of it, it wasn't that time, but I was there when he recorded the Mahler Second in Vienna. At that point I was conducting the Vienna Philharmonic's regular season concerts, and he used the orchestra during the same period to make the recording. For Columbia. I'm sure it was Columbia because my great friend John McClure, the Columbia producer, came to Vienna to do the recording. In other words, the orchestra was playing regular concerts with me and making records and TV tapes with guest conductors in their spare time.

MURAKAMI: When would that have been?

OZAWA: Hmm, it must have been early in 1972, just after my daughter, Seira, was born. Lenny was staying in the Sacher Hotel and we were in the Imperial. We always stayed in the Imperial because they gave discounts to people with the Vienna Philharmonic. Lenny came for a visit there to see the baby. He walked right in, picked Seira up, and tossed her into the air. He said he was especially good at communicating with babies this way. Boy, did Vera have a fit! [*Laughter.*] "After all I went through to bear this child!" she said.

MURAKAMI: Well, he doesn't seem to have done her much harm. She grew up okay. [*Laughter.*] I haven't seen the video of the recording with the Vienna Philharmonic. He made a video around that time of the Second Symphony, but in that case the orchestra was the London Symphony, and they taped it in England. I'm pretty sure John McClure produced that one, too. They recorded it live in a big church before an audience. There's no audio recording from CBS, though.

OZAWA: Well, maybe the tape they made in Vienna that time was for television, not a proper studio recording. But anyway, I'm quite sure that Bernstein performed the Mahler Second with the Vienna Philharmonic that time. His wife, Felicia, was there, too—a gorgeous woman, Chilean, with very fair skin. She had been an actress, a real beauty. She and Vera became very close friends. We were so poor then, she often gave Vera her dresses. "I know you like to wear pretty things," she'd say. Funny, they had the same build.

MURAKAMI: How was the performance?

OZAWA: Well, *I* thought it was excellent. But he was very nervous. Usually, we'd have dinner together and relax over drinks the night before, but that time was unusual, we didn't do that. We had a meal *afterwards*, though.

MURAKAMI: What kind of audience reaction was Bernstein getting from those passionate Mahler performances back in the sixties?

OZAWA: Just speaking of the Mahler Second I heard in Vienna, the audience reaction was terrific. I conducted the Second at Tanglewood after that, and that performance got a very good reaction from the audience, too. I remember thinking how great it was to get such a wonderful audience response doing Mahler. I think that may have been the first performance of the Mahler Second at Tanglewood.

MURAKAMI: How about with the New York Philharmonic?

OZAWA: Hmm, I don't remember very well. [*After some thought.*] Well, I think the newspapers were kind of split, pro and con. Unfortunately for Bernstein, there was this music critic for *The New York Times* named Sean Berg or something. He hated everything that Bernstein did.

MURAKAMI: That was Harold Schonberg. He was very famous. I read a book he wrote.

OZAWA: Funny, in 1960, when I was still a student, I conducted a student performance of Debussy's *La Mer* at Tanglewood. Three of us divided up the conducting duties, and I had the finale. Or maybe it was the Tchaikovsky Fourth Symphony. We divided that one up, too, among four of us, and again I did the finale. So then, the next day, Schonberg wrote about this in *The New York Times*. He was actually there for the Boston Symphony's concert, but he also wrote about the student performance. About me, he said, "People should keep the name of this conductor in mind."

MURAKAMI: That's fantastic!

OZAWA: Yes, it was a total surprise for me, but it gets even better! He telephoned the top person at the student orchestra, and he came to meet me face-to-face and told me I should come and see him if I was ever in New York. He was not the kind of guy who said things like that to people usually, I heard. So not long afterward, I had something to do in New York and went there for the first time in my life. And since I was there, I went to visit him at his office at *The New York Times*. He gave me a tour of the place—here's the print shop, here's the music department, here's the culture section . . . He spent a good two or three hours showing me around, and we even had a cup of tea together.

MURAKAMI: Amazing. He obviously liked you a lot.

OZAWA: It *is* amazing, isn't it? Lenny used to kid me about it after I became his assistant. "The guy dumps all over *me*, but he can't say enough about 'Say-jee.' " Really, Schonberg was *constantly* criticizing Bernstein. I'd see his stuff in the papers and felt he was overdoing it. He was just terrible to Lenny. He was always kind to me, though. Maybe he thought of me as a new star he had discovered.

MURAKAMI: The *New York Times* music critics and drama critics were tremendously influential.

OZAWA: It's true. I don't know about nowadays, but back then they were hugely influential.

MURAKAMI: After all the battering he took from the New York media, Bernstein was welcomed with open arms by both the public and the press when he went to Vienna. This made him happy, but at the same time it made him wonder, "What was *that* all about in New York?" That's why he shifted his base of operations to Europe in his later years. I read that in his biography.

OZAWA: I don't know much about that. My English was so bad, I hardly knew what was going on. I do know that he was tremendously popular, that his concerts were always sold out, that Columbia was bringing his records out one after another, the movie of *West Side Story* was a huge hit—all that spectacular stuff was what I was aware of. Whatever led up to it, he maintained a great relationship with the Vienna Philharmonic in his later years.

MURAKAMI: He never served as music director with any orchestra after the New York Philharmonic, did he?

OZAWA: No, that's true.

MURAKAMI: He was done with it, I suppose.

OZAWA: Ha ha, I wonder.

MURAKAMI: From what you tell me, though, by temperament he wasn't suited to management. He just couldn't use his position of authority to say no to anybody.

OZAWA: That's true, he found it tough to look somebody in the eye and give him an order or reprimand him. Basically, he would never do that. Quite the opposite: he would ask for others' opinions. When I was his assistant, he'd ask me after a concert, "Hey, Seiji, do you think the tempo of that Brahms Second was okay?" and stuff like that. I would be thinking, "What are you asking *me* for?" and I'd struggle to come up with an answer. So I always had to be very attentive at his concerts. I couldn't just loaf around in the back of the hall, half-listening, 'cause then I'd really be stuck if he asked my opinion afterwards. [*Laughter.*]

MURAKAMI: Was he really like that? He was honestly interested in other people's opinions?

OZAWA: Yes, always. Even with a beginner like me, as long as we were making music together, we were equals.

MURAKAMI: In any case, when it came to Bernstein's Mahler performances, opinions in New York were split, right?

OZAWA: That's how I remember it. But the orchestra gave it everything they had. I mean, Mahler is tough to perform. The musicians were all studying hard to master it. In those days, we used to play maybe three Mahler symphonies a year. I used to see how hard they worked at rehearsals. They'd give a concert, and right away they'd go to Manhattan Center and make a recording.

MURAKAMI: So two or three of those Mahler symphony records were coming out per year?

OZAWA: Yes, pretty much.

I Never Even Knew Music Like That Existed

MURAKAMI: Had you been listening to Mahler before Bernstein got you started?

OZAWA: No, not at all. When I was a student at Tanglewood, my roommate, the Uruguayan conductor José Serebrier, was studying the Mahler First and Fifth. Serebrier was a truly outstanding student. I still see him now and then. He'll drop in to visit me backstage, that sort of thing. I saw him in London, I saw him in Berlin. Well, anyway, back then I asked to look at the scores he was studying, and that was the first time in my life I found out about Mahler. Afterward, I sent for the scores of both those pieces and studied them. There was no way a student orchestra could play them, but I put tremendous effort into studying the scores.

MURAKAMI: Just the scores? You didn't listen to them on records?

OZAWA: No, I had never heard them on records. I didn't have the money to buy records then, and I didn't even have a machine to play them on.

MURAKAMI: What was it like, reading the scores for the first time?

OZAWA: It was a huge shock for me—until then I never even knew music like that existed. I mean, here we were at Tanglewood, playing Tchaikovsky and Debussy, and meanwhile there's this guy putting all his energy into studying Mahler. I could feel the blood draining from my face. I had to order my own copies right then and there. After that, I started reading Mahler like crazy—the First, the Second, the Fifth.

MURAKAMI: Did you *enjoy* just reading the scores?

OZAWA: Oh, tremendously. I mean, it was the first time in my life I had ever seen anything like them. To think there were scores like this!

MURAKAMI: Was it a completely different world from the music you had been playing until then?

OZAWA: First of all, I was amazed that there was someone who knew how to use an orchestra so well. It was extreme—his marvelous ability to put every component of the orchestra to use. And from the orchestra's point of view, the Mahler symphonies are the most challenging pieces ever.

MURAKAMI: So when was the first time you actually heard, with your own ears, the sound of an orchestra playing Mahler—was that with Bernstein?

OZAWA: Yes, the first time I ever heard Mahler was as Bernstein's assistant in New York.

MURAKAMI: What was it like for you, hearing the real thing for the first time?

OZAWA: It was a complete shock. At the same time, I felt overjoyed that I could be right there with him, in that time and place, when Bernstein was, quite literally, pioneering this kind of music. So I also did Mahler as soon as I got to Toronto. Then I could do it myself! And with the San Francisco Symphony, too, I played almost all of Mahler's symphonies.

MURAKAMI: What kind of response did you get from the audiences?

OZAWA: Good, I think. By then, Mahler was, well, not exactly popular—but among the kind of people who come to listen to symphonies, Mahler was getting a lot of attention.

MURAKAMI: But Mahler symphonies are hard work—not just to perform but to listen to!

OZAWA: True, but by then he was popular *enough*. It was already starting, thanks in large part to Bernstein's efforts. He put a huge amount of energy into getting the people of the world to listen to Mahler.

MURAKAMI: But still, for a long time, Mahler's music was not listened to very widely. Why do think that was?

OZAWA: Hmm, I wonder . . .

MURAKAMI: First you've got Wagner, then you go from Brahms to Richard Strauss, which more or less brings the German romantic line to an end. Then you go straight through from Schoenberg's twelve-tone music to, like, Stravinsky, Bartók, Prokofiev, and Shostakovich, and that's more or less how the history of music flows, without much room to squeeze in Mahler or Bruckner. At least that's how it was for a long time.

OZAWA: True.

MURAKAMI: But in Mahler's case, you get this miraculous revival a half-century after the composer's death. What's behind all that?

OZAWA: I suspect it probably started with the orchestra musicians themselves. Once they got a chance to actually play some Mahler, they found they liked it, and that led to the revival. And once the musicians started to think of Mahler as fun to play, the orchestras started vying with each other to perform the music. After Bernstein, orchestras from all over gladly adopted Mahler. Especially in the States, there came a point where you weren't considered an orchestra if you couldn't perform Mahler. And not just in America: in Vienna, too, they started playing Mahler like crazy, because, after all, they were

Mahler's home base.

MURAKAMI: Yes, but home base or not, the Vienna Philharmonic didn't play Mahler for a very long time.

OZAWA: That's true, they didn't.

MURAKAMI: Do you think that was mainly because people like Böhm and Karajan didn't take up the music?

OZAWA: Probably. Böhm especially.

MURAKAMI: Both of them often played, say, Bruckner or Richard Strauss, but they never touched Mahler. Mahler himself was the virtual music director of the Vienna Philharmonic for a long time, but I get the impression that the orchestra was cold toward his music for a *very* long time.

OZAWA: Yes, but the Vienna Philharmonic plays Mahler beautifully now. The orchestra and the music are really a perfect match. They can lay bare its very essence.

MURAKAMI: Last time we talked about this, you said that when the Berlin Philharmonic played Mahler, Maestro Karajan would often take a pass and hand the baton to you.

OZAWA: That's true. I conducted the Mahler Eighth in Berlin. I think it might have been the first time the Berlin Philharmonic played that symphony. Maestro

Karajan told me to do it. Normally, that's a piece that the music director would conduct himself.

MURAKAMI: Of course, it's such a big piece, a major event.

OZAWA: But for some reason, the task came to me, and I remember putting everything I had into it. They put together some wonderful soloists for me. And the chorus, too: it wasn't just the Berlin chorus, but they called in some top professional groups like the Hamburg Norddeutscher Rundfunk Chorus, and the WDR Radio Choir of Cologne, and made a huge production out of it. It was a truly special event.

MURAKAMI: Well, it's not the kind of symphony you can perform all the time.

OZAWA: I played it in Tanglewood, and then again in Paris—with the Orchestre National de France, in a place called Sandonie.

The Historical Evolution of Mahler Performance

MURAKAMI: The style used to perform Mahler has changed a great deal, hasn't it, from the sixties to now?

OZAWA: You could say that various different styles of performance have appeared. I was very fond of Lenny's Mahler.

MURAKAMI: You can listen to those recordings he did with

the New York Philharmonic today, and they're still fresh. I listen to them fairly often even now.

OZAWA: And Maestro Karajan's Ninth is just wonderful. He did it very late in his career, but it was great. The finale especially. I remember thinking how well suited the piece was to him.

MURAKAMI: The sound of the orchestra absolutely has to be beautiful and meticulous in that symphony.

OZAWA: Especially the finale. That and the finale of the Bruckner Ninth are really tough, the way they both quietly fade away.

MURAKAMI: You have to make the music of that piece in long units, or else you can't really scoop out everything it has inside—to put it more or less in terms of the "direction" we talked about before.

OZAWA: Right, right. Any orchestra without those long breaths can't play it. You could say the same thing about Bruckner.

MURAKAMI: The last Mahler Ninth you did with the Boston Symphony was breathtakingly beautiful, too. The one that's on DVD.

OZAWA: Because we put real feeling into it. Finally, Mahler appears to be written in this very complex way—and in fact it *is* written in a way that is very complex for the orchestra—but the essential quality of Mahler's music is such that (and here, I'm afraid the way I'm putting it will be misunderstood) if you do it with feeling, it's a fairly simple thing. By "simple" I mean something like the musicality of a folk song, something that everyone can hum. Lately, I've come to feel that as long as you capture that quality with truly superior technique and tone color and get the feeling into it, it's probably going to go well.

MURAKAMI: Hmm, it may be easy to *say* that, but isn't it hard to actually *do* it?

OZAWA: Yes, well, of course it's hard, but—look, all I want to say is that Mahler's music *looks* hard at first sight, and it really *is* hard, but if you read it closely and deeply, with feeling, it's not such confusing and inscrutable music after all. It's got all these layers piled one on top of another, and lots of different elements emerging at the same time, so in effect it *sounds* complicated.

MURAKAMI: You get these completely unrelated motifs— sometimes motifs that move in completely opposite directions—proceeding at the same time, with practically equal emphasis.

OZAWA: And they'll come very close to each other before moving on. When these things happen, the music sounds complicated. You can study it and still be left confused.

MURAKAMI: And it can be hard for listeners, too, almost schizophrenic, if you try to grasp the overall structure of a piece while you're listening to it.

OZAWA: That's true. It's the same with a later composer like Messiaen. He'll put in three simple melodies that proceed simultaneously and yet have absolutely nothing to do with one another. You pull out any one part and the thing itself is fairly simple. If you put feeling into it, you can perform it quite simply. Which means, in other words, that a musician performing one part just has to concentrate hard on doing that one part. A musician playing a different part puts just as much energy into that without any relation to the first. Put the two of them together at the same time, and the result is the kind of sound that we've been talking about.

MURAKAMI: I see what you're saying. The other day, for the first time in quite a while, I listened to a Bruno Walter performance of the "Titan" on a stereo LP, and it seems to me I could scarcely hear the grasp of Mahler's music, the separation of parts that you just described. Instead, I felt a kind of will to force the whole of Mahler's symphony into one massive frame, to bring it closer to the structure of a Beethoven symphony. But when you do that, you end up with a slightly different sound than the so-called "Mahler sound." Listening to the first movement of the "Titan," for example, I felt that I was hearing the Beethoven "Pastoral." That was the kind of sound that Bruno Walter was producing. But when I listen to your performance of the "Titan," the sound is so different. Finally, in Walter's case, it seems as if the traditional form of German music—something like the sonata form—is ingrained in him at the deepest level.

OZAWA: Uh-huh, for sure, that approach may not be very well suited to Mahler's music.

MURAKAMI: Of course it's very good as music, very high quality, and moving to listen to. Walter has his own idea of Mahler's world, and he constructs it in this very solid way. But I think the sound may be just a little different from what we now look for in Mahler's music, or what we take to be "Mahleresque."

OZAWA: In that sense, I think that Lenny's achievement was absolutely huge. He himself was a composer, so he was able to tell the performers, "Do this part this way. Don't think about the other parts, just concentrate on your own." When you perform it like that, the result is very convincing to listeners. It brings out the flow of the orchestra. Those elements were already present in the First Symphony, but they're even more pronounced from the Second onward.

MURAKAMI: But when I listen to records of Mahler performances from the sixties, I get the sense that the approach you're describing hadn't formed yet— the idea that if you forge ahead with the details, then the whole will emerge. Rather, what I think I may be hearing is a tendency to carry the music forward emotionally in a traditional fin-de-siècle Viennese way, accepting chaos as chaos. Isn't the kind of approach you're describing a relatively recent phenomenon?

OZAWA: Well, maybe so in terms of *performance*. But the fact is that Mahler was *writing his scores* the way I'm talking about. Before Mahler, if you had two motifs going at the same time—theme A and theme B—there was a clear distinction between primary and secondary. In Mahler, though, the two are completely equal. So the musicians who are playing theme A have to put their heart and soul into playing theme A; and the musicians playing theme B have to put *their* heart and soul into playing theme B—with feeling, with color, everything. It's the job of the conductor to put it all together so that the two themes proceed simultaneously. This is what you need to do with Mahler's music because *that's how it's written*—right there in the score.

MURAKAMI: Now, let's talk about the First Symphony, the *Titan*. So far, you have made three recordings of it: the first in 1977 with the Boston Symphony, then again with Boston in 1987, and the third in 2000 with the Saito Kinen Orchestra. The three recordings sound completely different from one another.

OZAWA: Oh, really?

MURAKAMI: It's shocking how different they are.

OZAWA: Hmmm.

MURAKAMI: In the simplest terms, the first Boston

performance has a very fresh feel to it overall. It's a young man's music that goes straight for the heart. The second Boston performance is terrific, with an added density that only the Boston Symphony could produce. But the newest one, with the Saito Kinen Orchestra, feels absolutely transparent to me—as though you can see every little detail. All the inner voices come clearly to the surface. I really enjoyed comparing the recordings and hearing these differences.

OZAWA: I myself changed, too, over that long a time. I've never sat down to do a comparison of the three recordings, but I'm pretty sure you're right about how they differ.

MURAKAMI: When I listen to Abbado's recent Mahler performances, I'm sure I feel that same kind of grasp of Mahler that you were talking about before. They give the impression of a very deep and meticulous reading of the score, as though he's become convinced that the more deeply you burrow into the score itself, the more naturally Mahler is going to emerge. I get the same kind of feeling from a conductor like Gustavo Dudamel. Of course it's important for the conductor to become emotionally involved with the music, but that's strictly something that comes later, as a result of the deep study of the score.

OZAWA: Maybe so.

MURAKAMI: But when you listen to Mahler performances

from the sixties, say, by someone like Rafael Kubelik, there's still a sense of compromise, as if the shift from a romantic grounding is not yet complete.

OZAWA: Yes, well, the musicians themselves probably had that sort of mind-set back then. But nowadays the players are changing. That's what I think. Their mentality has definitely been changing—their perceptions of what their roles are with regard to the whole. Recording techniques have also changed. In the old days, the dominant tendency was to record the overall sound. Things like the orchestra's overall resonance were important. They tried to capture the whole rather than the details. Most of the recordings made in the sixties and seventies were like that.

MURAKAMI: With digitalization, those tendencies have changed. Mahler is not that interesting to listen to anymore unless you can hear each of the individual instruments.

OZAWA: You're absolutely right about that. Digital recording made it possible to hear every little detail clearly, and that may have caused performances themselves to change. In the old days, we used to pay a lot of attention to things like how many seconds the reverberation lasted, but nobody talks about that anymore. Now, people aren't satisfied unless they can hear the details.

MURAKAMI: Maybe the recording technology has a lot to do with it, but you can't quite hear all those details in the Bernstein performances from the sixties, can you? The impression is more one of the sound of the orchestra en masse. So when you're listening to those records, emotional elements tend to be given far greater emphasis than the accumulation of details.

OZAWA: That's what the sound was like at the Manhattan Center, where they did the recording. Now they tend to record in performance halls, right up there on the stage. When they do that, you can hear the same reverberation from the record as you would at a concert.

Going Crazy in Vienna

MURAKAMI: Among musicians who perform Mahler— and maybe among his listeners, too—there are many who think a lot about the composer's life or his worldview or his times or fin-de-siècle introspection. Where do you stand with regard to such things?

OZAWA: I don't think about them all that much. I do read the scores closely, though. On the other hand, when I started working in Vienna more than thirty years ago, I made friends and started going to the art museums there. And when I first saw the work of Klimt and Egon Schiele, they came as a real shock to me. Since then, I've made it a point to go to art museums. When you look at the art of the time, you understand something about the music. Take Mahler's music: it comes from the breakdown of traditional German music. You get a real sense of that breakdown from the art, and you can tell it was not some half-baked thing.

MURAKAMI: I know what you mean. The last time I
went to Vienna, I went to a Klimt exhibit at an art
museum. Seeing the art in the city where it was
created, you really feel it.

OZAWA: Klimt's work is beautiful and painted with
minute attention to detail; but looking at it, don't you
think there's something kind of crazy about it, too?

MURAKAMI: Yes, it's certainly not what you'd call
"normal."

OZAWA: There's something about it, I don't know, that
tells you about the importance of madness, or that
transcends things like morality. And in fact, at the
time, morality really was breaking down, and there
was a lot of sickness going around.

MURAKAMI: A lot of syphilis and stuff. Vienna was
more or less pervaded with this kind of mental and
physical breakdown: it was the atmosphere of the
age. The last time I went to Vienna, I had some
time to kill, so I rented a car and spent four or five
days driving around the southern part of the Czech
Republic—the old Bohemian region where Mahler's
birthplace was located, the little village of Kalischt,
or Kaliště as they call it now. I didn't go there on
purpose, just happened to pass through. It's still
tremendously rural out there, nothing but fields as
far as the eye can see. It's not that far from Vienna,
but I was surprised at how different the two areas

were. "So Mahler came from a place like this!" I thought. What a huge turnabout in values he must have experienced! Back then, Vienna was not only the capital of the Austro-Hungarian Empire, it was a colorful center of European culture and probably ripe to the point of being overripe. The Viennese must have looked upon Mahler as a real country bumpkin.

OZAWA: I see what you mean.

MURAKAMI: And on top of that, he was a Jew. But come to think of it, the city of Vienna gained a lot of its vitality by taking in culture from its surroundings. You can see this in the biographies of Rubinstein and Rudolf Serkin. Viewing it this way, it's easy to see why popular songs and Jewish klezmer melodies pop up in Mahler's music all of a sudden, mixing into his serious musicality and aesthetic melodies like intruders. This diverse quality is one of the real attractions of Mahler's music. If he had been born and raised in Vienna, I doubt that his music would have turned out that way.

OZAWA: True.

MURAKAMI: All the great creators of that period—Kafka, Mahler, Proust—were Jews. They were shaking up the established cultural structure from the periphery. In that sense, it was important that Mahler was a Jew from the countryside. I felt that strongly when I was traveling around Bohemia.

There's Something Funny
About the Third and the Seventh

MURAKAMI: Now, regarding Bernstein's performances
of Mahler in the sixties, the emotional input seems
to be a major element in his case. He seems to be
projecting himself onto Mahler with enormous
passion.

OZAWA: Yes, the passion is there, no question.

MURAKAMI: He seems to have had tremendous empathy
for Mahler's music, a deep personal involvement. I'm
sure it was important to him that Mahler was a Jew.

OZAWA: Yes, very important, I think. Lenny felt that
element very deeply and was very conscious of it.

MURAKAMI: I get the feeling, though, that—for lack of
a better way of putting it—there's a kind of ethnic
quality that has tended to diminish in recent Mahler
performances. In yours, for example, or Claudio
Abbado's, such coloration is relatively pale.

OZAWA: It's not an area of special concern to me, but
Lenny felt that element very deeply and was very
conscious of it.

MURAKAMI: And not just because Mahler's music contains
what might be called Jewish elements, I suppose?

OZAWA: No, I don't think it was just because of that. In
Lenny's case, that kind of connection was probably

very strong. It was the same for the violinist Isaac Stern. And Itzhak Perlman, of course, though more so when he was young. It's the same with Daniel Barenboim, too. I'm close with all of these musicians, but there are areas deep down where I can't fully grasp what they're feeling or thinking. And I'm sure it's the same for them where I'm concerned—a guy like me with a Buddhist father and a Christian mother and practically no religious feeling of my own: I suspect they think they can't fully understand me!

MURAKAMI: But is there actually friction there, because of being just "Christians" and "Jews"?

OZAWA: No, none at all.

MURAKAMI: So you're just saying that Bernstein felt a strong Jewish tie to Mahler and his music, right? And of course, in Bernstein's case, there must have been a strong sense of commonality with Mahler in being both a conductor and a composer.

OZAWA: Looking back on it now, though, I feel I was in New York during the orchestra's most interesting period. I was able to be right there, by Bernstein's side as his assistant, when he was most feverishly grappling with Mahler. It was almost uncanny to see how he threw himself into the music—the total absorption. As I keep saying, I only wish I had had better command of English back then. He had so much to say during rehearsals, but I could only understand a fraction of it!

MURAKAMI: But you could tell how the sound of the orchestra would change when he gave them instructions, I'm sure.

OZAWA: Of course I could tell as I watched the rehearsal unfold, but in Lenny's case, he would often interrupt the rehearsal itself and talk to the musicians. Then I couldn't tell what he was saying. But you know, these talks of his were very unpopular with the orchestra members. There was only a certain amount of time for rehearsals, and the longer he talked, the less time there was to rehearse. So then you had a lot of irritated musicians who became even more annoyed if the rehearsal ran over.

MURAKAMI: What would he talk about? His opinions on the meaning of the music?

OZAWA: For the most part, he would talk about the meaning of the music, but then he would go off on tangents, like, "Oh, that reminds me, when I went to so-and-so's place last time . . ." and go on forever about stuff like that until people got fed up.

MURAKAMI: I guess he liked to talk.

OZAWA: He liked it and he was good at it, and he could be very convincing, which is why I still regret the fact that I couldn't really understand what he was saying.

MURAKAMI: I suppose you were right there with him, observing his rehearsals and taking notes.

OZAWA: That's right, but I'd get totally lost whenever he launched into his long monologues.

MURAKAMI: Did you ever find yourself in a situation where you had read the score and heard the music in your head, but then when you heard the actual music that Bernstein was making with the orchestra, it sounded totally different to you?

OZAWA: Oh, sure, that happened all the time. That's because I was still reading Mahler scores with the same mind-set as when I read Brahms. It could be a total shock to hear the orchestra playing what I'd read that way.

MURAKAMI: Whenever I listen to one of those long Mahler symphonies, I find myself thinking that if it were a Beethoven or a Brahms, I'd know pretty much how it was structured and it might not be that hard to learn the movements in order. But is it possible for a conductor to fit the entire complex construction of a Mahler piece inside his head?

OZAWA: In the case of Mahler, the important thing is not so much to learn it, as to immerse yourself in it. If you can't do that, you can't do Mahler. The works are not that hard to learn. The challenging thing is whether or not you can get inside a work once you've learned it.

MURAKAMI: I often find myself incapable of grasping the order in which the music unfolds. Take the fifth movement of the Second Symphony, for example.

It goes this way and that way and I start wondering why it does what it does at any one point . . . and before I know it my brain has turned to mush.

OZAWA: Yeah, there's no logic to it at all.

MURAKAMI: No, none at all. That never happens with Mozart or Beethoven.

OZAWA: Because their works adhere to certain forms. The point with Mahler was to destroy those forms, deliberately. So in a sonata form, where the piece is telling you, "Here, I want you to go back to this melody," he'll bring in a whole new melody. In that sense, of course, his works can be hard to learn— but if you study them properly and if you immerse yourself in the flow, his pieces are not that difficult. You *do* have to spend time on them, though, to get to that point—a lot more time than with a Beethoven or a Bruckner.

MURAKAMI: When I first started listening to Mahler, I used to wonder if he wasn't just fundamentally mistaken about how to go about creating music. I sometimes feel that way even now. Why is he doing *this* in *this* part of the composition? But over the years, those very passages have gradually become a source of pleasure for me. There will always be a kind of catharsis at the end of the process, but in the meantime, I'm often at a total loss.

OZAWA: That's especially true of the Seventh and the Third, even for those of us who are playing the music. If you don't concentrate hard and do things exactly right, you end up drowning along the way. The First is fine, the Second is fine, and so are the Fourth and Fifth. There's something a little strange about the Sixth, but ultimately, it's okay, too. But the Seventh, wow, that's a real problem. And the Third is another weird one. Once you get to the Eighth, you're already into the huge ones, and you can make it work one way or another.

MURAKAMI: There are still some inscrutable parts in the Ninth, of course, but, I don't know, with that one you're in a whole different category.

OZAWA: You know, I once traveled all over Europe conducting the Third and the Sixth. With the Boston Symphony.

MURAKAMI: Talk about an austere pair of symphonies!

OZAWA: The Boston Symphony was famous for its Mahler renditions at the time, and we got lots of invitations from Europe specifically to play Mahler. That was a good twenty years ago, though.

MURAKAMI: That was the time when Bernstein and Solti and Kubelik were the big names in Mahler performance. With you as conductor, the Boston became famous for having a somewhat different feel.

OZAWA: We were among the earliest orchestras to gain a reputation for performing Mahler. [*He eats a piece of fruit.*] Mmm, this is good. Mango?

MURAKAMI: No, it's a papaya.

Seiji Ozawa and the Saito Kinen Perform the *Titan*

MURAKAMI: At this point, I'd like to listen to the Saito Kinen Orchestra performing the third movement of Mahler's First Symphony, conducted by you. It's from a DVD performance taken at the Matsumoto music festival.

When the solemn (but in no way severe) funeral march, with its air of mystery, comes to an end, a traditional Jewish folk melody suddenly begins (2:29).

MURAKAMI: I always find this part—what?— extraordinary? It's certainly in no way ordinary.

OZAWA: You're right about that. The way this Jewish melody pops out after the funeral music: it's a crazy combination.

MURAKAMI: But think of what a shock it must have been to the Viennese of the day to have music like this played for them all of a sudden.

OZAWA: A huge shock, I'm sure! And in terms of technique, in something like this traditional Jewish musical passage, the violins play what they call *col legno*—striking the strings with the wooden part of the bow instead of the horsehair part—which produces a very crude sound.

MURAKAMI: Did other composers use the technique before Mahler?

OZAWA: Hmm, I wonder—certainly none of the symphonies of people like Beethoven, Brahms, or Bruckner used it. It may be there in Bartók, say, or Shostakovich.

MURAKAMI: Definitely, when you're listening to Mahler, you come across these passages where you have to wonder, "How are they making that sound?" If you listen closely to contemporary music, though, especially in movies, they use sounds like that every now and then—in John Williams's *Star Wars* music, for example.

OZAWA: That's the Mahler influence, I'm sure. But anyhow, just looking at this movement, it's packed full of all sorts of those elements. It's amazing that he was able to do that. Back then, his audiences must have been astounded.

The funeral march returns (4:30), and then (5:20) a beautifully lyrical melody makes its appearance, the same melody that concluded Mahler's Lieder eines fahrenden Gesellen.

MURAKAMI: Here again, the mood of the music undergoes a dramatic change.

OZAWA: Yes, this is a pastoral, finally, a song of paradise.

MURAKAMI: Yes, but it comes out of nowhere, without

any logical connection to anything that came before. There's no sense of inevitability to it.

OZAWA: No, none at all. Listen to that harp: it's supposed to be reminiscent of a guitar.

MURAKAMI: Oh, really?

OZAWA: The performers have to forget what they were just playing, adjust to a new mood, and completely immerse themselves in this new melody.

MURAKAMI: You mean to say that the people who are making the music aren't supposed to think about meaning or inevitability? They're just supposed to devote themselves to playing what's written in the score?

OZAWA: Well . . . hmm . . . let's see. How about thinking about it like this? First comes the heavy funeral march, then the part like a coarse folk song, and then the lovely pastoral. Then it changes dramatically again back to the grave funeral march.

MURAKAMI: So you mean we should just think about it in terms of that line of development?

OZAWA: No, maybe it's more like you just accept it as it is.

MURAKAMI: Not thinking about the music as a story but just accepting the whole thing—boom!—the way it comes?

OZAWA [*pausing to think*]: You know, talking about these things with you like this, it's gradually begun to dawn on me that I'm not the kind of person who thinks about things this way. When I study a piece of music, I concentrate fairly deeply on the score. And the more I concentrate, probably, the less I think about other things. I just think about the music itself. I guess I could say that I depend entirely on what comes between me and the music.

MURAKAMI: Not searching for meaning in the music or in each of its parts, but just accepting the music purely as music?

OZAWA: Exactly. Which is why it's so hard to explain to anybody. I have something that enables me to get completely inside the music.

MURAKAMI: Maybe it's a bit too much to be talking about "special powers," but there are these people who have the ability to simultaneously take in all parts of some complex object or some convoluted idea all at once, like taking a high-resolution photograph of it. Maybe you have something like that going on with music rather than understanding it through logical analysis.

OZAWA: No, I'm not saying that at all. It's just that when I stay focused on a score, the music quite naturally slips inside me.

MURAKAMI: So you have to take the time to concentrate on it.

OZAWA: That's right. Professor Saito used to tell us to concentrate on reading scores as if we had written them ourselves. For example, one time I was invited to the maestro's house along with my classmate the composer Naozumi Yamamoto. The first thing the maestro does when we get there is hand us some blank score sheets, and he tells us to start filling them in with the score of the Beethoven Second Symphony, which we've been rehearsing.

MURAKAMI: You mean, he wants you to write the full score?

OZAWA: The full score. It's a test to see how much we can write in one hour. We had kind of suspected that we might be asked to do such a thing, so we had more or less prepared ourselves beforehand, but this is a *very tough* assignment. Sometimes I'm knocked out before I can write twenty measures. I've got the French horn and trumpet parts all wrong, and there's no way I can write the viola and second violin parts correctly.

MURAKAMI: Is there really not much of a difference when it comes to memorizing relatively straightforward music like Mozart's and the convoluted music of someone like Mahler? Is it no different in terms of internalizing the whole?

OZAWA: No, not really. Of course, the ultimate purpose is not to memorize it but to understand it. There's a great deal of satisfaction when you finally come to understand a piece of music. The ability to understand is far more important for a conductor than the ability to memorize. After all, you can look at the score while you're conducting.

MURAKAMI: So for a conductor, memorizing a score is just one result of all this, but it's not that important in itself.

OZAWA: No, it's not that important. No one would ever say a conductor is great because he memorizes or bad because he doesn't memorize. The one good thing about memorizing the score, though, is that you can make eye contact with the performers. In something like opera, especially, you can watch the singers while you conduct, and you can trade signals with them.

MURAKAMI: I see.

OZAWA: Maestro Karajan used to have every note memorized, but he kept his eyes closed the whole time. I had a close-up view of him the last time he conducted *Der Rosenkavalier*, and he had his eyes tightly shut from beginning to end. You know how you've got the three female singers together at the end of the opera? Well, they had their eyes locked on the maestro in total concentration, and he never once opened his eyes.

MURAKAMI: Closed eye contact?

OZAWA: I wonder. The singers never took their eyes off him for a second. All three women might as well have had cords connecting their eyes with his. It was a very mysterious sight.

The funeral march emerges again at the end of the pastoral (7:00–7:14).

OZAWA: Here, this is another very difficult transition. The gong comes in [6:54–7:00], the three flutes do a quiet setup [7:01–7:12], and that first sad, simple melody of the funeral march comes back again [7:14].

MURAKAMI: And the shift from major to minor happens in the blink of an eye.

OZAWA: Right. Now, listen to this tiny little clarinet part [7:39–7:44]—*taa-ra-ra-ra, beep and, beep and.*

The clarinet adds an indefinably mysterious touch to the melody, the strange tones of a bird crying out a prophecy deep in the forest.

OZAWA: We've got a very simple piece of music here, but even in the simple way it's combined with the rest, it changes everything. Things like this were just inconceivable in the music that came before Mahler . . . but he's written in the score exactly how he wants it played.

MURAKAMI: He gives very detailed instructions, doesn't he?

OZAWA: He does. He knew the orchestra inside out, the

qualities of every single instrument. He brings out
the full power of the orchestra, and in a way quite
different from a composer like Richard Strauss.

MURAKAMI: In very simple terms, can you tell me some
differences in their orchestration?

OZAWA: The biggest difference is that Mahler's
orchestration is—how to put this?—kind of raw.

MURAKAMI: Kind of raw?

OZAWA: Yes, he draws something raw out of the
orchestra. In Strauss's case, it's all there in the score:
"Don't think, just play it exactly as it's written, and
you'll get the music." And in fact if you do perform
it as written, you get the music as it's supposed to be.
Mahler's music is not like that—it's much more raw.
Strauss has an all-string piece like *Metamorphosen*,
for example. It takes the fine-grained precision of
the all-string ensemble as far as it can possibly go,
in pursuit of an established form. Mahler probably
never even thought of going in that direction.

MURAKAMI: I guess you mean Strauss's orchestration
has more technically demanding parts. Certainly,
when you're listening to something like *Also
sprach Zarathustra*, it feels as if you're enjoying a
magnificent painting hanging on the wall.

OZAWA: I suppose so. But in Mahler's case, the individual
sounds rise up and come right at you. In the crudest
of terms, he throws this raw sound at you in its most

basic coloration. He can be very provocative in the way he draws out the individuality or idiosyncrasy of each and every instrument. By contrast, Strauss uses sounds after he has blended them together. I probably shouldn't be making such simplistic declarations.

MURAKAMI: When it comes to the techniques he employed in orchestration, it must have been a major factor that Mahler—and Strauss, too, for that matter—was also an outstanding conductor.

OZAWA: That's absolutely true. Which is precisely why his music makes such tremendous demands on the orchestra.

MURAKAMI: In the finale of Mahler's First, all of the horn players stand up at one point, don't they? Is that specified in the score?

OZAWA: Yes, right in the score it says, "All stand up holding instruments."

MURAKAMI: I mean, does that really have some effect on the sound?

OZAWA: Hmm. [*He pauses to think.*] I suppose there might be *some* difference in sound with the instruments held aloft like that.

MURAKAMI: I thought it was maybe just for show.

OZAWA: Well, that may be the case, too. But don't you

think the sound of the instruments would come through more clearly with them held in a higher position like that?

MURAKAMI: Seeing it happen is powerful enough. I'm fine with it being just for show. I recently heard this Mahler First in a concert by the London Symphony Orchestra conducted by Valery Gergiev. They had *ten* horns, and when they sprang to their feet all at once, it was tremendously powerful. Do you ever feel that there can be this element of showmanship in Mahler's music, a kind of lowbrow ornamentation?

OZAWA [*laughing*]: You may be right!

MURAKAMI: Come to think of it, wasn't there some kind of direction for the horn players to raise their horns in the finale of the Second Symphony?

OZAWA: Hmm, you're right, where they're supposed to turn the horns so the bells face upward.

The Directions in the Score Are Very Detailed

MURAKAMI: The directions are extremely detailed, aren't they?

OZAWA: Yes, tremendously detailed. Every little thing is written into the score.

MURAKAMI: You mean, like, how to use the bow and things like that?

OZAWA: Exactly.

MURAKAMI: So I guess there's not much to sort out when you're performing Mahler—no sections where you can't figure out how to play things?

OZAWA: No, there are very few places where the musicians have to wonder how to play their parts. Take a Bruckner or a Beethoven, for example— they're full of passages like that. But in a Mahler score, there are tons of little directives for every single instrument. Just look at this. [*He points at a large page in a well-worn score.*] We call these symbols "pine needles" or "hairpins." This one [<] indicates a crescendo, where the volume grows gradually louder, and this one [>] indicates a decrescendo, where the volume grows gradually softer. There are hundreds of these things. This line goes *taa-ra-ra, taritara, raaa-ra.* [*He sings the line aloud.*]

MURAKAMI: I see.

OZAWA: Beethoven wouldn't put in so many directives. He'd just write "espressivo" in a passage like this. Now, here, you see this line. It's not just a *legato* marker to make the notes link smoothly. It means play it like this: *taa-aa-ri, rari-rari, raaa-ba.* [*He sings expressively.*] Having this many directives means that the range of choice given to us performers is narrowed way down.

MURAKAMI: But won't there be passages where you can't agree with the directive, or where you wonder why it should be played that way?

OZAWA: There are some, especially where horn players think, "It couldn't possibly be that way."

MURAKAMI: But if that's what the score says, I suppose the musician feels obliged to at least try to play it the way it's written.

OZAWA: That's what we all do, because we have to.

MURAKAMI: Are you talking about passages that are technically difficult?

OZAWA: There are lots of those. And there seem to be some in particular that musicians find impossible to play.

MURAKAMI: But impossible or not, if the score contains such detailed instructions that the performers are given hardly any choice, how are there so many different kinds of performances of Mahler with different conductors at the helm?

OZAWA: [*He takes a long while to think this one over.*] Hmm, that's an interesting question. By which I mean that I've never thought of it before. As I said earlier, a Mahler score gives so much more information than a Bruckner or a Beethoven, so it only stands to reason that it should offer a narrower range of choice—but in actual practice, it doesn't really work out that way.

MURAKAMI: No, I'm sure it doesn't, because listening to all these various performances, I can tell that one sounds very different from another. The sound itself is different.

OZAWA: But still, I really have to think about it. You know, ultimately, the more information a composer supplies, the more each conductor has to agonize over how to put all that information together—over how to balance the various pieces of information.

MURAKAMI: You mean, for example, in instances where you're given detailed instructions regarding two different instruments that are playing at the same time?

OZAWA: Sure, that's it. How do you prioritize? Or rather, how do you bring the best out in both instruments? In Mahler, especially, you have to help both instruments rise to their full potential. But you get into rehearsals with your orchestra and you hear what it actually sounds like and you sense that you can't bring both out to the fullest—so then you've got to strike a balance. So even though there is no composer who gives as much information in his scores as Mahler, there is also no composer whose sound changes as much depending on who is conducting.

MURAKAMI: It's a real paradox, isn't it? It seems that the richer the information given to your conscious mind, the more subconscious choices you have to make. I suppose that means that you, as the conductor, don't take these bits of information as restrictions?

OZAWA: That's true.

MURAKAMI: In fact, maybe you'd rather have some restrictions.

OZAWA: Well, sure. That would make the music easier to understand.

MURAKAMI: But even if you had some restrictions, you'd still have the sense of being free.

OZAWA: I think that's true. It's our job as conductors to convert the music exactly as it's written into actual sound; and so execute these restrictions accurately. But above and beyond what is written, we are free.

MURAKAMI: If you think of being free as something that happens above and beyond the accurate transfer of the score into sound, then there's no difference in the performer's ability to be free, either. This would hold true whether we're talking about the music of Beethoven—which has relatively few restrictions written into the score—and that of Mahler, which has a lot.

OZAWA: That is true, but only to an extent. Strauss, for example, provides information that is very consistent and indicates a single direction in which the music is meant to move. But Mahler is not like that at all. His instructions are often inconsistent and sometimes contradictory. He even has a few that may make perfect sense to him but not to anyone else. All are "restrictions" of one kind or another, but they can be very different in character.

MURAKAMI: I see what you mean. But for a composer who puts so many restrictions into his scores, Mahler has surprisingly little to say about metronome settings.

OZAWA: It's true, he doesn't write them in.

MURAKAMI: Why do you think that is?

OZAWA: There are all kinds of theories. Some people say he figures he's given you so many detailed instructions that the tempo will take care of itself. Others say he wants to leave the tempo, at least, up to the judgment of the performers.

MURAKAMI: And yet with Mahler's symphonies, you don't find such extreme differences in tempo from one conductor to the next.

OZAWA: You may be right about that.

MURAKAMI: I can't seem to recall any performances that struck me as extremely fast or extremely slow.

OZAWA: Recently, though—say, in the past five or six years—a few such performances have begun to emerge. When I was in Vienna in 2006 I came down with a case of shingles and couldn't conduct for a while, so I started listening to other people's performances. I think it was about that time that you began to hear these more extreme performances. Maybe some conductors were doing it just to be different, adopting tempos that hadn't been used by people who had made recordings up to that point—by Bernstein, for example, or Abbado—or by me.

MURAKAMI: But since the tempos aren't specified, the conductor is free to choose his own.

OZAWA: That is correct.

MURAKAMI: Mahler himself was both a composer (the one who gives the instructions) and a conductor (the one who interprets them). So balancing one against the other might have been quite a struggle for him. Speaking of interpretation, the funeral march that comes at the beginning of this third movement really varies in sound, depending on who conducts it: it can be full of an emotional heaviness, or have an academic feel, or even be somewhat comical. In your performance it can feel more neutral, given your more fine-grained treatment from a purely musical standpoint. Then comes the passage of traditional Jewish music which, as I said before, Jewish musicians have tended to imbue with a kind of klezmer sound; while others have taken a cooler approach. Such questions of interpretation are also choices for the performer, I presume.

OZAWA: That traditional Jewish section uses an actual klezmer melody—so you have some conductors who strongly emphasize its Jewish sound, and others who deal with it as one motif in the context of the overall long movement. In the latter case, the conductor will give the theme a precisely nuanced performance when it first appears, and when it is developed again later, they will not add any particular flavor and will tie it in with what follows. That's another way to do it. The score contains no instructions when it comes to making choices like these.

MURAKAMI: I seem to recall that the movement is labeled "Feierlich und gemessen, ohne zu schleppen," which translates as "Solemnly and measured, without dragging."

OZAWA [*looking at the score*]: Correct, that is what it says.

MURAKAMI: When you start thinking about it, those are difficult instructions.

OZAWA: Yes. [*Laughing.*] Very difficult!

MURAKAMI: It starts with a double-bass solo. But is the conductor the one who establishes the sound in this case—like "That's a little too heavy," or "Lighten it up a little"?

OZAWA: Well, yes, but it would be mainly the character of the bass player's tone that would determine that. The conductor can't say a lot where such things are concerned. Come to think of it, though, before this point, it was unheard of for a symphonic movement to begin with a long double-bass solo. The very fact of having a bass solo was unusual enough, but to put

it at the very beginning of the movement! Mahler
was really an oddball.

MURAKAMI: Personally, I like this part, but the way the
solo is played kind of sets the mood for the whole
movement, so it must be hard to perform. All alone
like that for such a long passage.

OZAWA: It *is* hard, so often I'll talk one-on-one with
the soloist about it offstage rather than during
rehearsal—like, could you play it a little softer, or
raise the intensity a bit, or tone it down just a little?

MURAKAMI: This solo must be the chance of a lifetime for
a bass player, I would think. Really nerve-wracking!

OZAWA: Sure, it's a tremendous responsibility. Which is
why we always have a bass player perform it during
an audition. How the person plays this solo can
determine whether or not he's invited to join the
orchestra.

MURAKAMI: I see!

OZAWA: Behind the double bass, the timpani are going
ton-ton-ton, like this.

MURAKAMI: In fourths, counting off the same
monotonous rhythm all the way through.

OZAWA: Yes, *re-la-re-la*—keeping up the sound of a
heartbeat, so to speak, setting up a solid framework
for the music. And just as the heartbeat won't wait

for anyone, the timpani won't wait, so the double bass has to do its best to keep up, taking breaths or one thing or another to fit into the framework. Look, here's a comma in the score.

MURAKAMI: Yes, what's that for?

OZAWA: It means "Take a breath here." *Rii-rari-raa, raa.* [*He sings the double bass's melody.*] (??:??){243.3} Things like this are all written in. Of course, you can't actually "take a breath" on a double bass—it's not a wind instrument—but it means that the bassist should momentarily cut the sound, as if taking a breath, rather than keep the sound going without a break. Mahler is very careful to provide these detailed directions.

MURAKAMI: Amazing.

OZAWA: So then, you see, when the oboe enters with its *ryat-tatari-ran, ran* [*he sings with a bouncing rhythm*], then the phrase comes to life. And then later, (??:??){243.10} he writes in these accents for an instrument like the harp, whose softer sound is more difficult for the audience to hear. And then he adds a staccato mark on all of the following notes.

MURAKAMI: Oh, I see. It's incredibly detailed. What a job it must have been to write a score with so much information in it!

OZAWA: That's why the performers are so nervous to do this one.

MURAKAMI: I can see where they'd be kind of stressed out playing this stuff, the way it never ceases to demand that they concentrate on every little thing.

OZAWA: Exactly. There's a lot of stress involved. Take this part, for example: you can't play it as you ordinarily would—*tori-raa-yaa-tataan*—but rather *toriira-ya-tta-tan*. The instructions are very precise. You can't relax.

MURAKAMI: This instruction, "mit Parodei"—does it really mean you're supposed to play it with a sense of parody?

OZAWA: It does.

MURAKAMI: That's another difficult bit of direction.

OZAWA: You have to have a spirit of parody here.

MURAKAMI: But I imagine you can overdo it and destroy the dignity of the music.

OZAWA: You're right. All it takes is one teaspoon too much or too little, and you can change the whole flavor of the music. That's what's so interesting.

MURAKAMI: Even given all this direction, I'm sure there are still times when a musician supposedly playing it as written produces a sound that is different from what you imagined.

OZAWA: Yes, of course, that happens. When a musician

produces a sound that is different from the sound
I have in my head, I'll work hard to bring the two
closer together—either bv verbal instruction or via
hand signals.

MURAKAMI: Are there musicians who don't get the point?

OZAWA: Yes, of course, all the time. It's the conductor's
job, during rehearsals, to find compromises, or to
keep pushing until the musicians come around.

What Makes Mahler's Music So Cosmopolitan?

MURAKAMI: Just listening to this third movement of the
First Symphony, it seems pretty clear to me that
Mahler's music is filled with many different elements,
all given more or less equal value, used without
any logical connection, and sometimes even in
conflict with one another: traditional German music,
Jewish music, fin-de-siècle overripeness, Bohemian
folk songs, musical caricatures, comic subcultural
elements, serious philosophical propositions,
Christian dogma, Asian worldviews—a huge
variety of stuff, no single one of which you can
place at the center of things. With so many elements
thrown together indiscriminately (which sounds
bad, I know), aren't there plenty of openings where
a non-Western conductor such as yourself can make
his own special inroads? In other words, isn't there
something particularly universal or cosmopolitan
about Mahler's music?

OZAWA: Well, this is all very complicated, but I do think there are such openings.

MURAKAMI: I remember when we talked about Berlioz and you said that his music had openings that a Japanese conductor could exploit, because it was "crazy." Can't you say pretty much the same thing about Mahler?

OZAWA: The big difference between Berlioz and Mahler is that Berlioz doesn't put in all these detailed instructions.

MURAKAMI: Ah, I see.

OZAWA: So we performers are a lot freer when it comes to Berlioz. We have less freedom with Mahler, but when you get to those final, subtle details, I think there exists a sort of universal opening. We Japanese and other Asian people have our own special kind of sorrow. I think it comes from a slightly different place than Jewish sorrow or European sorrow. If you are willing to attempt to understand all of these mentalities, and make informed decisions after you do so, then the music will naturally open up for you. Which is to say that when an Easterner performs music written by a Westerner, it can have its own special meaning. I think it's well worth the effort.

MURAKAMI: You mean you have to dig down to something deeper than superficial Japanese emotionalism to understand it and internalize it?

OZAWA: Yes, that's it. I like to think that a performance of Western music that also makes full use of Japanese sensibilities—assuming the performance itself is excellent—has its own raison d'être.

MURAKAMI: Earlier we listened to Mitsuko Uchida playing Beethoven's Third Piano Concerto, and I don't think it would be wrong to say that her performance is very Japanese with regard to the transparency of her piano or her perfect placement of those moments of silence. I don't think she is deliberately aiming for such things but rather that they emerge quite naturally as a result of her pursuit of the music itself. In that sense, they are not superficial at all.

OZAWA: You may be right about that. There may be uniquely Eastern ways of playing Western music. I would like to go on believing in that possibility.

MURAKAMI: I guess you could say that Mahler was a person who, half consciously but also half unconsciously, departed from what you might call orthodox German music.

OZAWA: It's true. Which is precisely why I want to think that there is plenty of room for us non-Europeans to cut our way inside. Professor Saito had some very helpful things to tell us in that regard. "You youngsters are blank slates at the moment. So when you go to other countries, you will be able to absorb their traditions. But traditions are not always good. There are both good traditions and bad traditions. That's true of Germany, of France, and of Italy. Even in America now there are both good traditions and bad traditions. You'll have to learn to distinguish between the two, and when you go to those countries, you should absorb their good traditions. If you can do that, you will find there is a role for you as Japanese, as Asians."

MURAKAMI: If you ask me, I would guess that, for a very long time, conductors like Karajan had an almost visceral intolerance for the hybridity, the vulgarity, the disunity of Mahler.

OZAWA: I see what you mean. It's probably fair to say that.

MURAKAMI: We talked before about Karajan's performance of the Mahler Ninth Symphony, and I agree it's a wonderful performance. It practically drips with beauty. But if you listen to it carefully, it's—how should I put it?—it's not really Mahleresque Mahler. He's playing Mahler with the same tone he might use for a Schoenberg or a Berg or some other early work of the New Viennese school. In other words, it sounds to me as if Karajan is performing Mahler by dragging him into the area where he himself is at his best.

OZAWA: That is exactly right. It's especially true of the final movement. Even during the earliest rehearsals, he gave the orchestra the orders he always gave them and made the same kind of music he always did.

MURAKAMI: Instead of producing a Mahleresque sound,

he was borrowing the "Mahler" container and filling
it with his own music.

OZAWA: Which is why the only Mahler symphonies he
played were the Fourth, the Fifth, and this Ninth
we're talking about.

MURAKAMI: I'm pretty sure he did the Sixth, too, and *Das
Lied von der Erde*.

OZAWA: Oh, really? He did the Sixth, too, did he? So that
means the ones he *didn't* do were the First, Second,
Third, Seventh and Eighth.

MURAKAMI: Which is to say that he chose to record the
containers—the works—that were best suited to
his own musicality. Maybe he couldn't quite accept
the deep, truly Mahleresque parts of Mahler's
music, which were, in other words, incompatible
with orthodox German music. Böhm might have
had a tough time with those qualities in Mahler,
too. In Germany, especially, Mahler's music was
quite literally wiped out over the twelve long years
following 1933, when the Nazis took power, to the
end of the war in 1945. That's a huge gap that put it
at a great disadvantage. "A bad tradition" doesn't
begin to encompass the things that happened.

OZAWA: Hmm.

MURAKAMI: Afterwards, it fell to America, and not
Europe, to become the powerhouse for the current
Mahler revival. In that sense, in some ways, the

advantage was given to performers *outside* of the European home base, or at least the music of someone like Mahler was under no *dis*advantage there.

OZAWA: It's not "someone like Mahler"—it *is* Mahler. He was special in that sense.

MURAKAMI: Speaking of "special," when I'm listening to Mahler, I always think that there are deep layers of the psyche that play an important role in his music. Maybe it's something Freudian. In Bach or Beethoven or Brahms, you're more in the world of German conceptual philosophy, where the rational, unburied parts of the psyche play the most important role. In Mahler's music, though, it feels as though he is deliberately plunging down into the dark, into the subterranean realm of the mind. As if in a dream, you find many motifs that contradict one another, that are in opposition, that refuse to blend and yet are indistinguishable, all joined together almost indiscriminately. I don't know whether he's doing this consciously or unconsciously, but it is at least very direct and honest.

OZAWA: Mahler and Freud lived at just about the same time, didn't they?

MURAKAMI: Yes. Both were Jewish, and their birthplaces were not far apart, I think. Freud was a little older, and Mahler came to Freud for a consultation when his wife, Alma, had an affair [with the architect Walter Gropius, whom she married after Mahler's death]. Freud is said to have been deeply respectful of Mahler. That kind of straightforward pursuit of the underground springs of the unconscious may make us cringe—but I think it is probably what helps to make Mahler's music so very universal today.

OZAWA: In that sense, Mahler rebelled singlehandedly against the sturdy mainstream of German music, from Bach through Haydn to Mozart, and from Beethoven to Brahms—at least until the emergence of twelve-tone music.

MURAKAMI: When you stop to think about it, though, twelve-tone music is extremely logical, in the same sense that Bach's *Well-Tempered Clavier* is logical music.

OZAWA: That's true.

MURAKAMI: Twelve-tone music itself has hardly survived, but different elements of it were absorbed into the music that came afterwards.

OZAWA: Indeed.

MURAKAMI: But this is really quite different from the kind of influence that Mahler's music has had on later generations. I think you can say that, don't you?

OZAWA: I do.

MURAKAMI: In that sense, Mahler was really one of a

kind.

Ozawa and the Boston Symphony
Play the "Titan"

MURAKAMI: Now I'd like to listen to the same third movement of the First Symphony on a CD you recorded in 1987 with the Boston Symphony.

After the double-bass solo, the funeral march continues with an oboe solo.

MURAKAMI: The sound of the oboe is so different from the one on the Saito Kinen recording we just heard! I'm amazed.

OZAWA: Well, the Boston player doesn't have that "Miyamoto" sound we talked about before. This one is much milder.

Not just the solo oboe but the whole orchestra sounds much milder than the Saito Kinen.

OZAWA: This part is very mild, too, isn't it?

MURAKAMI: The sound is unified, and the quality of the playing is high.

OZAWA: Yes, but it could use a little more flavor.

MURAKAMI: I think it's expressive, and it really sings.

OZAWA: But it's missing a certain heaviness—a feeling from the countryside.

MURAKAMI: You mean it's too clean and neat?

OZAWA: The Boston Symphony may have a tendency to make sounds that are too nice.

MURAKAMI: You talked before about bringing out all the little details. Maybe the sound that the Saito Kinen produces is closer to your current conception of this piece.

OZAWA: That's true. Each individual musician of the Saito Kinen is consciously playing with that in mind. The Boston musicians are thinking about the overall sound of the orchestra.

MURAKAMI: Listening to their sound, I can see exactly what you mean. This is very good-quality, high-level teamwork.

OZAWA: No one does anything to depart from the orchestra's overall sound. But that's not necessarily the right way to play Mahler. Getting the proper balance between the two is extremely hard.

MURAKAMI: Maybe that's why it seems to me so thrilling and interesting these days to hear Mahler played by the irregularly constituted orchestras such as your Saito Kinen or Abbado's Lucerne Festival Orchestra or his Mahler Chamber Orchestra.

OZAWA: That's because the members of such orchestras can be bolder. From the moment they get together, each individual of the Saito Kinen is showing off his or her own art: they want the others to see what they can do.

MURAKAMI: So each one is in business for himself.

OZAWA: Of course, this can have its good aspects and its bad aspects. But it fits with Mahler.

MURAKAMI: I guess when the Saito Kinen gets together, it's like, "All right! This year we're gonna do the Mahler Ninth!" and they're all set to go.

OZAWA: Exactly. They arrive with a clear sense of purpose. Almost everybody has studied the score closely.

MURAKAMI: There's no sense of the routine work of a standing orchestra doing a different program every week.

OZAWA: No, there's none of that with the Saito Kinen. They're always fresh. But they may be missing some of the cohesion of a standing orchestra where the members bond together as a unit and can almost read each others' minds.

MURAKAMI: How does the whole orchestra build a consensus on a piece of music—by going over all the details?

OZAWA: Yes, of course. Most problems can be solved just by the musicians playing their instruments— especially when you've got outstanding musicians. An outstanding musician will have a bunch of pockets to draw from. He'll be watching the conductor and think, "Oh, so *that's* how he wants to do this part," and pull something out of this pocket over here, and it's kind of like he's saying to the conductor, "Okay, then, let's go with *this*." A young musician might not have so many pockets to draw from, of course.

MURAKAMI: Are there some orchestras that are better suited to playing Mahler than other orchestras?

OZAWA: Yes, I think there are. Some orchestras out there are just not up to it technically, where not all the members can play that well. Nowadays, though, I think there are more and more orchestras that can easily handle anything—Mahler, Stravinsky, Beethoven. It didn't used to be like that. Back when Bernstein was doing Mahler in the sixties, there was very definitely an attitude of "What? He's doing *Mahler?* Whoa, that's *tough stuff*!"

MURAKAMI: You mean technically difficult?

OZAWA: Yes. In the string sections alone, the demands made on the players push them to their technical limits. So Mahler was composing with an eye on the distant future, writing music like that even though orchestras of his day were probably not of such high quality. He saw his music as a challenge

to orchestras, like, "Here, see if you can play *this*!"
So everybody must have been sweating when
they performed his music. Nowadays, though,
professional orchestras have more of an attitude of
"Mahler? Sure, we can play that."

MURAKAMI: Performance skills have improved that much,
have they—even compared with the 1960s?

OZAWA: Absolutely. Over the past fifty years, orchestral
technique has advanced to a whole new level.

MURAKAMI: Not just instrumental performance skills
but musicians' ability to read scores closely has also
improved?

OZAWA: Yes, I think so. Take me, for example. There was
a very definite change in my ability to read a score
after I had started reading Mahler in the early sixties,
as compared to before.

MURAKAMI: So for you, reading a Mahler score was very
different from reading others?

OZAWA: Yes, that's true.

The Effectively Avant-Garde Nature
of Mahler's Music

MURAKAMI: What is the biggest difference between
reading a score by Richard Strauss, for example, and
reading a score by Mahler?

OZAWA: At the risk of oversimplifying it, I'd say that if you traced the development of German music from Bach through Beethoven, Wagner, Bruckner, and Brahms, you could read Richard Strauss as part of that trajectory. Of course, he's adding all kinds of new layers, but still you can read his music in that stream. But not Mahler. You need a whole new view. That's the most important thing that Mahler did. There were also composers like Schoenberg and Alban Berg in his day, but they didn't do what Mahler did.

MURAKAMI: As you said a minute ago, Mahler was opening up very different areas than twelve-tone music.

OZAWA: He was using the same materials as, say, Beethoven or Bruckner, but building a whole different kind of music with them.

MURAKAMI: Fighting his battles while always preserving tonality?

OZAWA: Right. But still, in effect he was headed in the direction of atonality. Clearly.

MURAKAMI: Would you say that by pursuing the possibilities of tonality as far as he could take them, in effect he confused the whole issue of tonality?

OZAWA: I would. He brought in a kind of multi-layering.

MURAKAMI: Like, lots of different keys in the same

movement?

OZAWA: Right. He keeps changing things around.
And he'll do stuff like using two different keys
simultaneously.

MURAKAMI: He doesn't discard tonality, but he causes
confusion from the inside, really shakes things
up. That's how he was, in effect, heading toward
atonality. But was he striving for something different
from the atonality of twelve-tone music?

OZAWA: Yes, it was different, I think. It might be closer
to call what he was doing polytonality rather than
atonality. Polytonality is one step before you get
to atonality—it means that you use more than one
key at the same time. Or you keep changing keys
as the music flows. In any case, the atonality that
Mahler was aiming for came out of something quite
different from the atonality and twelve-tone scale
that Schoenberg and Berg were offering. Later,
somebody like Charles Ives pursued polytonality
more deeply.

MURAKAMI: Do you think Mahler thought he was doing
something avant-garde?

OZAWA: No, I don't think so.

MURAKAMI: Schoenberg and Alban Berg were certainly
very conscious of being avant-garde, though.

OZAWA: Oh, very much so. They had their "method."

Mahler had no such thing.

MURAKAMI: So he flirted with chaos, not as a methodology, but very naturally and instinctively. Is that what you're saying?

OZAWA: Yes. Isn't that exactly where his genius lies?

MURAKAMI: There was a development like that in jazz, too. In the 1960s, John Coltrane kept edging closer and closer to "free jazz," but basically he stayed within the bounds of a loose tonality called "mode." People still listen to his music today—but "free jazz" is little more than a historical footnote. What we're talking about may be kind of like that.

OZAWA: Wow, so there was something like that in jazz?

MURAKAMI: Come to think of it, though, Mahler had no clear successors. The main symphonic composers who came after him were not Germans but Soviet Russians, like Shostakovich and Prokofiev. Shostakovich's symphonies are vaguely reminiscent of Mahler.

OZAWA: Yes, very much so. I agree. But Shostakovich's music is very coherent. You don't feel the same kind of craziness you do in Mahler.

MURAKAMI: Maybe for political reasons it wasn't easy for him to let anything like craziness come out. There's also something deeply abnormal about Mahler's music. If I had to put a label on it, I'd call it schizophrenic.

OZAWA: Yes, it's true. The art of Egon Schiele is like that, too. When I saw his pictures, I could really see how he and Mahler were living in the same place at the same time. Living in Vienna for a while, I got a strong sense of that atmosphere. It was a tremendously interesting experience for me.

MURAKAMI: Mahler says in his autobiography that being director of the Vienna State Opera was the top position in the musical world. In order to obtain that position, he went so far as to abandon his Jewish faith and convert to Christianity. He felt the position was worth making such a sacrifice. It occurs to me that you were in that very position until quite recently.

OZAWA: He really said that, did he? Do you know how many years he was director of the State Opera?

MURAKAMI: Ten years, I think.

OZAWA: For somebody who spent such a long time conducting opera, it's amazing that he never wrote one of his own. I wonder why not. He wrote all those Lieder, and he was very conscious of the combination of words and music.

MURAKAMI: That's true, now that you mention it. It's too bad. But given the kind of person he was, it might have been hard for him to choose a libretto.

The Boston Symphony continues playing.

MURAKAMI: Hmm, listening to them playing like this, the sheer quality of the Boston Symphony Orchestra is almost overwhelming.

OZAWA: Well, I did spend all those years polishing it to make it a world-class orchestra, so the quality ought to be high! The Boston, the Cleveland . . . the technical accomplishment of orchestras of that caliber is fantastic.

The string section gives elegant voice to the beautiful "pastoral" passage.

MURAKAMI: You can't get a sound like that out of the Saito Kinen?

OZAWA: Well, after all . . .

MURAKAMI: It's just a different sound.

OZAWA: It depends on what the listener is looking for—a harmonious, thoroughly beautiful, finished performance; or one that is not so perfect but has a touch of danger. Such differences can easily arise in Mahler's case—and especially in this movement, which is so full of such passages.

Ozawa studies the score intently.

OZAWA: Oh, I see, this piece was first performed in Budapest.

MURAKAMI: And was very poorly received, I gather.

OZAWA: I would imagine that the performance was not very good.

MURAKAMI: Maybe the orchestra couldn't really understand how it ought to be played.

OZAWA: The first performance of Stravinsky's *Rite of Spring* was a fiasco, too, you know. Of course the work itself was partly to blame, but it could well be that the orchestra wasn't fully prepared to perform it. The piece is full of musical acrobatics. I wish I had asked Pierre Monteux about it directly. We were fairly close for a while.

MURAKAMI: Now that you mention it, Monteux conducted that first performance, didn't he?

The music comes to the section where the strings and the wind instruments clash head-on and become entangled, like the tails of several complicated dreams. (8:43–9:01)

OZAWA: This part is a little crazy, isn't it?

MURAKAMI: It does contain a kind of madness, doesn't it?

OZAWA: But in the Boston Symphony's performance, it all comes together smoothly like this.

MURAKAMI: That's part of the orchestra's DNA, isn't it, to calm down the chaos and fill in the gaps?

OZAWA: The members listen to each other and adjust quite naturally. This is, of course, one of the Boston's outstanding features.

MURAKAMI: I think it's very difficult for performers to grasp the similarities between the dissociation in Mahler's music and the general dissociation experienced by those of us living in the present day. But if you were to perform this same piece with the Boston Symphony right now, don't you think it would sound very different?

OZAWA: It certainly would. I myself have changed, and. . . .

The Boston Symphony's performance of the third movement ends.

MURAKAMI: I don't know, this performance was kind of like making a leisurely tour in a chauffeur-driven Mercedes-Benz.

Ozawa laughs.

MURAKAMI: By contrast, the Saito Kinen was like zipping around in a sports car with a nice stick shift.

OZAWA: Listening to it like this, the performance has that steadiness you'd expect from the Boston Symphony, doesn't it?

Ozawa Continues to Change

OZAWA: These conversations with you have made me realize how much I've changed over the years. Just recently, as you know, I went to Carnegie Hall with the Saito Kinen to perform the Brahms First, the Berlioz *Symphonie fantastique*, and Britten's *War Requiem*, and that experience changed me quite a bit.

MURAKAMI: I'm sure you're changing even now.

OZAWA: Even at my age, you change. And practical experience keeps you changing. This may be one of the distinguishing features of the conductor's profession. The work itself changes you. Of course the one thing that any conductor has to do is to get sounds out of the orchestra. I read the score and create a piece of music in my mind, after which I work with the orchestra members to turn that into actual sound, and that process gives rise to all kinds of things. There are the interpersonal relationships, of course, and also the musical judgments you make when you decide which particular points of the work you want to emphasize. There are times when you look at the music and really focus on the long phrases, and, conversely, times when you split hairs over the tiny phrases. You also have to decide which of these various tasks you are going to favor. Each of these experiences will change a conductor. I got sick, went into the hospital, and stayed away from conducting for a long time. But then recently I went to New York and had a burst of conducting. Then I came back to Japan, and because I had nothing else to do at New Year's, I listened to recordings of those Saito Kinenperformances over and over again. I learned a lot from them

MURAKAMI: You learned a lot . . . ?

OZAWA: It was the first time in my life that I had ever listened to recordings of my own performances with such intense concentration.

MURAKAMI: The first time in your life? Don't you always listen closely to recordings of your performances?

OZAWA: No, I don't. Ordinarily, by the time a disc is ready, we're already into the next piece of music. Of course when the recording is going to be released commercially, I'll give it a listen, but on any one day I'm usually thinking about the music I have to perform that evening, so it's simply impossible for me to listen closely to a recording of something I'm already done with. In this case, however, I had nothing else planned, and I was able to listen with the memory of the performances still ringing in my ears. So I really did learn a lot from them.

MURAKAMI: Can you give me a concrete example of what you learned?

OZAWA: Well, it was like looking at myself in the mirror. I could see every little detail with frightening clarity. You can do something like that when the sound of the live performance is still in your ears—or in the very tissues of your body.

MURAKAMI: When you get into another piece of music,

your mind is completely focused on that one—so if you listen to a piece you've already finished, you can't really get into it?

OZAWA: That's right. We conductors are constantly moving from one piece to the next. We work with different orchestras, and sometimes we're involved in long, grueling opera rehearsals. There's a big difference between finding a little time between rehearsals to listen to a recording you've made and listening when you've got all the time you need and the music of the original performance is still in your ears: the music enters you in an entirely different way.

MURAKAMI: You mean you hear things in the recording that give you pause, that make you wish you had done them differently?

OZAWA: There are those moments, of course. But there are also passages where you think, "Hey, that was pretty good," or "We're really together here"—that kind of thing.

MURAKAMI: How about in the Saito Kinen performances we're discussing here? Can you tell me what strikes you as some of their best features?

OZAWA: In the simplest terms, I can hear there's more depth to the performance than before. More concretely speaking, the character of each section of the orchestra has deepened—or, rather, the potential has emerged for each section to go deeper. When

that potential emerges, all of the musicians want
to give it their best . . . and when that happens, the
performance gets deeper and deeper. Because we've
got a really outstanding group of musicians there.

MURAKAMI: Are you saying that when the Saito Kinen
Orchestra performed at Carnegie Hall, it was in
some ways different from usual?

OZAWA: Yes, without a doubt. We were working under
so many constraints—we had hardly any time for
rehearsals, I was still convalescing and, in addition,
had caught a terrible cold—and yet we were able
to bring off such powerful performances. There's
nothing normal about that. The Brahms and the
Berlioz were truly wonderful. And everybody just
threw themselves wholeheartedly into the *War
Requiem*—the orchestra, the soloists, the chorus—it
was incredible.

MURAKAMI: The *War Requiem* I heard in Matsumoto was
an astounding performance.

OZAWA: No, this one was even better. I brought the
whole Matsumoto chorus and the boys' chorus
with me, and having them there was very moving.
You know, Japan has some of the best brass bands
and choruses in the world, and this performance
gave people a good taste of those high standards.
The orchestra, too, had a thorough understanding
of the music, so much so that a very difficult
composition didn't sound difficult at all. Meanwhile,
I'm up there with that awful cold, in another world,

coughing so much, it must have been terrible for
the people around me. [*Laughter.*] But you know,
when everybody's into it with their hearts and
souls, the conductor doesn't have to do a thing—
just direct traffic a little so as not to obstruct the
flow of the music. Things work out perfectly like
this every once in a while. It can happen with an
orchestra, and it can happen with an opera. Then
the conductor has no need to crack the whip. All he
has to do is maintain the momentum. Everybody
was determined to do his best in that performance
because they knew the conductor was sick and
needed help—which is exactly what I got.

MURAKAMI: But you had pneumonia! It's incredible you
lasted the full eighty minutes.

OZAWA: It's true I had a pretty high fever, but I was too
scared to take my temperature. [*Laughter.*] I couldn't
do the whole thing in one go, though, so I had them
insert an intermission.

MURAKAMI: The original work doesn't have an
intermission?

OZAWA: No, I requested it. I seem to remember having
done that once before somewhere. See, I've got
"Pause" written into my score. But I can't remember
where I did that. It might have been Tanglewood. It's
a long piece, it was outdoors, some people need to go
to the bathroom, that kind of thing. And maybe the
weather was hot.

MURAKAMI: So far the only thing I've heard from your Carnegie Hall recording is the Brahms, but it's an incredibly tight performance.

OZAWA: That's probably because there was a lot of tension behind that performance. It gave me a very good feeling.

MURAKAMI: It just occurred to me that you've never once recorded *Das Lied von der Erde* in your whole long career.

OZAWA: No, I never have.

MURAKAMI: It's surprising. Why is that? You've recorded the First Symphony three times.

OZAWA: Hmm, why is that? I don't know, either. I wonder if it was just that I couldn't get two outstanding singers together at the same time. You need a tenor and an alto or mezzo-soprano for that. Sometimes it's done with two male singers. In concert, I've performed it with Jessye Norman a lot.

MURAKAMI: I've always thought that *Das Lied von der Erde* is the one Mahler piece in which an Asian conductor could bring out its special flavor.

OZAWA: That's absolutely true. Now that you mention it, I once broke a finger conducting *Das Lied von der Erde*. Right here! [*He extends his little finger.*]

MURAKAMI: Is it possible to break a finger *conducting*?

OZAWA: Do you know the Canadian tenor Ben Heppner?
He's a very big guy, and he was singing on my right
side, and Jessye Norman was singing on my left.
We rehearsed for two days, and Ben held the score
in his hands the whole time. When it came time for
the actual performance, though, he suddenly said
he wanted to have both hands free and asked to
have a music stand set up in front of him. It's always
dangerous to do things differently in performance
than you did in rehearsals. Because he's such a big
guy, I knew the music stand would have to be a
tall one; and if something like that fell off the stage
it could injure a member of the audience and then
we'd have a real mess on our hands. So instead of a
regular music stand, we brought in big lectern kind
of thing—you know, a heavy piece of furniture like
a minister uses to deliver a sermon. I don't know, I
just didn't feel good about it, and sure enough, when
I swung my arm hard in a forte passage, my little
finger got caught under the edge of the lectern, and
snap! My little finger broke.

MURAKAMI: Ow, that must have hurt!

OZAWA: You have no idea. I went on conducting in pain
for another half hour or more, but by the time I was
finished, my finger had swelled up. I went straight to
the hospital and had it operated on.

MURAKAMI: Conducting can be a tough job in all kinds
of ways, with danger lurking in places you'd never
imagine. [*Ozawa laughs, amused.*] In any case, I find
it a shame that you have no recording of *Das Lied*

von der Erde. I'd love to hear the latest performance by the ever-changing Seiji Ozawa!

From Chicago Blues
to Shin'ichi Mori

MURAKAMI: Do you listen to any music other than classical?

OZAWA: I like jazz. Blues, too. I used to go three or four times a week to listen to blues when I was staying in Chicago for the Ravinia Festival. I was *supposed* to be studying scores— early to bed, early to rise—but instead I was heading out to the clubs because I liked the blues so much. They started to recognize me as a regular and let me in a side door instead of making me wait in line with everybody else.

MURAKAMI: At that time, weren't the blues clubs located in not the safest neighborhoods in Chicago?

OZAWA: True, they're not the best. But I never had anything unpleasant or scary happen to me. They all seemed to know I was conducting at Ravinia. I used to drive there myself, a half hour each way. After I had my fill of blues, I'd drive back to the house I was renting in Ravinia. I played a lot with Peter Serkin while I was in Chicago, and he'd come to the blues joints with me once in a while. He was still a minor in those days, though, so they wouldn't let him in. They can be very strict about such things in America. They won't let you in without an ID. He'd stand outside by the window the whole time I was inside listening, trying his best to hear what he could. [*Laughter.*]

MURAKAMI: Poor guy.

OZAWA: That happened a few times.

MURAKAMI: Chicago blues—that's deep music.

OZAWA: There was a guy named Corky Siegel playing there. A harmonica player. He was the only white guy. Later, I did a recording with him. But boy, the Chicago blues back then were so great! Heavy, intense! There were lots of good players and lots of different kinds of bands. It was a fantastic experience for me. Another thing I did in Chicago was go to hear the Beatles. Somebody gave me a ticket. It was a really good seat, but I couldn't hear a thing. It was an indoor venue, and the screams blotted out all the music. So I got to see the Beatles but not hear them.

MURAKAMI: Kind of pointless.

OZAWA: Completely pointless. It was a total shock. I enjoyed the band that opened for them, but once the Beatles came on stage, you couldn't hear a thing.

MURAKAMI: Did you go to jazz clubs?

OZAWA: Not much. In New York, though, when I was an assistant conductor at the New York Philharmonic, one of the violinists—the only black member of the orchestra—heard that I liked jazz, so he took me to some Harlem jazz clubs a few times. They were great. There was usually a strong smell of soul food coming from the kitchen. Oh, that reminds me, we once invited Louis Armstrong—they called him Satchmo—and Ella Fitzgerald to Ravinia. This was something I pushed for. I just loved Satchmo. Until that time, Ravinia was an all-white music festival, and this was the first time jazz performers appeared. And what a great concert it was! I was so excited, I went to visit them backstage. It was tremendous fun. That special style of Satchmo's was indescribable. You know how we talk about artistic *shibumi* in Japan, when a mature artist attains a level of austere simplicity and mastery? Satchmo was like that. He was already getting along in years, but his singing and trumpet playing were at their peak.

MURAKAMI: It sounds as if your blues experience left the strongest impression.

OZAWA: I'd have to agree with that. I didn't know anything about the blues until then. Also, at Ravinia, I was getting a decent salary for the first time in my life. We could finally have proper meals, go to restaurants, live in a nice house. It just so happened I learned about the blues just as I was getting to a point where I could afford to do things for a change, and that coincidence was a major factor in the way my interest developed. Until then, I could never afford to pay to go hear music ... By the way, do they still play the blues in Chicago?

MURAKAMI: They sure do! I don't know that much about it, but I think it's gotten very active again. Still, I suspect the first half of the 1960s was probably when the Chicago blues were at their best. That's when they were having their greatest influence on the Rolling Stones.

OZAWA: I think there were three good blues clubs back then, all within a few blocks of each other. New bands would come to each one every two or three days, so I was going there constantly.

MURAKAMI: Oh, that reminds me, you and I went to a Tokyo jazz club together once or twice.

OZAWA: True, true.

MURAKAMI: The first time we heard Junko Onishi on the piano, and then Cedar Walton.

OZAWA: Yes, that was a lot of fun. I'm glad there are good clubs like that in Japan, too.

MURAKAMI: I'm a big fan of Junko Onishi. The quality of her playing and that of other young Japanese jazz musicians is tremendously high. Twenty years ago, there was nothing like their technical mastery.

OZAWA: You're probably right. Now that you mention it, though, I heard Toshiko Akiyoshi sometime in the late sixties in New York. I thought she was amazingly good.

MURAKAMI: Such a clean touch! Decisive, assertive.

OZAWA: Like a man's.

MURAKAMI: Like you, she was born in Manchuria. I think she's a little older, though.

OZAWA: Do you think she's still performing?

MURAKAMI: Yes, I'm pretty sure she is. She had a big band of her own for a long time.

OZAWA: A big band? Incredible! Later, when I was in Boston, I heard Shin'ichi Mori a lot. And Keiko Fuji.

MURAKAMI: No kidding? You listened to *enka*?

OZAWA: They were both wonderful singers.

MURAKAMI: Keiko Fuji's daughter is very active nowadays as a singer.

OZAWA: Oh, really?

MURAKAMI: She calls herself Hikaru Utada. When I was a student, I worked in a little record shop in Shinjuku, and one day Keiko Fuji came in. She was a small woman, very simply dressed, and didn't stand out in any way. She introduced herself to us with a smile and thanked us for selling her records. Then she gave us a little bow and left. I remember being very impressed that such a big star would go to the trouble of making the rounds of the record stores like that. That would have been around 1970.

OZAWA: Yes, yes, it was exactly that time that I was listening to *enka*—Shin'ichi Mori's "Harbor Town Blues" ("Minato-machi burūsu"), Keiko Fuji's "Dreams: At Night They Open" ("Yume wa yoru hiraku"), that kind of thing. I had them on cassette and would listen whenever I was driving between Boston and Tanglewood. Vera and the kids were back in Japan, I was living alone, and really homesick for Japan. I used to listen to *rakugo* storytelling, too, whenever I had time to kill—people like Shinshō.

MURAKAMI: When you've been living abroad for a long time, you can build up a real hunger to hear Japanese spoken, can't you?

OZAWA: Naozumi Yamamoto had that TV show of his, *The Orchestra Is Here!* [*Oukesutora ga yatte kita*], and when he asked me to appear as a guest on it I said I'd do it if they'd have Shin'ichi Mori on the same show. He really came! I conducted the orchestra accompanying him for one song, which maybe didn't go all that well. Some famous novelist dumped all over me for that one. [*Laughter.*]

MURAKAMI: What was bothering him?

OZAWA: Well, he said, "Just because you understand classical music doesn't mean you understand *enka*."

MURAKAMI: Aha.

OZAWA: Of course I didn't say anything at the time, but I do have my own response to such a criticism. Everybody says that *enka* is unique to Japan, a form of music that only Japanese can sing and only Japanese can understand. But I don't believe it. Basically, *enka* comes from Western music, and it can be fully explained using Western music's five-line musical staff.

MURAKAMI: Aha.

OZAWA: The special *kobushi* vocal ornamentation of *enka* can be written in Western musical notation as vibrato.

MURAKAMI: So you're saying that, if written down correctly in a score, an *enka* song can be sung properly even by someone who has never heard one—by a Cameroonian musician, for example?

OZAWA: Exactly.

MURAKAMI: That's a most unusual view. At least in terms of music theory, even *enka* can be a universal form of music. I see what you mean.

The Joys of Opera

This conversation took place on March 29, 2011, when both of us happened to be staying in Honolulu. It was eighteen days after the gigantic earthquake and tsunami struck the Tohoku region of Japan, when I was working in Hawaii. Unable to return to Japan, all I could do was follow the situation as it unfolded each day on CNN. The news that came in brought one painful fact after another. Discussing the joys of opera in such a situation seemed strangely out of place, but opportunities to grab the busy Seiji Ozawa for an organized discussion did not come around all that often. And so we spoke about opera, interspersing our musical conversation with such pressing questions as what would happen with the nuclear power plant breakdown and where Japan was headed.

Nobody Was Farther Removed
from Opera Than I Was

OZAWA: I conducted opera for the first time in my
life after I became music director of the Toronto
Symphony in 1965. It was a concert performance
of *Rigoletto,* done without stage sets. I was so
happy—or should I say fulfilled—to have my own
orchestra. I could perform Mahler if I wanted to.
I could perform Bruckner. I could even perform
opera.

MURAKAMI: I imagine that conducting opera would be
very different from conducting ordinary orchestral
works. Where did you study the techniques for
conducting opera?

OZAWA: Maestro Karajan insisted that I conduct opera
and he had me assist him when he did *Don Giovanni*
in Salzburg in 1968. So I learned the opera well
enough to play all parts of it on the piano. That was
the beginning of my opera study. The next year he
had me conduct *Così fan tutte,* which was the first
stage production I conducted myself.

MURAKAMI: Where was that?

OZAWA: Salzburg again. Before that, a good friend of
mine, the African-American tenor George Shirley,
suggested that we do an opera together. He wanted
to do *Rigoletto,* which is how I came to do the
complete work in Toronto. That was a lot of fun. In
Japan, I did *Rigoletto* at the Tokyo Bunka Kaikan

with the Japan Philharmonic. That was a concert performance, too. Come to think of it, I still haven't done *Rigoletto* as a fully staged opera. In the spring of 2013, I'm scheduled to be doing it for the stage at the Seiji Ozawa Music Academy, with David Kneuss directing. I've been working with David for thirtyy years now. He directed all the operas I conducted at Tanglewood.

MURAKAMI: I'm looking forward to it.

OZAWA: So anyway, that's how *Così fan tutte* turned out to be the first opera I conducted for the stage. The director was Jean-Pierre Ponnelle. He was a marvelous director, but tragically he fell backwards into the orchestra pit when he was working on a production in 1988. I think he injured his back or something, and he died not long afterward. Karl Böhm was supposed to have conducted *Così fan tutte*, but he had health problems, so I took his place. I'm pretty sure he was having eye surgery.

MURAKAMI: Catapulting the obscure young conductor into prominence.

OZAWA: Right. I think they were really worried about putting me in charge. [*Laughter.*] I mean, it was my first staged opera, after all. Both Maestro Karajan and Maestro Böhm attended a performance because they were worried about how I'd do. They also came to rehearsals. Come to think of it, Claudio Abbado conducted *The Barber of Seville* on the same stage in Salzburg the year before. That was his Salzburg opera debut. Of course, he had probably conducted operas in Italy before that.

MURAKAMI: Abbado is a little older than you, isn't he?

OZAWA: Yes, a year or two, I think. I worked as Lenny's assistant just a bit before he did.

MURAKAMI: How well received was your *Così fan tutte*?

OZAWA: I'm not sure, but it couldn't have been too bad. I was invited to conduct the Vienna Philharmonic after that, and I started hearing now and then from the Vienna State Opera, too.

MURAKAMI: Did you enjoy conducting a staged opera for the first time in your life?

OZAWA: Oh, man, it was *so* much fun! And the cast was superb. We worked like one big, happy family. I conducted *Così fan tutte* again at Salzburg the following year. At Salzburg, you perform the same piece two or three years in a row. I was invited to Salzburg again, yearsafter that, to conduct *Idomeneo,* another Mozart. We performed *Così fan tutte* in the small theater, the Kleines Festspielhaus, and *Idomeneo* in the Felsenreitschule, the theater they built in an old stone quarry. Come to think of it, most of my experience conducting opera took place in the Palais Garnier opera house in Paris and Milan's La Scala. And also the Vienna opera house. Those three. I've never conducted opera in Berlin.

MURAKAMI: Were you conducting opera on the side while you were Boston Symphony's music director?

OZAWA: Yes. I would take a break from my work in Boston and go to Europe. Working on an opera takes a month at the very least. So that's how long my break from Boston would be. Which meant I could never do any new productions. They're too time-consuming. I did work on some new productions in Paris, though—*Falstaff* and *Fidelio*, for example. But the *Turandot* I did there was an old production. Later, I did *Tosca* with Domingo. And the Messiaen *Saint François d'Assise*, which I did in 1983, was a world premiere.

MURAKAMI: Opera has been a major part of your career for many years, hasn't it?

OZAWA: You know, to tell you the truth, nobody was farther removed from opera than I was! [*Laughter.*] By which I mean that Professor Saito never taught me a thing about opera. So as long as I stayed in Japan, I had nothing to do with it. Except, while I was still in school, Maestro Akeo Watanabe conducted Ravel's *L'Enfant et les sortilèges* with the Japan Philharmonic. I'm pretty sure that was in 1958.

MURAKAMI: That's a short opera, isn't it?

OZAWA: Yes, short, maybe an hour-long piece. I remember they did it in concert form, not staged. I sometimes stood in for the conductor during rehearsals—Maestro Watanabe was so busy with his duties as music director. That was truly my first opera experience.

MURAKAMI: Where was it performed?

OZAWA: Hmm, I'm not sure . . . Sankei Hall? Maestro Watanabe used to do an opera every couple of years. I'm pretty sure he did Debussy's *Pelléas et Mélisande* after I went abroad. He chose somewhat unusual pieces.

MURAKAMI: So the first time you really grappled with opera, you were conducting under Karajan?

OZAWA: That's right. He gave me some very good advice. "The symphonic repertory and opera," he said, "are like two wheels on a single axle. If either of the wheels is missing, you can't go anywhere. In the symphonic repertory, you have concerti, symphonic poems, and so forth, but opera is utterly unlike such forms. If you were to die without ever having conducted an opera, wouldn't that be like dying without ever having really known Wagner? Of course it would. That is why, Seiji, you absolutely *must* study opera. Puccini, Verdi: you can't say a thing about them without touching on their operas. Even Mozart poured half his energy into operatic works." When he told me this, I knew that I would have to do an opera.

MURAKAMI: So that's how you made up your mind to do *Rigoletto* in Toronto?

OZAWA: Correct. And I reported my plans to Maestro Karajan. So when I was leaving as music director of the San Francisco Symphony to move to Boston, he suggested that I wait, and take a leave of absence to work with him. He would give me thorough training in the conducting of opera.

MURAKAMI: How kind of him!

OZAWA: Indeed. He seemed to think of me as one of his direct disciples. I was supposed to be resigning as director of the Ravinia Festival and taking over the Tanglewood Music Festival that summer, but I asked Boston to let me postpone for a year and spent the summer studying with Maestro Karajan instead. That was the Salzburg *Don Giovanni* I mentioned earlier, when I assisted him. He not only conducted the opera but he directed it, too. He even worked on the lighting himself.

MURAKAMI: Amazing.

OZAWA: He didn't go so far as to do the costumes, of course, but the maestro was tremendously busy, so I got to do a lot of conducting in the rehearsals.

Mirella Freni's Mimi

OZAWA: The title role was sung by Nicolai Ghiaurov, a bass from Bulgaria. Mirella Freni sang Zerlina. I accompanied their rehearsals on the piano almost every day. Before long, they were a couple and they

ended up getting married in 1978. They were like
family to me. [*Laughter.*] Afterward, I invited them
to Tanglewood, and we did the Verdi Requiem. He
appeared for me in Mussorgsky's *Boris Godunov* and
Tchaikovsky's *Eugene Onegin*. Of course Mirella
Freni sang Tatiana in *Onegin*. For years, we made it a
habit to dine together after the opera. Unfortunately,
Ghiaurov died in 2004.

MURAKAMI: So Freni could sing opera in Russian?

OZAWA: Yes, she often appeared in *The Queen of Spades*.
Ghiaurov's repertory included a lot of Russian
operas, so she had to learn a lot of them, too, if they
were going to work together as husband and wife.
They were always together, on and off the stage.

MURAKAMI: So Freni made Russian opera one of her
specialties.

OZAWA: Because I was lucky enough to meet her in
Salzburg, I got to do a lot of different operas. We
worked together on five or six of them, but the one
she most wanted to do was *La Bohème*.

MURAKAMI: Singing Mimì. It's one of her signature roles.

OZAWA: For years, she would say to me, "Let's do *La
Bohème* together next time, Seiji." But for some
reason, we never did it. I don't know if I should be
telling you this, but around that time, Carlos Kleiber
brought La Scala to Japan and did *La Bohème*. I saw
a performance and said to myself, "I could never do

that. He's just too good. There's no hope for me. I could never top that."

MURAKAMI: That was the 1981 Japan tour, wasn't it? The tenor was Peter Dvorský.

OZAWA: And Mimì was Mirella Freni. I finally got to do *La Bohème* some years later, but by then Mirella was no longer singing. Now she's back in her home town of Modena teaching voice. The timing just never worked out for us.

MURAKAMI: That's really a shame.

OZAWA: Her Mimì was so beautiful, you'd never want to hear anyone else do it. You know how, in drama, an actor might appear as if he's not acting at all? You ask him about it, and he'll tell you, "It may not look it, but I'm out there acting as hard as I can." As far as you can tell, though, as an observer, he's barely working. He just seems to *be* there, naturally, entirely as is, no technique, nothing. Mirella's Mimì was just like that.

MURAKAMI: *La Bohème* is an opera that won't work unless Mimì makes the audience cry, don't you think?

OZAWA: That's quite true.

MURAKAMI: And Freni could do that naturally.

OZAWA: You can tell yourself, "I'm not going to cry today," but you can't help yourself. I'm thinking I'll go visit her in Modena next time I'm in Florence.

He drinks hot tea.

OZAWA: This is sugar, isn't it?

MURAKAMI: Yes, it is.

About Carlos Kleiber

MURAKAMI: Was Carlos Kleiber's *La Bohème* really so wonderful?

OZAWA: You know, the conductor was totally enveloped in the play. All questions of technique had simply vanished somewhere. I asked him afterwards how he could manage to do such a thing, and he said, "Hey, Seiji, what are you talking about? I could conduct *La Bohème* in my sleep!"

MURAKAMI [*laughing*]: Amazing!

OZAWA: I had Vera with me at the time, so I wondered if he was showing off for her, but it's true, he had been conducting *La Bohème* since his youth—enough times to be sick of it.

MURAKAMI: He had every last detail of it in his head, I suppose. But Kleiber had a rather limited repertory, didn't he?

OZAWA: Yes, he didn't have that many operas—or even

symphonic pieces—in his repertory.

MURAKAMI: Funny, though, in a book I read recently, Riccardo Muti recalls a time when he was conducting Wagner's *Ring* and Kleiber came to visit him backstage. They started talking, and Muti was astonished to realize that Kleiber had every last detail of *The Ring* engraved in his mind. He had never once performed *The Ring*, but he had studied the score with meticulous attention to detail.

OZAWA: Yes, Kleiber was a very studious conductor, and he knew his pieces well, but he could be a bit of a troublemaker. When he was conducting the Beethoven Fourth in Berlin, there was so much wrangling, they never knew from day to day whether he would actually go on. I knew him well and had an intimate view of the situation, but it appeared to me as though he was looking for an excuse to quit conducting the piece.

MURAKAMI: Have you ever cancelled an engagement?

OZAWA: Sure, with all my recent illness. But if I'm just running a little fever or something, I tend to tough it out and go on.

MURAKAMI: How about getting into a fight, to the point where you pack up and go home?

OZAWA: That happened just once. I think it was my second year as guest conductor with the Berlin Philharmonic. You know the Argentine composer

Alberto Ginastera?

MURAKAMI: No, never heard of him.

OZAWA: Well, anyhow, I was conducting his 1941 composition *Estancia,* which is performed with a big orchestra. Maestro Karajan had chosen it for some reason, not to conduct it himself, but to have me study and perform it. I don't know why, but I guess the orchestra was supposed to perform an Argentine piece. So I did what I had to do and studied it as hard as I could. I think the second part of the program was a Brahms symphony. I don't remember which one. When I started rehearsing this *Estancia,* it turns out the percussion part is tremendously difficult. You need seven percussionists. Because it was so hard, I had only the percussionists rehearse their parts, letting the other musicians wait. But the rhythms were too complicated, and as we worked on it, we got bogged down completely. It was impossible. So then one of the percussionists, a young guy, laughed out loud. That made me furious, and I yelled at him, "What the hell is this? You're *laughing?*" But he just sat there without apologizing, and that made my blood boil. So I yelled again, "You're supposed to be the great Berlin Philharmonic, aren't you? What's going to happen in two days when you've got to perform this thing?" That just made it even more impossible to play. I was so mad, I left the score there, yelled one word, "Break!" and got the hell out of the room.

MURAKAMI: Wow.

OZAWA: So then I called my manager, Ronald Wilford, in New York. I said, "I'm coming home. I can't work in this place anymore. No way. I want you to apologize to Maestro Karajan for me." Then I notified the orchestra managers that I was returning to America and went straight back to the Kempinski Hotel. In those days, though, Berlin was still divided between East and West, and there were no direct flights from West Berlin to New York. You had to transfer somewhere. So I had the hotel order a ticket for me and started packing.

MURAKAMI: You were pretty worked up, weren't you?

OZAWA: I checked out and was getting ready to leave the hotel when the orchestra's president, Rainer Zepperitz, a double-bass player and a man deeply trusted by Maestro Karajan, came with several other members of the orchestra to apologize. "Our behavior was inexcusable. Ever since you left, the percussionists have been working hard to master the part they were unable to play before. Won't you please come to rehearsal once tomorrow, if only to see what kind of progress they are making?" Well, when they put it that way, I really had no choice but to go, don't you think?

MURAKAMI: Yes, I guess so.

OZAWA: So I called Wilford again and said I'd give it one more day, and I had the hotel cancel the ticket. That was the one little drama I had. It was a pretty famous incident.

MURAKAMI: So did you perform *Estancia,* in the end?

OZAWA: We did. I went back and conducted it.

MURAKAMI: I bet Kleiber would never have gone back.

OZAWA: No, I'm sure you're right! [*Laughter.*] In my case, though, the lack of direct flights to New York was a big factor.

MURAKAMI: They won you over while you were waiting for the transfer to be worked out. [*Laughter again.*]

OZAWA: By the way, Rainer Zepperitz was the lead double bassist in the Saito Kinen Orchestra for twenty-some years, from the time of its inception. I'm afraid he passed away just recently.

MURAKAMI: To get back to Kleiber's Japan performance of *La Bohème.*

OZAWA: Right, right.

MURAKAMI: It seems to me that Carlos Kleiber is a conductor who at times can bring out a whole new pattern from even the most familiar compositions— the Brahms Second, for example, or the Beethoven Seventh—and give the listener a fresh sense of discovery, as if hearing for the first time something that was always hidden deep inside the music. There are lots of very fine conductors, truly gifted musicians, but there aren't many who can do what he does.

OZAWA: Yes, I see what you mean.

MURAKAMI: I imagine that it takes a very deep reading of the score to accomplish something like that.

OZAWA: Yes, he was an incredible reader. The unfortunate thing for him was that his father was such a great conductor.

MURAKAMI: Erich Kleiber.

OZAWA: I think that's what made him so nervous. It was pretty extreme. But he seemed to like me and always treated me with affection. I wonder why. He was also fond of Vera and was fairly chummy with her. He came to several of my concerts and bought me dinner on more than one occasion. When I was appointed music director of the Vienna State Opera, Carlos was the first to send me a congratulatory telegram—a very long one!

MURAKAMI: He sounds like a difficult character.

OZAWA: Oh, tremendously difficult. He was famous for his cancellations—he'd cancel at the drop of a hat. Later, he also gave me a call to congratulate me on my appointment, so I took the opportunity to ask him if he'd come to conduct in Vienna once in a while now that I was there. I mean, it was so hard to get him to come anywhere. So he said to me, "Hey, I didn't send you that telegram because I was looking for an invitation!" [*Laughter.*]

MURAKAMI: Meaning, the two had nothing to do with one another.

OZAWA: I also invited him to conduct the Saito Kinen. He was definitely interested in the orchestra—enough to come to a concert we gave in Germany. But he wouldn't commit himself one way or the other. I invited Maestro Karajan, too, when he was in his last years. I couldn't get him to come, though. He was supposed to conduct the Boston Symphony for me. He had conducted the Chicago Symphony in Salzburg at Solti's request. He said he couldn't travel all the way to Boston, but he wouldn't mind conducting the Boston Symphony if the orchestra ever came to Europe. He died, though, before we could make it happen.

MURAKAMI: That's too bad.

OZAWA: He never gave me a clear answer as to whether he would conduct the Saito Kinen or not, but he did invite us to Salzburg. That time, I told him I would conduct one piece and leave another one for him, but I never got a clear yes or no from him. He passed away the following year. I'm sure he had already weakened considerably.

MURAKAMI: I wish I could have heard Kleiber or Karajan conduct the Saito Kinen!

OZAWA: Maestro Karajan was very interested in the Saito Kinen. Which is why he made it a point to invite us to Salzburg. It's no easy matter to invite a whole orchestra to the Salzburg Festival!

Operas and Directors

MURAKAMI: Come to think of it, you told me there was once a plan for you to do an opera with Ken Russell directing.

OZAWA: Right, right. We were supposed to do *Eugene Onegin* in Vienna with Mirella Freni. This was before I moved to Vienna, when Lorin Maazel was still music director. I met with Ken several times to discuss it. But then, I don't know what happened—there was a big fight with the opera house and he got out. I had nothing to do with that.

MURAKAMI: If it had come to fruition, I'm sure it would have been a wild production.

OZAWA: No doubt. His earlier *Madama Butterfly* had caused a lot of controversy with its big background photo of the atomic bomb exploding, a giant Coca-Cola bottle on the stage as a symbol of America . . . When I met him, he impressed me as a radical sort of person.

MURAKAMI: His movie *Mahler* was pretty far out.

OZAWA: Yes, he showed it to me back then. We met in some kind of club in the middle of London, a weird, dark place where only men were admitted. That's where we talked. He said that in Pushkin's original, the protagonist, Onegin, is portrayed as a more repulsive character. In Tchaikovsky's opera, he is certainly weak and vacillating, but is not presented as the all-out womanizer he is in the original. Russell said he wanted to emphasize this dark side in his production.

MURAKAMI: I'll bet that would have caused an uproar. [*Laughter.*] But anyhow, the project never happened.

OZAWA: No, that was the end of it.

MURAKAMI: It must be tough to choose a director.

OZAWA: The director I first teamed up with on *Così fan tutte*, Jean-Pierre Ponnelle, was truly wonderful. I still think of him as a genius. He understood the music so well! The first thing you do with an opera is to rehearse the bare music, without stage sets or anything, just piano accompaniment. But he pointed out to me that even then, the music would be more natural if the singers went through the gestures and movements they would be performing on the stage. This was my first experience with conducting a staged opera and a totally new discovery for me. So I asked him how he was able to do such a thing. He said he would listen to the music over and over until he became completely immersed in it. I'm sure he had a special understanding of music.

MURAKAMI: So he wasn't one of those people who would crank out a stage set before he's actually heard the music?

OZAWA: No, no, not at all. He and I were on the same wavelength. When I met him in Paris just before he died, we talked about doing *The Tales of Hoffmann* together. He was working on a new production of *Hoffmann* at the Paris Opéra-Comique, but he suggested we move it into a larger venue. I was all for it, but a short time later he died. It was such a shame! To me, he was truly a marvelous director.

MURAKAMI: Just recently, I saw, on NHK, a stage production of *Manon Lescaut* that you conducted in Vienna in 2005. The one with a modern-day setting.

OZAWA: The director of that was Robert Carsen. Of all the many operas he directed, the most wonderful one was Richard Strauss's *Elektra*. It was a tremendously modern setting, but he did a fantastic job. And one other one—Janáček's *Jenufa:* it was flawless. He also did *Tannhäuser.* You know how that's the story of a song contest: he changed it into a painting contest.

MURAKAMI: You can do stuff like that?

OZAWA: Yes, a picture contest. I conducted that one—at Tokyo Opera Nomori, and again in Paris. The reception in Japan was kind of lukewarm, but the production was very well received in Paris. I guess the French are fond of art.

MURAKAMI: When you put out the money to mount a new opera production, I suppose you can't make up your expenses unless it's performed a certain number of times.

OZAWA: In fact, from the theater's point of view, they'd
like to do the same production of a work for ten
or twenty years to get their investment back. For
example, the Vienna State Opera still has Zeffirelli's
production of *La Bohème*. That must be going on
thirty years by now. At the very least, the theater
assumes it will keep a production it's mounted
for three years. If it performs the opera for three
years, say, a dozen or so times a year, that's about
forty performances. Then they can recoup their
investment. After that, they can make a profit
renting the sets out to somewhat lesser opera houses.

MURAKAMI: So theaters can make a profit that way?

OZAWA: That's right.

MURAKAMI: Some years ago, you conducted Beethoven's
Fidelio in Japan. Were those borrowed sets?

OZAWA: Yes, of course. They were brought over on a
ship. But that time was a little different. It was a
tour performance of the Vienna State Opera, so
the theater didn't have to rent the sets. Next they're
going to do Tchaikovsky's *The Queen of Spades*, and
all the sets will be shipped from Vienna.

MURAKAMI: So what you're saying is that stage sets or the
production itself becomes an opera house's asset?

OZAWA: Correct. In Japan, though, even though we
might want to store a stage set, we've got no place
to put them. In Vienna, there's a great big storage

facility out in the suburbs. The theater got a big piece of property from the government, and they keep all their sets there. They bring them back and forth to the theater by truck. The Vienna opera house can't hold the equipment for more than two operas at a time, so the trucks are hauling sets back and forth between the theater and the storehouse almost every day.

Booed in Milan

MURAKAMI: I guess it's safe to say that opera is the very essence of modern European culture. It has always borne the most colorful and brilliant part of European culture on its shoulders, from the age when it was patronized by the royalty and aristocracy through the time when it secured the feverish support of the bourgeoisie, to our own period of corporate sponsorship. Do you think there has been some sense of resistance to the idea of a Japanese conductor invading such territory?

OZAWA: Yes, of course. I was treated to some intense booing when I first appeared at La Scala [in 1980]. I was conducting *Tosca* with Pavarotti. He and I got along well, so he invited me to come to Milan. He was very eager for us to work together, and I liked him, so I finally took the bait [*Laughter.*]. Maestro Karajan was totally opposed to the idea. "It's suicide," he said. "They'll kill you!"

MURAKAMI: Who would kill you?

OZAWA: The audience. The La Scala audiences are famous for being tough on performers, and, sure enough, they booed me like crazy. I conducted seven performances, but after the first three, I suddenly noticed they weren't booing me anymore, and the rest went off without a hitch.

MURAKAMI: They do a lot of booing in Europe, don't they?

OZAWA: A lot—especially in Italy. There's never any in Japan, though.

MURAKAMI: None at all?

OZAWA: Well, maybe a little, but nothing like the mass howling they do in Italy.

MURAKAMI: I used to see that in the papers all the time when I was living in Italy. Like "Ricciarelli Roundly Booed Last Night in Milan." I was shocked to see what big news they could make of opera-house booing in Italy.

Ozawa laughs.

MURAKAMI: There seems to be a culture of booing. As a novelist, I'm used to having my books trashed in print, but if I don't want to see bad reviews, I just don't have to read them. I don't have to get angry or depressed. But a musician does his stuff right there in front of an audience, so if they boo him to his face, he can't run away from it. That must be awfully hard, isn't it? I always think how tough it would be.

OZAWA: I got booed for the first time in my life when I was conducting those *Toscas* at La Scala, and that was exactly the time my mother came all the way from Japan to Milan. Vera couldn't be there because the kids were still small, so my mother came in her place to cook me Japanese food. She came to the theater for the first performance, and when she heard all the booing around her, she figured they must be yelling "Bravo!" [*Laughter.*] It was so loud, she assumed people must be enjoying the performance. When we got back to the hotel, she said, "Wasn't that wonderful? There was so much cheering for you!"

MURAKAMI: Ha, ha, ha.

OZAWA: So I explained to her that they weren't saying "Bravo!" but "Boo!" She had never heard anything like that in her life, so she just didn't get it.

MURAKAMI: That reminds me of the time I went to a Red Sox game at Fenway Park, and every time the third baseman Kevin Youkilis came out, the crowd would start yelling "Youuk!" at the top of their lungs. At first, I thought they were booing him, but I couldn't figure out why. They were "You-ing" him, not booing him.

OZAWA: True, they sound a lot alike! But anyway, when I got booed in Milan, Pavarotti tried to comfort me. "When they boo you here, Seiji, it means you've

made it into the top ranks of the music world."
And some of the orchestra members told me that
no conductor had ever appeared there without
being booed. Even Toscanini had been booed at La
Scala. But no matter what they said, I didn't find it
comforting at all. [*Laughter.*]

MURAKAMI: Still, it sounds as if everyone was very
concerned for you.

OZAWA: My manager, too. "You've got nothing to
worry about," he said, "because the members of
the orchestra are on your side. That's the most
important thing. If a conductor gets booed and he
doesn't have the support of the orchestra, he's done.
So don't worry, just put up with it for a little while. I
guarantee you it will all go well." And he was right:
I did have the musicians behind me. Sometimes they
would even boo right back at the audience. I saw it
happen.

MURAKAMI: So it worked out all right?

OZAWA: It did. The booing died out after a few days.
It got weaker and weaker, and then one day it was
gone. From that point to the end of the run, I had no
booing at all. But, boy, if it had gone on to the end, it
might have done me in. I've never had it that bad, so
I really can't say what I would have done.

MURAKAMI: And you've conducted lots of operas at La
Scala since then, haven't you?

OZAWA: Yes, quite a number: Weber's *Oberon,* Berlioz's *The Damnation of Faust,* Tchaikovsky's *Eugene Onegin* and *The Queen of Spades,* and a bunch of others I can't remember offhand.

MURAKAMI: And you were never booed after that first time?

OZAWA: Hmm, no, I don't think I was. Maybe a few times by individual audience members, but never again by the whole house like that.

MURAKAMI: Do you think there was some resistance to the idea of an Asian conducting Italian opera at La Scala?

OZAWA: Well, look, don't you think it was just that the music sounded a little different from what they were expecting? The sound I gave to *Tosca* was not the *Tosca* that they were used to. I think that's what it was. And also, of course, to some extent, as Italians, they had a hard time accepting the fact that an Asian conductor could come and conduct *Tosca.* Sure.

MURAKAMI: Back then, weren't you the only Asian conducting at a first-class European opera house?

OZAWA: Yes, I suppose I was. But as I said before, I had the enthusiastic support of the orchestra members at La Scala, and of the chorus, for which I was very grateful. It was the same thing at Chicago. The first year I was appointed music director at the Ravinia Festival, the newspapers tore me to bits. The music critic at the most influential paper just didn't like me, I guess, or maybe there was something else going on behind the scenes, but he wrote these scathing reviews of my performances. It was the same as when Lenny was lambasted by the *New York Times* music critic Schonberg. But the orchestra members gave me their full support, and at the end of the first season, they even gave me a shower.

MURAKAMI: A shower?

OZAWA: I had never heard of such a thing, either, at the time. You know how the conductor withdraws from the stage at the end of the last number and then comes out again for a bow? At that point, the musicians all make random noises with their instruments—the trumpets, the strings, the trombones, the timpani all together make one big *fwaaan* or *gaaaan* sort of noise. You see what I mean?

MURAKAMI: I see.

OZAWA: That's called a "shower." It took me totally by surprise, I didn't know what was going on. So the second violinist, who was the orchestra's personnel manager, came over and explained it to me and said I should keep it in mind for the future. In other words, this was kind of like the orchestra's musical protest to the critical reviews

MURAKAMI: Oh, I get it.

OZAWA: That was my first and last shower experience.

The Chicago papers were trying to destroy me,
to get rid of me. But I contracted with the Ravinia
Festival for the following summer and, let's see, how
many years was I with them? Five years altogether, I
think. They didn't manage to destroy me.

MURAKAMI: I guess you have to bear up under such
external pressure and survive.

OZAWA: Maybe you could say that. But to some extent I
was already used to that kind of stuff. In Vienna, in
Salzburg, in Berlin—the reviews were scathing at
first. So I was pretty accustomed to getting dumped
on.

MURAKAMI: Scathing reviews? What would they say?

OZAWA: I don't know, I couldn't read the papers! But
people used to tell me they were really bad.

MURAKAMI: Maybe it was like a baptism of fire that all
newcomers have to go through.

OZAWA: No, I'm sure it wasn't that. There are lots of
people who never experience it. Take Claudio
Abbado, for example. I don't think he ever got a bad
review. He was recognized as a gifted conductor
right from the start.

MURAKAMI: In those days, there weren't any Asian
musicians active in Europe. Do you think that made
the headwinds against you all the stronger?

OZAWA: Well, it was very big news back then when the Japanese viola player Kunio Tsuchiya became a member of the Berlin Philharmonic in 1959—an epoch-making event. Nowadays, it would be hard to imagine a major European or American orchestra without Asian string players. Things have really changed.

MURAKAMI: I suppose they assumed back then that an Asian musician couldn't understand Western music.

OZAWA: That might have been part of it. I really don't remember what they were saying about me exactly. The orchestra performers themselves, though, welcomed me warmly. I think that to some extent, they felt sorry for me. Here's this young guy who comes from faraway Asia all by himself and everybody's giving him a hard time, so let's get behind him. That kind of thing.

MURAKAMI: That kind of support from your fellow musicians must be very encouraging when the media are being so negative.

The Fun Far Outstripped the Hardships

OZAWA: Anyhow, Maestro Karajan seems to have made up his mind that he was going to get very serious about teaching me how to conduct opera.

MURAKAMI: When you're conducting an opera, you have to relate not only to the orchestra but to the singers, too. You have to direct them both. Isn't it hard to get used to doing that?

OZAWA: Well, it's all a matter of contact. You have to make contact with the orchestra and with the singers at the same time.

MURAKAMI: Unlike members of an orchestra, singers are more or less in business for themselves—they're the stars—so aren't they harder to handle?

OZAWA: There are some difficult personalities, of course, but once you start working on a piece and asking them to "sing this part like this" or whatever, there's really nobody who is going to object. Everybody wants to do the right thing.

MURAKAMI: So you haven't had that much trouble with opera singers?

OZAWA: That *Così fan tutte* in Salzburg was the first staged opera I had ever worked on in my life, and I did absolutely nothing to hide that fact. Before we started, I announced to everybody, "This is my very first opera," so they all pitched in and very kindly taught me everything—from the singers on down to the assistant conductor. Maestro Karajan, of course, guided me through several parts, and even Claudio Abbado showed up and taught me things—like how to make the sound of the orchestra work with the singers' voices.

MURAKAMI: Nobody was mean to you?

OZAWA: Mean? I wonder. Maybe somebody did something mean, but I didn't know it at the time! [*Laughter.*] We got along very well. It was like one big, happy family. I invited everybody over for a potsticker party.

MURAKAMI: So it was less a matter of everyone's confronting the challenge of putting on an opera together than just enjoying the whole thing?

OZAWA: Yes, it was much more like that. Of course, I had a very strong sense that I had a lot of hard, serious work to do, but mainly it was fun. Opera was something that came later—a special added treasure that came to me after my career was well underway. Even now, I'm hoping for the chance to do more and more opera. There are still tons of them that I've studied but have never actually worked on.

MURAKAMI: The invitation for you to become the music director of the Vienna State Opera was rather sudden, wasn't it?

OZAWA: Yes, very sudden. I had been going practically every year to conduct in Vienna, not just with the Vienna Philharmonic, but I did a lot of opera there, too. And then all of a sudden they asked me to become music director. By then, I had been in Boston for twenty-seven years, and I was starting to think that thirty years in the same place was too long, that it was time for me to quit. I figured that working in the opera house might be a little easier than working as the Boston Symphony's music

director. I'd have more free time, and maybe I could
have longer stays in Japan. But it didn't work out
that way. Working on new material was very time-
consuming, especially in Vienna, where they put
a lot of time into preparation. And I had to travel
more, going all over the place with the company.
We did concert performances everywhere we went,
rather than staged productions.

MURAKAMI: So you were just as busy in Vienna as you
had been in Boston?

OZAWA: Yes, very busy. But it wasn't so stressful.
Everybody was worried that I'd be working too
hard, but it wasn't that bad. I had a lot of fun. And I
learned a tremendous amount. I just kept wanting to
do more and more. If I hadn't gotten sick . . . it was
really a shame, I had so much I wanted to do.

MURAKAMI: You know, as a layman, I would have
expected a place like the Vienna State Opera, just
dripping with history, to be a hotbed of conspiracy
and intrigue.

OZAWA [*laughing*]: That's what everybody says. But
it's not like that at all. Or maybe I'm just especially
unaware of such things.

MURAKAMI: You mean to say there wasn't a lot of political
maneuvering?

OZAWA: Oh, that. I try not to let myself get involved in
such things. In Boston, too, I kept as far away from

that stuff as I could. I don't do it anywhere, not even in Japan. And in Vienna, it was probably a good thing that my German was so bad. Of course, it can be inconvenient when you don't know the language, but it can be all the more convenient at times, too. So my eight years in Vienna were truly enjoyable. I could do practically any opera I wanted, and I was constantly surrounded by different productions of operas to see.

MURAKAMI: You were in opera heaven.

OZAWA: Yes, but—I hate to admit it—I almost never saw an opera from beginning to end. I used to go for the high points and leave. [*Laughter.*] It was terrible of me, I know.

MURAKAMI: What a waste! On the other hand, operas do tend to be very long.

OZAWA: I would go just for the high points and go back to my office in the opera house and work. Of course, I probably should have sat there for the whole thing, but I was so busy during the day that I just couldn't spare that much time. I had rehearsals with the Vienna Philharmonic, and studio rehearsals for the next opera. A "studio rehearsal" is just a session with piano accompaniment. With three hours of one in the morning and three hours of the other in the afternoon, I was exhausted by the end of the day and didn't have the energy for another three hours or more of a whole opera. I needed to eat, too! [*Laughter.*]

MURAKAMI: Well, sure, opera was originally intended
for persons of leisure. A few years ago, while you
were still music director, I went to Vienna and saw
a whole series of operas. I'd see an opera, I'd go to
a Vienna Philharmonic concert, and then to another
opera, and there were some matinee performances. It
was sheer bliss. Please get well and do more opera in
Vienna!

In a Little Swiss Town

I had the privilege of being present at nearly all the activities of the Seiji Ozawa International Academy Switzerland from June 27 to July 6, 2011. The academy is a seminar for young string players directed by Seiji Ozawa and based in the little town of Rolle on the banks of Lake Geneva near Montreux. It is held over a ten-day period every summer, and this was its eighth year.

Outstanding string players, mostly in their twenties, are brought together from all over Europe for a retreat, during which time they receive instruction. They live and practice together in a kind of cultural center run by the town. The facilities are quite luxurious for such a small town. The center is situated by the lake in an extensive, lush green property. The buildings appear to be old, and they have a rich history. Beyond the wide-open windows, ferry boats occasionally cross the lake waters, with the flags of the countries they connect—France and Switzerland—fluttering pleasantly on each boat's bow and stern.

Under Seiji Ozawa's direction, such world-class string players as Pamela Frank (violin), Nobuko Imai (viola), and Sadao Harada (cello) guide the students; and Robert Mann, a truly legendary figure who played first violin with the Juilliard String Quartet for half a century, comes from America as special instructor. Of course there is no end to the number of applicants who want to participate in such an illustrious seminar, and thus a rigorous audition process is held in advance to ensure that only truly outstanding talents are admitted—the cream of Europe's young musicians.

The string quartet is the focus for instruction. Three members of the faculty circulate from one quartet to another, listening to each rehearsal and offering advice on subtle points of tempo or tone or balance. This is not so much instruction as it is valuable advice from older professional colleagues who are not there to suggest that their young charges "do it this way," but rather that "it might be better to do it like this, don't you think?" As far as "instruction" is concerned, the young musicians gathered here have (probably) received more than enough. What they require is something a step above instruction. This is the shared recognition that underlies the entire seminar—it is about the comradeship of fellow musicians. Ozawa also attends from time to time and offers his own pieces of advice.

Robert Mann provides yet another level of special guidance in the form of master classes. The large room in which these classes are held is always filled to capacity. What occurs here is not so much democratic instruction as the sharing of secrets of the musical art, in concentrated form. Practically all the faculty and students gather for these events, giving their full attention to every word uttered by this great mentor of chamber music. I was allowed to attend all of the master classes, and though I know very little about stringed instruments, I found these exchanges profoundly interesting, full of valuable suggestions for the understanding and appreciation of music.

During the day, the students devote themselves to practicing their particular string quartets in the culture center, and then in the evening they walk ten minutes down the lakeshore with their instruments to an old stone building with a tower. This place is called "the Castle." In the old days it was probably the mansion or manor house of the lord of the domain, while nowadays it is apparently preserved by the town. The rehearsals of the large ensemble pieces played by the entire student body are held in this high-ceilinged, lavishly decorated hall where the lord likely held fancy balls. Its walls are covered in portraits and, during my visit, its many windows were usually thrown open to the summer light.

The orchestra's rehearsals are open to the citizens of Rolle. Many people show up every night to enjoy the spectacle, seated in the folding chairs that have been arranged just for them. Against the still-bright sky beyond the windows, swallows soar past each other in such numbers that, in *pianissimo* passages, the cries of the birds are louder than the music. After an hour or so of rehearsal, the audience sends warm applause to the musicians who have entertained them. Such appears to be the intimate tie between the academy and the people of the town. Music has taken root as a fixed part of their everyday lives.

The orchestra is conducted by Ozawa and Mann. The pieces chosen for performance this year are Mozart's Divertimento K. 136, conducted by Ozawa, and the third movement of Beethoven's String Quartet no. 16, conducted in a string-orchestra version by Mann. They have also readied the first movement of Tchaikovsky's Serenade for Strings for use as an encore piece. This one is conducted by Ozawa.

In this way, the academy's students are honing their musical skills from morning to night with hardly a break, literally immersed in music every day. These are all young men and women in their twenties (slightly more women than men), so although they are busy, they also manage to find time to enjoy their youth. They take their meals together, chattering throughout, and when rehearsals are finished, they head out to the bars for fun and relaxation—and, naturally enough, there seems to be a little romance in the making, too.

I was being allowed to participate as a kind of "special guest." Maestro Ozawa told me, "You should absolutely come to Rolle and see with your own eyes what we do there. It will change the way you listen to music." And so I had set out for Switzerland, intrigued, but not quite convinced that the experience would "change the way" I listened to music. I flew into the Geneva airport, headed for Rolle in a rental car, and attended the seminar from its second day on. There were no hotels where I could stay in Rolle (the number of hotels in such a small town is quite limited), so I ended up staying in Nyon, another town on the lakeshore, about a fifteen-minute drive away. There were several excellent restaurants near the hotel that served fish taken directly from the lake. The town on the opposite shore was in France. Far off to the right, in sharp outline, were the snow-capped Alps.

Switzerland is a pleasant place to be in the summer. The sun can be hot during the day, but the plateau's air is cool under the trees, refreshing breezes sweep across the lake, and you need a light jacket after sunset. Even without air conditioning, the musicians can concentrate on their rehearsals without breaking into a sweat. Each morning, after waking, I went running for an hour, jogging along the shore and cutting through a quiet wooded nature trail before returning to the hotel. That kind of sweat felt good. I sat at my desk for a while getting some work done, and then drove to Rolle, with sunflower fields and vineyards stretching into the distance on either side of the road, and not a billboard nor a convenience store nor a Starbucks anywhere in sight. I joined everyone for a buffet lunch in the courtyard at one o'clock, enjoying a healthy meal filled with fresh local vegetables.

After lunch, I circulated among the rooms listening to the various rehearsals, and in between, I chatted with students. Most of the young people were French-speaking or Eastern European, but the common language in the music world tends to be English, so we could understand each other pretty well. They were usually a little shy at first, but that didn't last very long. All of them found it odd to have this writer wandering around where they were making music, but once I explained that I was writing a book with Seiji Ozawa, they had no trouble accepting me as a "special guest." Some asked my opinion of the performance I had just heard. I was pleased to find that not a few of them had read some of my books.

Being there enabled me to hear a variety of valuable talks—by the regular instructors, of course (Pamela

Frank, Nobuko Imai, and Sadao Harada)—but also on occasion by Robert Mann. Because this was a kind of "temporary community," you were able to have free and frank conversations with all kinds of people once you were inside of it. I was extremely grateful for this opportunity.

Of greatest interest to me in attending this seminar was the *process* whereby good music is created. We are all used to the experience of being moved by good music and disappointed by not-so-good music: it's the most natural thing in the world. But I know almost nothing about the *process* of making good music. I can pretty well imagine what's involved in performing music of an individual nature—a piano sonata, for example—but I could never quite grasp what went into putting an ensemble together: what kind of rules were involved, what kind of guidelines were based on experience. These might be obvious to professional musicians, but they were not entirely clear to a general listener like me.

One of my roles was to observe, chronologically, what kind of music could be created as a result of gathering together, in one place, a number of young musicians who barely knew each other—and then giving them meticulous guidance by world-class performers. To do so, I spent as much time as I could attending rehearsals. Ozawa and the other instructors checked the performances closely against the scores, but for me, as someone who could barely read music, all I could do was sit and listen with an open mind. I had never before spent day after day like this, completely immersed in music. As a result, I can still hear the pieces I listened to then, echoing in my ears.

Let me list here the pieces that I heard the students rehearsing. Perhaps if I do so, the reader can grasp, to some extent, the sort of music I still have ringing in my ears:

1. Haydn: String Quartet no. 75, op. 76, no. 1
2. Smetana: String Quartet no. 1 ("From My Life")
3. Ravel: String Quartet in F Major
4. Janáček: String Quartet no. 1 ("Kreutzer Sonata")
5. Schubert: String Quartet no. 13 ("Rosamunde")
6. Beethoven: String Quartet no. 6
7. Beethoven: String Quartet no. 13

As a general rule, the students rehearsed the entire work, but in the concerts that concluded the week, they performed only one movement. There was simply not enough time to perform all the works in their entirety. The instructors chose which movements would be performed. The first and second violinists changed places from movement to movement. The concerts were held in Geneva and Paris, with different movements performed in each venue and different musicians performing the first violinist's part. Again due to time constraints, the Beethoven Thirteenth was not performed at either concert.

Another feature of the concluding concerts is that the three instructors and five outstanding students (four of whom worked on the Beethoven Thirteenth) joined together to perform the Mendelssohn String Octet in E-flat Major, which happens to be a particular favorite of mine; Mendelssohn composed it when he was only sixteen years old. The rehearsals for this particular piece were held in parallel with the quartet rehearsals.

On the first day I attended the seminar, I found myself growing a little nervous when I heard the students playing. Their performances sounded rough and awkward. Of course, this was only the second day since their group had begun making music together. I knew that it was unreasonable to expect polished performances under the circumstances, but still I had to wonder if they would go on to produce a concert-level performance in only one week. What I was hearing was very far from what we call "good music." Wasn't a week too short a time to bring this up to the level of a finished product, even for a mentor of Seiji Ozawa's abilities? These were not seasoned professionals, after all, but students.

"Don't worry, they'll get better every day," Ozawa declared with a smile, but I had my doubts. At that point, all I could hear were the imperfections, both in the string quartets and in the string orchestra. The Haydn didn't sound like Haydn, the Schubert didn't sound like Schubert, and the Ravel didn't sound like Ravel. They were playing all the right notes, but they weren't making *that* music.

Still, I continued to drive my somewhat underpowered Ford Focus wagon to Rolle every day. I made the rounds of the classrooms scattered throughout the property, listening intently to the young string players perform. I came to know all the movements of the seven string quartets and observed how they changed from day to day. I learned the names and faces of the students, and got to know their individual styles. Their progress seemed terribly slow at first, as if some kind of soft, invisible wall were blocking their way, and I worried that they would not be ready in time for the concert.

But then one day, in the brilliant summer light, some kind of silent spark seemed to leap among them. In both the daytime quartets and the evening ensemble, their sound suddenly began to come together. It was like a mysterious rising of the air. The performers' breathing started subtly to match, and their instruments sent beautiful reverberations through the air. The Haydn sounded more and more like Haydn, the Schubert like Schubert, the Ravel like Ravel. Each musician was no longer simply performing his or her part in isolation: they were all listening to each other. Not bad, I thought: not bad at all. Something was definitely coming out of this.

It was, however, still not "good music" in the true sense. There were still one or two thin membrane-like things left covering the music, preventing it from directly moving into people's hearts. I had experienced such membrane-like things in many different situations, unfortunately—in music, in writing, and in other artistic forms. Stripping off that last membrane can be a very difficult thing to do. But unless you manage to strip it off, a work of art has no—or almost no—meaning.

This was the stage at which Robert Mann joined the seminar, holding master classes in which he listened to and commented on the performances of each group, sometimes quite harshly.

For example, after he had listened to the first movement of the Ravel quartet, he said, "Thank you. That was a wonderful performance. Quite well done. But"—and here he grinned—"I didn't like it at all." Everyone in the classroom laughed, but I'm sure the performers themselves didn't feel like laughing. I knew what he meant, though. The music they were playing still didn't really sound like Ravel. It didn't create true musical empathy. That was clear to me, and it must have been clear to the others in the room. Robert Mann had simply stated that fact honestly, directly, without sugar coating. It was an extremely important fact, because there was not enough time available to indulge in pointless euphemisms—not enough time for the students and not enough time for Robert Mann. In effect, he was performing the function of the bright, precise mirror of a dentist, a mirror meant not to blur and flatter but to focus directly on the affected area and bring out the problem. I had the feeling that only someone like Mann could carry this off.

Mann provided detailed guidance on the smallest matters, as if tightening all the screws of a machine. His advice was always very concrete, his intentions perfectly clear to everyone. He avoided all ambiguity, so as to make maximum use of the limited time available. The students clung desperately to every word of Mann's rapid-fire advice. His guidance continued for more than half an hour—a very tense, even suffocating, half hour. The students must have been worn out by the end of it, but Mann—who was then ninety-two years old—must have been exhausted too. When he spoke about the music, however, Mann's eyes were lively and youthful, not the eyes of an old man.

The Ravel I heard at the Geneva concert a few days later was a marvelous performance, almost unrecognizably so in comparison with the rehearsal. It practically dripped with that special beauty found only in Ravel. Yes, every last screw had been tightened as needed. The race with time had been won. Of course, it was not a per-

fect performance. There was still room for a deeper maturation. But it definitely had that sense of urgency that
has to flow through all genuinely "good music." More
than anything, what it had was an earnest, youthful joy.
The last membrane had been stripped off.

The students had, then, learned a great deal and had
grown in little more than a week. And having witnessed
the transition, I felt that I, too, had learned much and
grown. This was true not only in the case of the Ravel.
Listening to each of the six groups performing in the
concert hall, I came to feel that there was something they
all shared to a greater or lesser degree. It was something
heartwarming and, quite simply, moving.

The same could be said about the orchestra—which is
made up of the entire student body and is conducted by
Ozawa—the centripetal force of which increased daily.
At one point all of a sudden, like a stalled engine catch-
ing fire, they began to exhibit an autonomous sort of
movement, like a single community. I felt almost as if I
were witnessing the birth of a new kind of animal into
a world of darkness. Each day they got better at moving their limbs and tail, their ears and eyes, and utilizing
their senses. Their initial confusion gave way to increas-
ingly natural movements executed with genuine grace
and beauty. It was as if the animal had begun to understand instinctively what kind of sounds Ozawa had in
mind, what kind of rhythms he was looking for. He was
not so much training them as he was using a special kind
of communication to elicit empathy from them . . . and,
as a result, they were beginning to discover in that act
of communication the rich meaning and natural joy of

music.

Ozawa, of course, gave detailed instructions to the orchestra regarding each part of the composition—on tempo, dynamics, timbre, bowing—and he repeated the same passage over and over again until he was satisfied, as if making minute adjustments on a precision instrument. He did not issue his instructions as orders but rather as proposals: "Why don't we try it like this?" he would say. He'd tell a little joke, and everyone would laugh, and the tension would ease a little, but his sense of the music remained a constant. There was no room for compromise. The jokes were just jokes.

I had no trouble understanding each of Ozawa's instructions to the orchestra members, but I was simply incapable of seeing the connection between these small, concrete instructions and the overall shape of the music. How did these many little orders accumulate in such a way to create something so vivid, so that the sound and direction of the music became something shared by everyone? This was a kind of black box for me. How was it even possible?

Surely this was one of Seiji Ozawa's "professional secrets"—the secrets of a man who had been active as one of the world's great conductors for over half a century. Or maybe not. Maybe it was not a secret or a black box or anything of the sort. Maybe it was something that was obvious to anyone but which only Seiji Ozawa could actually do. Whatever it might be, all I knew was that it was really and truly magical. The two things needed for "good music" to come into being were, first of all, a spark, and secondly, magic. If either was missing, "good music" wouldn't happen.

This was one of the things I learned in that little Swiss

town.

The first concert took place in Geneva's Victoria Hall on July 3rd, and the second (and final) concert took place on July 6th in Paris's Salle Gaveau. In spite of the rather austere program (chamber music and a student string orchestra), both were sold out. Of course, most people were there to see Seiji Ozawa. And no wonder: it had been six months since he last took the podium, at the Carnegie Hall concert.

The first half of the program consisted of performances by the six string quartets, each playing one movement of the compositions they had studied. The second half began with the Mendelssohn String Octet, and then the full orchestra took the stage. Robert Mann conducted the Beethoven, making truly beautiful music. Next, Seiji Ozawa conducted the Mozart and the Tchaikovsky encore.

Both concerts were wonderful and memorable, the quality of playing extremely high and deeply felt. The music was played with real urgency, but it was nevertheless spontaneous and filled with pure joy. The young players gave everything they had on stage, and the results were truly superb. The concluding Tchaikovsky, especially, was the hit of the evening, filled with an emotional, limpid beauty. Everyone in the hall was on their feet at the end, applauding endlessly. The response of the Paris audience was especially intense.

Much of the applause, to be sure, came from music fans eager to encourage Seiji Ozawa in his successful comeback. Ozawa has long had many fans in Paris. The applause, too, was undoubtedly meant in part as praise for the student orchestra's outstanding efforts, which far surpassed anything normally expected of a "student orchestra." But quite simply, as well, what we were hearing was the pure, unstinting, heartfelt applause for genuine "good music." It didn't matter who had conducted or who had performed. They had produced unmistakable "good music," with that indispensable spark and magic.

When I spoke with some of the students after the concert, before their excitement had cooled, they said things such as "The tears were pouring out of me during the performance" and "I'm pretty sure you don't get to have too many experiences this amazing in one lifetime." Seeing them so deeply moved, and seeing the audience's feverish reaction, I began to grasp how Ozawa felt pouring his heart and soul into the activities of this academy. Nothing could ever take its place for him. To hand genuine "good music" on to the next generation; to convey that intense feeling; to stir the hearts of young musicians in such a pure and fundamental manner: these surely gave him a joy that was fully as profound as that to be gained from conducting such world-class orchestras as the Boston Symphony and the Vienna Philharmonic.

At the same time, to see him mercilessly driving his body, which had yet to fully recover from several major operations, to see him literally grinding himself down as he grappled with the nurturing of these young musicians for virtually no compensation, made me feel that no matter how many bodies he might have to devote to this work, he would never have enough. I couldn't stop myself from sighing, because it was, quite frankly, painful to see him like this. I found myself wishing I had the power to find him a spare body or two to keep him going.

"There's No Single Way to Teach. You Make It Up as You Go Along."

This interview originally took place on July 4, 2011, aboard the express train heading from Geneva to Paris for the second concert presented by the Seiji Ozawa International Academy Switzerland. This one time, there were problems with the recording (thanks to my carelessness), and so supplementary interviews took place in Ozawa's Paris apartment before and after the concert. Ozawa visibly showed his exhaustion in the two days between concerts. His expression retained some of the excitement from the success of the first concert, but the energy he had expended so unstintingly on stage had yet to return. His strength was reviving, but only little by little, as he urged himself on little by little, supplementing that with fleeting naps and furtive nourishment. In spite of all this, Ozawa came over to where I was sitting on the train and said, "Let's talk!" When the subject turned to the education of young musicians, he spoke with far greater eloquence than when discussing his own music.

MURAKAMI: I had a chance to talk with Robert Mann yesterday between rehearsals, and he said that this year's students are doing better than any in the seven years he's been attending this event.

OZAWA: I think so, too. And why is that? Last year, as you know, I was too sick to attend, and that seems to have had a good effect, paradoxically. I really think so. I mean, here I am, supposedly the main promoter, and I'm always there, but the fact that I couldn't be there probably made both the teachers and the students get serious about doing a really good job. Before, I was going around to all the sessions from morning to night, attending every rehearsal, observing them very closely. But last year I couldn't come at all, and this year I just peeked in at a few of the sessions, leaving all the hard work to the teachers.

MURAKAMI: This year's teachers are the same as last year's, aren't they?

OZAWA: Exactly the same. They've been the same from the start. But if you ask me, both Sadao Harada and Nobuko Imai have made huge strides as teachers over the years. Pamela Frank has always been good, but all of them are much better now in their teaching. Plus we've got such high-level students, a lot of them coming back year after year.

MURAKAMI: Which makes teaching them that much more worthwhile.

OZAWA: Exactly.

MURAKAMI: Are all the young performers who come here actually students?

OZAWA: Most of them are, but not all. We've got a few who are already active on stage as professional musicians. We had a rule at first that nobody could attend for more than three years, but after a while we let that go, and now there are no limitations. As long as you can pass the audition, you can come as many years as you like. So now the number of repeats has gone up, and so has the overall quality of the group. We've still got an age limitation, but I'm thinking of doing away with that, too, next year. So then you'll be able to come back when you want, no matter how old you get.

MURAKAMI: At this point, the oldest musician is twenty-eight, and the youngest is nineteen, with most of the students in their early twenties.

OZAWA: Right. I'm thinking of changing that so people can keep coming into their thirties or forties. They just have to pass the audition. We also have a few special honor students who don't have to audition— the violinists Alena and Sasha and Agata. They can attend any time they'd like, without preconditions. We'll probably have one more of those next year.

MURAKAMI: So there's a solid nucleus forming. But isn't there some set maximum number of students you can take?

OZAWA: Well, actually, six string quartets—twenty-four students—should be the limit, but the way things worked out this year, we ended up with seven quartets. You really can't put more than six quartets on stage in a concert setting, though, so we added the Mendelssohn Octet to this year's program, combining the teachers and the four extra students so they could perform, too. Also, if I wasn't able to attend again this year, we were going to drop the orchestra performance and do the Mendelssohn instead. But here I am, I made it, and so did Robert Mann, who was saying he probably couldn't.

MURAKAMI: As a result of which, you ended up with a musically rich program—a very interesting concert the way it was put together. I was speaking with Mrs. Mann, who told me that her husband really enjoys teaching.

OZAWA: Yes, it's true. And he and I are a good match, personality-wise. To tell you the truth, he is constantly being invited by all these famous places—Vienna, Berlin—but he turns them down so he can work with me—here in Rolle, and in Matsumoto, too. People tell me all the time that they envy me for being able to get him to come.

MURAKAMI: At ninety-two, though, he's really getting on in years. To be blunt, there's no way to know how long he's going to be able to keep coming to these events. Won't his absence create a huge gap to fill? I mean, his presence is obviously a major factor in this academy.

OZAWA: Yes, we've talked about that, and we've decided not to even try to replace him but to go on with just the current teachers—Pamela and Sadao and Nobuko. Finally, there *isn't* anybody who could take his place. We've thought about it a lot, but can't come up with anybody among living performers who could fill his shoes. Which reminds me—the only reason that he has taken to conducting orchestras lately is because I pushed him to do it. He refused at first, insisted he didn't know how, but I nagged him to try, and he finally did it for the first time, in Japan. He seems to conduct with a lot more confidence these days.

MURAKAMI: Is he still playing the violin?

OZAWA: Very little, hardly at all. But he is going to play for us in Matsumoto—a Bartók quartet with Sadao Harada and the others. He won't be conducting, just performing in the quartet. He was originally supposed to play in the Mendelssohn Octet here, but he ended up just conducting. He found it too demanding to do both, so he chose to conduct. Which was great for me.

MURAKAMI: I'm sorry he didn't play in the Mendelssohn, though. I would have loved to hear him perform. I've been a fan of the Juilliard String Quartet since my teens. Observing the students here, though, maybe it's because they come from all different parts of the world, but each one seems to have developed a distinctive character in his or her music.

OZAWA: That's very true. Which makes it all the more worthwhile and interesting for us to be teaching them.

MURAKAMI: Especially in string quartets, you've got very individualized voices interacting with one another, so it can be thrilling when each voice has its own clear-cut character. Of course, that can work well in some cases and quite the opposite in others.

OZAWA: That's true.

MURAKAMI: Now, turning to the orchestra, you conducted the Mozart Divertimento K. 136 and, for the encore, the first movement of Tchaikovsky's Serenade for Strings. I assume the selection is different every year.

OZAWA: Yes, every year we play different pieces. Let's see . . . what have we done in the past? I remember playing the complete Serenade for Strings, but that's a bit too long. We also did Grieg's *Holberg Suite*. And Bartók's Divertimento for String Orchestra. I've conducted for six years here, always something different. I'd like to do Schoenberg's *Verklärte Nacht* sometime, but that's pretty long, too. It would have been too much this year, unfortunately.

MURAKAMI: Listening to your list of selections, it seems

to overlap almost perfectly with the repertoire you were taught by Professor Saito back when you were a student.

OZAWA: Hmm, that's true. Every piece I've just mentioned was something that Professor Saito taught me back then. Even *Verklärte Nacht*. I definitely want to play that next year. My health just wasn't up to it this year, unfortunately. He also taught me Dvořák's Serenade for Strings. I'd like to do that sometime, too. And Hugo Wolf has an all-string piece, *Italian Serenade*.

MURAKAMI: I don't know that one.

OZAWA: Most professional musicians don't know it, either. It's a beautiful piece, though.

MURAKAMI: I think Rossini had some all-string piece.

OZAWA: Yes, there is one. Professor Saito used to teach that one, too. It's pretty light, though, maybe too light.

MURAKAMI: It sounds to me as though you are taking what Professor Saito taught you when you were young and passing it on to the next generation in your own way.

OZAWA: That's true, now that you mention it. Professor Saito put a lot of emphasis on both the Bartók and the Tchaikovsky's Serenade for Strings.

MURAKAMI: But the Toho Gakuen orchestra was not all strings, was it? You had a few wind instruments, too.

OZAWA: Yes, at times there were some. But we did way more all-string pieces than anything else because there was hardly anyone playing wind. I remember doing Rossini's overture to *The Barber of Seville* with exactly one oboe and one flute. We had to do a whole new arrangement, and what a job that was! We had the viola playing some of the woodwind notes.

MURAKAMI: Talk about making do! Which reminds me, yesterday's Tchaikovsky was a marvelous performance, but I felt there would have been a stronger bass sound if you had had one or two more double basses playing. The one double bass sounded a little lonely by itself.

OZAWA: Well, that's the way Tchaikovsky had it in the original score.

MURAKAMI: Still, listening to the concert, I felt it would have been a perfectly adequate performance for an established professional orchestra. It had an urgency beyond anything you might expect from a "student orchestra."

OZAWA: It's true, you could take a performance like last night's anywhere in the world. If you increased their repertory, there are several musicians in that group who could handle a solo well enough to perform a concerto, and the orchestra would work in Vienna or Berlin or New York. You could perform there without the least embarrassment.

MURAKAMI: The overall level is so high, after all. You know the expression "not a hair out of place." Well, there really wasn't one.

OZAWA: No, there's not one second-rate musician in that group. This year, everybody is terrific. It's no accident, though. The more we work on the group, the better they get. Each year, the auditions have become more demanding, and the teaching has become more thorough.

MURAKAMI: To tell you the truth, the first time I heard them playing—I think it was the second day of rehearsals—I had some real doubts about what they could accomplish. The Ravel didn't sound like Ravel, and the Schubert didn't sound like Schubert. I never imagined they would come this far in a little over a week.

OZAWA: Well, they were still getting to know each other at that point.

MURAKAMI: The main thing I felt then was that they sounded so *young*! The *forte* passages were messy, and the *piano* passages shaky. But as I listened to each day's rehearsals, the *forte* started coming together, and the *piano* sections developed into clear, even lines of music. I was impressed! So *that's* how musicians get good.

OZAWA: Every once in a while, we get a few students who

play their instruments extremely well and produce truly beautiful, natural sound, but who don't yet really understand what music is. They have talent but no depth. They don't think about anyone but themselves. When the teachers encounter students like that at their auditions, they have trouble making up their minds. Should they admit these students? Wouldn't they just disrupt the others' harmony? As far as I'm concerned, though, that is the very kind of person we want to admit. If the sound is that natural and wonderful, you should bring the student in and really drill the music into them. If you do that—and if everything goes well—a person like that can become a marvelous performer. There aren't that many born musicians who can produce such a natural and beautiful sound.

MURAKAMI: You mean, you can't teach that innate talent, but you can teach someone how to approach music and how to think about it.

OZAWA: Exactly.

MURAKAMI: Among the student quartets I heard, the one that played the Janáček was the best—really wonderful. I had never heard that piece before.

OZAWA: Yes, that was terrific, really wonderful. The first violinist in that quartet, Sasha, was the one who begged to play the Janáček. Usually it's the teacher who assigns the work, but this time the request came from the student.

MURAKAMI: With a little more cooking, that group would be good enough to appear as a professional string quartet, wouldn't you say?

OZAWA: Yes, they could maybe make a living at it even now. But the students we get all want to be soloists.

MURAKAMI: There aren't that many young musicians who want to play chamber music, are there?

OZAWA: No, maybe not. There are hardly any people who say they want to work this hard on chamber music. But still, if they do study chamber music as closely as they do here, they're going to last longer as musicians. At least I think that's true.

MURAKAMI: Robert Mann has concentrated on chamber music for his entire career, hasn't he? Don't you think it's a matter of personality? I mean, there are some people who want to do chamber music and others who are only interested in becoming soloists. Or is it just that you can't make a living doing only chamber music?

OZAWA: That may be part of it. So everybody aims to become a soloist, and if that doesn't work out, they can always join an orchestra.

MURAKAMI: And after they do join an orchestra, there's a tradition of forming quartets with their colleagues and becoming active in chamber music that way. The Vienna Philharmonic, the Berlin Philharmonic . . .

OZAWA: True, true. Their orchestra work gives them a regular income, and they perform chamber music in their spare time—music for themselves. No, it's not easy to make a living with chamber music.

MURAKAMI: And isn't the audience for it rather limited?

OZAWA: Maybe so. People who love chamber music really love it, but there probably aren't that many of them. I do hear that their numbers are increasing these days, though.

MURAKAMI: In Tokyo, there's been a gradual increase in the number of small halls suited for chamber music—places like Kioi Hall or Casals Hall, though that one's gone now.

OZAWA: True, there weren't many places like that in the old days. They used to perform chamber music in the old Mitsukoshi Theater—Professor Saito, or the violinist Mari Iwamoto. And there was Dai-ichi Seimei Hall.

MURAKAMI: Why does the Ozawa Academy concentrate so heavily on string quartets?

OZAWA: Well, this year's program doesn't have any quartets by Mozart or (among more modern composers) Bartók or Shostakovich—but all the great composers, from Haydn to the present day, have written string quartets. Mozart, Beethoven, Schubert, Brahms, Tchaikovsky, Debussy—all of them have put tremendous energy into their quartets, so by performing the string quartets they wrote, you're able to gain a deeper understanding of those composers. Especially Beethoven: you can't really understand him unless you know his late quartets. So for that reason, we put a lot of emphasis on the string quartet. It's one of the foundations of music.

MURAKAMI: But the late quartets of Beethoven seem difficult for musicians in their early twenties. This year's more advanced group worked on his String Quartet no. 13 (Opus 130).

OZAWA: Yes, some people say you can't perform the late Beethoven unless you've got a lot of living behind you. Because they're so complex. But the students themselves asked to do it, and I think that's a very good thing.

MURAKAMI: They were certainly giving it their best. But how about something other than string quartets— like, say, a Mozart quintet, with an extra viola in the mix? Don't you want to have students work on something like that?

OZAWA: Yes, of course we do. For example, we're talking about doing a Brahms sextet next year. And we did that Dvořák quintet with the part for the double bass. We invited the double bassist to join us for the ensemble piece, so it would have been too sad for him if he had nothing else to do.

MURAKAMI: Yes, it is a little sad for him. I asked him what he did while the others were rehearsing their quartets. "Just practicing all by myself," he said. [*Laughter.*] Oh, another good piece would be that Schubert quintet with the two cellos.

OZAWA: Yes, of course, we do provide for variation. But the main thing we concentrate on is the string quartet. It's the foundation.

MURAKAMI: Are you the one who came up with the idea for the current system, half string quartets and half ensemble?

OZAWA: Well, I guess you could say it was me, but that was how we had done it for years at the Okushiga Kogen ski resort summer concerts that I organized. So we just brought the same approach to Switzerland. At Okushiga, too, my first thought had been to perform only string quartets . . . but since we had brought all these musicians up into the mountains, we started performing as an ensemble just for fun after dinner. We needed a conductor, and there I was! Hmm, I think the first piece we played was the Mozart Divertimento. That became part of the program. From then on we started doing a different ensemble piece every year.

MURAKAMI: So the "system" came about spontaneously. How long have the Okushiga concerts been going on?

OZAWA: Well, let's see, this program in Switzerland has been going for seven years, so the one in Okushiga must be going on nearly fifteen years.

MURAKAMI: So you put the system in place in Okushiga and imported it whole to Europe.

OZAWA: That's it. Robert Mann came to Okushiga and started saying how we ought to do something like it in Europe. That's how we got started.

MURAKAMI: Still, it seems a little strange to me that an orchestra conductor would establish a program organized around the string quartet. How do you explain that?

OZAWA: That's what everybody says, but under Professor Saito I studied pretty much the main string quartet repertory, and that's been tremendously useful to me. But I have a lot of homework to do when, like this year, the students are playing stuff I don't know— the Janáček, say, and the Smetana. I mean, even with Haydn, there are lots of pieces I don't know, so I have to study them. Anyhow, my most important job in this academy is to choose good teachers. If that goes well, everything else will work out one way or another. It's the same in Japan and in Europe.

MURAKAMI: So what you do is circulate from room to room, watching the teachers in action and offering advice when necessary.

OZAWA: Yes, and sometimes I just sit there listening and only speak when somebody asks my opinion. Finally, it's the teachers who are doing the actual teaching.

MURAKAMI: And only teaching string?

OZAWA: Well, after all, the idea from the start was that the string quartet would be the basis for all we do. I've thought about adding wind instruments, and I've spoken to some flute and oboe teachers, but once you start branching out like that, it can be really tough. The scale of things gets too big.

MURAKAMI: And no piano?

OZAWA: No, no piano. You start adding piano, and the whole feeling changes. In a piano trio, say, you've pretty much got three soloists. In a string quartet, the ensemble is the basis.

MURAKAMI: When I was observing the academy in action, one thing I found very interesting was the way the first and second violins would trade places from one movement to the next. Ordinarily, I suppose, the stronger player, the one with the richer experience, takes the first chair—but not here.

OZAWA: Yes, that's a terrific approach. We started doing it that way in Okushiga and adopted the practice here. We have all our violinists take both the first and the second parts regardless of their ability.

MURAKAMI: And how about for you? Do you find that guiding people in string quartets contributes something to your own musical activity?

OZAWA: Hmm, I suppose it probably does. For one thing,

it makes you look closer and closer at every little detail in the score. There are only four voices, after all. Which is not to say that because it's a quartet, the music is simple. All kinds of musical elements are crammed in there in a very concentrated form.

MURAKAMI: Watching Robert Mann's master classes, I noticed that his advice to the students is very consistent. He gave detailed guidance to each of the seven groups, but he had pretty much the same thing to say in each case, which was that they needed to bring out the inner voices more clearly. In a string quartet, striking that kind of balance is tremendously important, I suppose.

OZAWA: That's true. In Western ensemble music, the inner voice is a very important element.

MURAKAMI: In orchestras, too, bringing out the inner voice has come to take on much greater significance lately, hasn't it? So orchestral music has become more like chamber music.

OZAWA: Yes, it's true. All the good groups are doing it. You have to if you want to bring out the flavor of the music.

MURAKAMI: But students go to music schools hoping to become soloists, don't they? That's why they concentrate on playing the main melody and rarely take responsibility for producing the inner voices. Which makes it all the more meaningful for them to occupy the second chair in a string quartet.

OZAWA: I think you're right. By playing the inner voice, you get to see the interior of the music. And that may be the most important thing. It nurtures your ear. Viola players and cellists, too. Of course, unlike the violin, their instruments are designed to be part of the overall ensemble. When they come here they learn to look more deeply at those parts of the music.

MURAKAMI: Another thing that Robert Mann mentioned frequently was that the instruction to play *piano* doesn't mean to play weakly. Any number of times I heard him say, "*Piano* means half as strong as *forte*, so play at a lower volume but play with *strength*."

OZAWA: He's right about that. When we see *piano* in a score, we tend to soften everything up, but what he's saying is, even if the volume is lower, make those notes clearly audible. Give even the weaker sounds their proper rhythm and emotional force. Balance tension and release. He has gained this faith from over half a century of playing string quartets.

MURAKAMI: The sound of the Juilliard String Quartet is just like that—clear, utterly analytical, contrasting tension and release. Europeans may not be too fond of that approach.

OZAWA: No, Europeans would say it's better to keep things a little vague and atmospheric. But Mann suggests you perform the music exactly as the composer intended, in order to deliver those precise notes to the ears of the audience. That's what he strives for—a faithful performance that glosses over nothing.

MURAKAMI: Another thing he said a lot was "I can't hear you!"—like at the end of a diminuendo if the notes became inaudible. It must be difficult to play such quiet passages solidly.

OZAWA: Yes, it is. He often tells the students that, in order to make sure that those weak notes come out properly, you make the notes just before them a touch stronger. If you make the earlier notes weak, you've got nowhere to go. He's got all those things figured out.

MURAKAMI: He also said, "I can hear those notes in this place, but not in a big auditorium."

OZAWA: Yes, that's the result of years of experience. Even if you're playing in a small space, you always anticipate the sound you'll need in a big hall.

MURAKAMI: I asked Sadao Harada about that. He said that the true sound is one that can be heard properly in either kind of place, big or small. There are musicians who play differently depending on the size of the hall, but that's probably not the right way to perform.

OZAWA: That's probably the best way to put it. It's tough to actually *do* it, but that's the best way to put it.

MURAKAMI: The academy's two concerts took place in Geneva's Victoria Hall and in Paris's Salle Gaveau, places with totally different acoustics. The students seemed to be quite confused by the difference.

OZAWA: You're right about that. They had to rehearse well if they wanted to hear each other.

MURAKAMI: Oh, another thing that Robert Mann said a lot was "Speak!" Not "sing," but "speak," "talk to each other."

OZAWA: Yes, he was talking about something more than just "singing" back and forth to each other with their instruments. When you sing, you just go *ta-daaaa!* [*He stretches his arms out wide.*] Of course, the musicians have to sing to each other, but in addition they also have to signal to each other clearly when they are going to start singing or stop singing. I think he's telling them to be conscious of each of those stages as they play.

MURAKAMI: Another thing he said in that connection was that each composer has a unique language, and the students should "speak" to each other in that language.

OZAWA: He's talking about the composer's style. You have to internalize the composer's unique voice.

MURAKAMI: At the same time, he said that Smetana has expressions that "speak" Czech, and Ravel has expressions that "speak" French, and the musicians ought to keep such things in mind. I thought that was a very interesting point. Robert Mann is

obviously very clear in his opinions, and he gives
voice to them over and over. He doesn't change his
teaching method from one student to the next. He
has his own unique philosophy, and he holds to it
firmly and consistently.

OZAWA: Again, this is something that comes from his
long experience. He has his own unique way of
looking at things. After all, he's been exclusively
devoted to chamber music longer than anyone, and
he has richer experience than anyone.

MURAKAMI: I suppose there are components to his
instruction that conflict with what the permanent
faculty teach—people like Pamela Frank or Nobuko
Imai or Sadao Harada.

OZAWA: Of course, that's only natural. I always say
that to the students—that it's natural for different
teachers to have different opinions. I say that to
the instructors and to Robert Mann, too. That's
just music—it's what makes music so interesting.
Different teachers have different things to say, but
they may arrive at the same point. Or not!

MURAKAMI: Can you give me some concrete examples of
differences that have emerged?

OZAWA: Well, here's something that happened the other
day when Robert Mann was offering guidance on
the Ravel Quartet. The score indicates this long slur.
Most violinists and cellists interpret this to mean
that they should play those linked notes without

reversing the bow. In other words, they take it as a practical instruction concerning how to move the bow. Some composers, though, use the slur to indicate a musical phrase, which is how Mann was interpreting it, and he told the students to stop the bow.

MURAKAMI: In other words, it was okay for them to stop and reverse the bow in the middle of the slur.

OZAWA: Right. But before that, Pamela had given them the opposite instruction: since the composer had made a point of writing in the slur, they should try drawing the bow across the strings without reversing. It was completely the opposite. Pamela immediately followed Mann's instruction, pointing out that she had just told them to do it the other way.

MURAKAMI: Oh, so that's what that was about. It was a matter of technique, so I didn't quite get it.

OZAWA: The way Pamela saw it, the students should at least try to play it the way the composer wrote it, even if there might be some difficulty involved.

MURAKAMI: So she was telling them to respect the original score and at least try to draw the bow in a single stroke from grip to tip, even if that's hard to do. But in Mann's opinion, there was no need to do anything so difficult.

OZAWA: No need at all. As long as they produced the sound the composer was aiming for, it was no problem if they reversed the bow. The bow has a certain fixed length, so there was no point in trying too hard. That was his opinion. Both were correct. The students should try doing it both ways and choose the way they believed to be right.

MURAKAMI: I suppose different people will arrive at different conclusions.

OZAWA: The same way different singers will sing the same phrase differently depending on whether or not they have the lung capacity. Do they have to take a breath or not? Some violinists can play the phrase with a single stroke of the bow and some cannot.

MURAKAMI: Now that you mention it, Mann said a lot about the breath. When people sing, they have to take a breath at some point. But "unfortunately," he said, string instruments don't have to breathe, so you have to keep the breath in mind as you play. That "unfortunately" was interesting. He also talked a lot about silence. Silence is not just the absence of sound: there is a sound called silence.

OZAWA: Ah, that's the same as the Japanese idea of *ma*. The same concept comes up in gagaku, and in playing the *biwa* and the *shakuhachi*. It's very much like that. This kind of *ma* is written into the score in some Western music, but there is also some in which it's not written. Mann has a very good understanding of these things.

MURAKAMI: Another thing that surprised me was that he

had very little to say about bowing or fingering. I
figured that as a specialist, he would give a lot more
detailed instruction on those matters.

OZAWA: The students who come here have already gone
past that point, I suppose. His teaching is at a level
above that. Bowing and fingering are not a problem
anymore. That's what I think.

MURAKAMI: He did, though, have a lot to say about
certain technical matters, like "You should play
this closer to the bridge," or "Play this on the
fingerboard."

OZAWA: Well, that would change the sound. It softens
when you play on the fingerboard and becomes
clearer when you play near the bridge. Certainly,
that's something he would talk a lot about.

MURAKAMI: I'm not a musician, but I learned a lot from
watching his instruction.

OZAWA: I'm sure that's true. Being able to watch such a
thing is a rare and valuable opportunity, an excellent
learning experience. We recorded it all on video so
people can see it later.

MURAKAMI: Robert Mann is a person who is very clear
about his method: he knows exactly what he wants
to do. But I felt that you were rather different as
a mentor. You change your approach in different
situations.

OZAWA: That's true. Professor Saito was very much like Robert Mann. He always had a very clear method. But I always resisted that. They know exactly what they're going to say. It's all fixed for them. But I've always felt that that's not all there is to music. I've always made a point of doing things differently.

MURAKAMI: You mean, like, doing the opposite of what you were taught when you were young?

OZAWA: Yes, in both my conducting and my teaching. I don't approach either with preconceived ideas. I don't prepare beforehand but decide on the spot when I see who I'm dealing with. I respond then and there when I see how they are handling things. Somebody like me could never write an instruction manual. I don't have anything to say until I've got a musician right in front of me.

MURAKAMI: And then, depending on who that musician is, it changes what you say. It must be good for the students to have the two of you in combination: you, with your flexible approach, and Robert Mann, with his unwavering philosophy. I bet it works out very well.

OZAWA: Yes, I think so.

MURAKAMI: When did you begin to take an interest in training young people?

OZAWA: Hmm, let's see, it was shortly after I went to Tanglewood, so it must have been around ten years after I signed on as music director of the Boston Symphony. People tried to get me to teach before that, but I wasn't much interested in doing it. Just after I went to Boston, Professor Saito kept pressing me to teach at Toho Gakuen, but I turned him down again and again because, as I told him, I just didn't like doing that kind of thing. Finally, though, I said okay, but right after I got started, Professor Saito died. Maybe that made me feel I had a responsibility to teach, because after he died I started doing it quite seriously and started guiding students at Tanglewood, too.

MURAKAMI: In conducting?

OZAWA: No, not in conducting. I was training the orchestra. And finally, at Tanglewood, too, I started teaching string quartets on the assumption that if you can't do string quartets you can't do anything. I wasn't doing it as seriously as we do here, but it was pretty much the same sort of thing.

MURAKAMI: You know, I write novels, and producing my own work is just about all I do. Twice, though, I taught university classes. Once at Princeton and once at Tufts, I gave courses in Japanese literature, but preparing for classes and grading student papers took *so* much time and effort, I knew for sure it wasn't for me. Working with young students was lots of fun and very stimulating, but it made it impossible for me as a practicing writer to do what I really wanted to do. Do you ever feel that way?

OZAWA: I certainly did at Tanglewood, and I hated it. I had a concert to give every week; teaching on top of that was a tremendous effort. It was the same when I started teaching at Matsumoto in addition to running the Saito Kinen Festival. So I moved the teaching to Okushiga, where I could concentrate on it as something quite separate from the conducting. Of course, that way, I have no break at all!

MURAKAMI: Yes, there goes your summer vacation.

OZAWA: Really. The Saito Kinen took most of it, and Okushiga finished it off. Oh, well, it's for the teaching. It's really too much, though, trying to teach in addition to being a full-time performer.

MURAKAMI: Are there other top professional conductors who do that?

OZAWA: I don't know. Maybe not too many.

MURAKAMI: Pardon me for asking, but is the teaching something you do on a volunteer basis, without compensation?

OZAWA: As a rule, yes. The teaching staff are paid, but I usually work without compensation in both Switzerland and Okushiga. This year is a little different, though, following my illness. I'm not conducting, and I'm here in Switzerland just for this, so for the very first time I'm collecting a salary.

MURAKAMI: Ordinarily, the teaching is its own reward,

I suppose. Your teaching method, though, is totally different from what you received from Professor Saito, isn't it? And the teachers here at Rolle: they all approach their instruction calmly, without raising their voices.

OZAWA: No, they do raise their voices sometimes. At one rehearsal, Sadao Harada really yelled at a student, and everybody froze and the place went absolutely silent. These things happen once in a while. Professor Saito used to yell at us constantly, though. [*Laughter.*]

MURAKAMI: You've got nothing but the most elite students here, people who are used to being number one in their class. I would think you get a few who don't follow orders all that willingly.

OZAWA: Yes, of course, we have some of those. Which is why we have to have very capable instructors. We're teaching some very confident individuals.

MURAKAMI: Of course they have to be strongly competitive, or they can't make it as professional musicians.

OZAWA: That's true.

MURAKAMI: It must be quite a job to divide them up into six or seven groups and assign each unit a piece of music to work on.

OZAWA: Sadao Harada does all of that himself. It's a huge

job. I used to help a little, but it's too much for me. I leave it entirely up to him. I mean, after all, he is a chamber-music specialist.

MURAKAMI: You weren't able to participate in this program last year after your surgery, but do you think that had some impact on the academy?

OZAWA: I was sorry to miss it, but the young conductor Kazuki Yamada took over for me to some extent, and as I said before, there were several ways in which my absence paradoxically had a good effect on the program. I suspect that the shock of my not being present made both the instructors and the students more determined to stand on their own and take more responsibility for making the academy a success. That's why this year we've got several units who weren't satisfied to be given assignments but instead made their wishes known to work on particular pieces—the Beethoven, the Janáček, the Ravel. I think that's a very good thing rather than leaving the decision up to the instructor.

MURAKAMI: The Ravel group was especially interesting, with two members from Poland, one from Russia, and only one French musician, the viola player. I asked Agata, the violinist, why such a group had made a point of choosing a work by a French composer. She said, "I wanted the challenge. I didn't want to do Szymanowski just because I happen to be Polish but rather to try someone so utterly French, like Ravel."

OZAWA: Oh, so that's what she was thinking! That was something that only you could get away with asking her. If one of us had tried, we never would have gotten such an honest answer. You're an outsider, not one of the teachers, so she opened up to you, I'm sure.

MURAKAMI: That group did a truly beautiful job of producing the Ravel sound. I was so impressed, I just let the question pop out.

OZAWA: No, I never could have asked her that, and she never would have given me such a straightforward answer.

MURAKAMI: But it's a good thing, isn't it, for such a desire to come out in the open? It means they've gone up a level in ability.

OZAWA: You know, teaching like this is not my true profession. Even now, after running such programs here and in Okushiga for some fifteen years, I'm still just groping my way forward. We've been rehearsing here now every day, but still there's no single way to teach. You make it up as you go along; you figure out, in each case, how to best explain what you are thinking to the students. But you know, that's good for us, too. That way, we can get back to basics.

MURAKAMI: So even world-class professionals like you can learn from teaching.

OZAWA: We can definitely learn from teaching. But tell

me honestly, what do you think? Watching what we
do here, do you think it has any meaning?

MURAKAMI: Yes, I think it's very important and
meaningful. A diverse group of young performers
from all over the world come together to learn
important things from active, first-class veteran
musicians. You help them to go on stage to perform,
collectively, before an audience, and then they go
back in all directions to their home countries. I
have found it moving to think that many wonderful
performers of the future will have come through
this program. I also found myself imagining them
congregating for a kind of reunion someday,
spontaneously forming a "superorchestra" like the
Saito Kinen, a magnificent performing body free of
nationality or politics.

OZAWA: There have been suggestions that I take this
orchestra on tour. My manager and others think
I ought to have them perform more widely, since
we've gone to all the trouble of whipping them
into such superb shape. Currently we just have the
two recitals in Geneva and Paris, and I agree it is a
kind of a waste. It would make sense to put a tour
together and perform in Vienna or Berlin or Tokyo
or New York. But so far I've turned down all such
suggestions. I just don't see the need for it. Of course
it's not entirely out of the realm of possibility. It
might be conceivable sometime in the future.

MURAKAMI: That's a hard thing to decide. If the orchestra
were to become firmly established, your educational

objectives might suffer. I suppose the ways in which you guide and conduct this kind of student orchestra are very different from the way you "train" a first-class orchestra such as the Boston Symphony or the Vienna Philharmonic.

OZAWA: Yes, very different, both in attitude and in techniques. In the case of a professional orchestra, you've got three days to whip a whole concert's worth of material into shape. You've got a fixed schedule with absolutely no wiggle room. In the case of this orchestra, though, the number of pieces is far more limited, so you can pour a lot of time into rehearsing each one. Take the rehearsals we're doing now: we probe very deeply into each piece. And the more you rehearse, the more difficulties come to the surface.

MURAKAMI: You mean, the more time you spend rehearsing, the more difficult become the various hurdles that need to be cleared?

OZAWA: That's right. You may get them to where they're all breathing together, but still the parts are not perfectly synced. The nuances of sound are a little off, say, or the rhythms are not quite together. So you put lots of time into refining each of these tiny details. That way, tomorrow's performance should be at an even higher level. So then you demand even more from them. This process teaches *me* an awful lot.

MURAKAMI: What is it that you learn?

OZAWA: Well, it brings out my own greatest weaknesses.

MURAKAMI: Your greatest weaknesses?

OZAWA: Yes, they come out right away when we're concentrating on such tiny details.

Murakami note: He spends some time thinking more about this, but finally does not provide concrete examples.

MURAKAMI: Of course, I have no idea what your weaknesses might be, but one thing I can say for sure is that each day you work with the orchestra, the more *its* sound becomes *your* sound. I think it's amazing that you can actually make such a thing happen.

OZAWA: It just goes to show the high caliber of these musicians.

MURAKAMI: In observing the academy, I realized for the first time how much hard work it takes to create an orchestral sound that has individuality and direction and presence. But you said earlier that your ability to play music becomes even better when you've played in a string quartet. Can you give me some concrete examples of exactly how this works?

OZAWA: Well, look, let me put this as simply as possible. When you're playing with an ensemble—as opposed to when you're performing by yourself—your ears are open in all directions. This is very important for a musician. It's the same when you're playing in an orchestra, of course, in the sense that you have to keep listening to what the others are doing. But in a string quartet, you can have more intimate communication among the instruments. While you play, you listen to the others. You think, "Hey, that's very nice, what the cello is doing now," or "My sound doesn't quite match the viola's." Also, the musicians are able to speak to each other and exchange their personal opinions. You can't have that in an orchestra; there are just too many people. But when there are just four of you, you can voice your opinions to each other directly. You have that kind of easy interaction. And so the musicians are able to listen to each other's playing very closely, as a result of which you can clearly hear their music getting better and deeper. It really works.

MURAKAMI: I see what you mean. But still, as an outside observer, I couldn't help noticing that everybody's playing with this confident look on their faces, like "Hey, I'm the best one here!"

OZAWA [*laughing*]: It's true, we do get some of that. Especially among the Europeans. It's a little different in Japan.

MURAKAMI: You mean, Japanese musicians don't show their confidence so openly? You've been running this same kind of program in Okushiga and Switzerland, but I would guess you find yourself teaching in subtly different ways in the two places.

OZAWA: Hmm, maybe so. Japanese musicians have their

own strengths—they work well together, and they study very hard. In Okushiga, this can assert itself in both positive and negative ways. When people are openly self-assertive in Japan, we say . . . uh, what's that expression?

MURAKAMI: You mean *"Deru kugi wa utareru"* [The nail that sticks out gets hammered down]?

OZAWA: Yes, maybe that, or something like it. You're not supposed to say or do anything that makes you stand out, or sounds as if you're nosing into someone else's business. Respect the consensus. Practice restraint. If you're squeezed into a commuter train in the morning, don't say a thing. Just shut up and bear it. Behavior like that can be good in a program like ours, but also not so good. If I took these European students to Tokyo and put them on an eight o'clock commuter train, they'd explode! [*Laughter.*] They wouldn't be able to stand being pushed around that way.

MURAKAMI: I can imagine it! [*Laughter.*]

OZAWA: In any case, self-assertion is perfectly normal here in Europe. It's the only way to survive. In Japan, though, people think and think and think about things until they finally take action—or take no action at all. So we've got that major difference to deal with, and I'm not sure which mentality is better. In the case of a string quartet, though, the European way is definitely superior. You get the best results when each member asserts his opinion. That's why

in Japan I find myself yelling "Don't hold back!"
until I'm blue in the face.

MURAKAMI: Because they do hold back.

OZAWA: You've watched our practice sessions in
Switzerland. Next you should come to Okushiga.
You'll see the difference immediately. It's like
night and day. Unfortunately we couldn't hold
the Okushiga academy this year because of the
earthquake. I was hoping to have you come.

MURAKAMI: I'm very much looking forward to the next
one. But about these European students: they talk
back when they're not convinced by the teacher's
instructions. "Here's what I think we ought to do,"
they'll say. Even with a superstar like Robert Mann,
if they don't understand what he's telling them,
they'll just say they don't get it. A Japanese student
couldn't do such a thing. If a young Japanese student
talked back to a distinguished teacher, he'd get cold
stares from the other students: "What a disrespectful
jerk! Who do you think you are?"

OZAWA: I think you're right.

MURAKAMI: It's true in just about any field in Japan.
Maybe even in writers' circles. People can't do
anything until they've gauged the opinions of the
other people present. They look around, they absorb
the atmosphere, and only then do they raise their
hands and say something unobjectionable. That way,
there's no progress where it matters, and the status

quo becomes set in stone.

OZAWA: You know, recently, among young musicians in Japan, there's a growing chasm between those who get out of the country as soon as possible and those who stay in Japan even when they have an opportunity to go abroad. In the old days, a lot of people wanted to go abroad but couldn't, because they didn't have the money. These days, it's fairly easy to go if you want to, but the number of people who choose not to go seems to be increasing.

MURAKAMI: You left Japan back in the days when there were still travel restrictions. You were going to get out no matter what, money or no money.

OZAWA: Yes, it's true, and I was pretty reckless about it. There used to be these Symphony of the Air programs with the old NBC Symphony Orchestra. When I heard them, I knew there was no point in staying in Japan. I had to get out, period. And that's what I did.

MURAKAMI: So now you've come full circle and you find yourself with a strong desire to come back to Japan and educate young musicians.

OZAWA: Yes, but that desire didn't take shape until much later.

MURAKAMI: And now that you're back and guiding young musicians in your own special way, you're finding that some members of the musical-education establishment are saying that your methods are all wrong, that what you're doing is not really education, isn't that the case?

OZAWA: Yes, I suppose there are a few people like that. I hear about them once in a while.

MURAKAMI: Don't the students find it a little confusing when your methods diverge from the musical education they've received so far?

OZAWA: Well, you know, when you're all out there in the mountains living together, you get to know each other pretty well. We're fellow musicians, after all, so we become friends before we know it. And that's what a music academy is all about. The more we rehearse together, the better we understand each other.

MURAKAMI: Watching how the students' music progressed and deepened every day, I was truly amazed. I wasn't living with them, but I saw them every day, and learned their names and their individual performance styles, which made their transformations all the more profound for me. I was impressed—or should I say "moved"?—to realize that *this* was how outstanding music was made.

OZAWA: It really is something wonderful. It's the power these young people have. I do this every year, but I still find it hard to believe the speed with which they improve during those last three days. It's awe-inspiring. You have to see it to believe it.

MURAKAMI: Yes, it has been a rare opportunity for me. I'm a writer, a lone craftsman in the true sense, so it was very touching for me to witness a communal work of art in the making. I enjoyed it thoroughly.

Afterword by Seiji Ozawa

I have lots of friends who love music, but Haruki takes it way beyond the bounds of sanity. Jazz, classics: he doesn't just love music, he *knows* music. Tiny details, old stuff, musicians—it's amazing. He goes to concerts, and to live jazz performances, and he listens to records at home. It really is amazing.

My daughter, Seira, the only member of the family who can write, is great friends with Haruki's wife, Yoko, and that's how I got to know Haruki.

Haruki came to observe my Seiji Ozawa Music Academy, a project very dear to me, that we hold every year in Kyoto. He and I went out to enjoy the Kyoto night life under the fascinated gazes of my fellow teachers and the students. This was a first for both of us.

We had our first conversation in a little bar that the two of us went to for the first time in Ponto-cho, Kyoto's entertainment district. We talked about what he had seen at the academy, and I'm sure we talked about music in general, too.

Back home in Tokyo, I told Seira about the evening I had spent with Haruki. She said, "If you found it so interesting to talk about music with him, you two ought to get together and record your conversations," but I didn't give it much thought at the time. After my major surgery for esophageal cancer, though, when I had nothing but time on my hands, we were invited as a family to visit the Murakami home in Kanagawa. While the others were gabbing in the kitchen, Haruki and I went into another room and listened to the records that Haruki had set out.

They were recordings by Glenn Gould and Mitsuko Uchida. Memories of Glenn Gould came flooding back to me, though fifty years had passed in between.

Until my surgery, I was too busy making music every day to think about the past, but once I started remembering, I couldn't stop, and the memories came back with a nostalgic surge. This was a new experience for me. Not all things connected with major surgery are bad. Thanks to Haruki, I was able to recall Maestro Karajan, Lenny, Carnegie Hall, the Manhattan Center, one after another, and I spent the next three or four days steeped in those memories.

I was scheduled to conduct the Saito Kinen Orchestra accompanying Mitsuko Uchida in the Beethoven Third Piano Concerto in New York, but I aggravated a back problem, and so, with great regret, I ceded the baton to Tatsuya Shimono. It still rankles me terribly. We'll do it next time, Mitsuko!

If there's anything good about a major illness, it's that it gives you more time than you know what to do with. Thank you, Seira! You made it possible for me to meet Haruki.

Thank you, Haruki! You brought out so many memories for me. And I'm not sure how you did it, but you really got me talking. Thank you, Yoko, for always putting out those nutritious snacks!

Haruki and Yoko, thank you both for coming all the way to Switzerland. I had always felt that no one could really grasp the beauty of that academy without seeing it in person.

I'm only sorry, Haruki, that you weren't able to observe the music-making at Okushiga this year. We'll do it next year for sure.

Let's talk about any differences you find between the young musicians of Europe and the East.